William Browne, Arthur Henry Bullen

The Poems of William Browne of Tavistock

Vol. II

William Browne, Arthur Henry Bullen

The Poems of William Browne of Tavistock
Vol. II

ISBN/EAN: 9783744714020

Printed in Europe, USA, Canada, Australia, Japan

Cover: Foto ©Thomas Meinert / pixelio.de

More available books at **www.hansebooks.com**

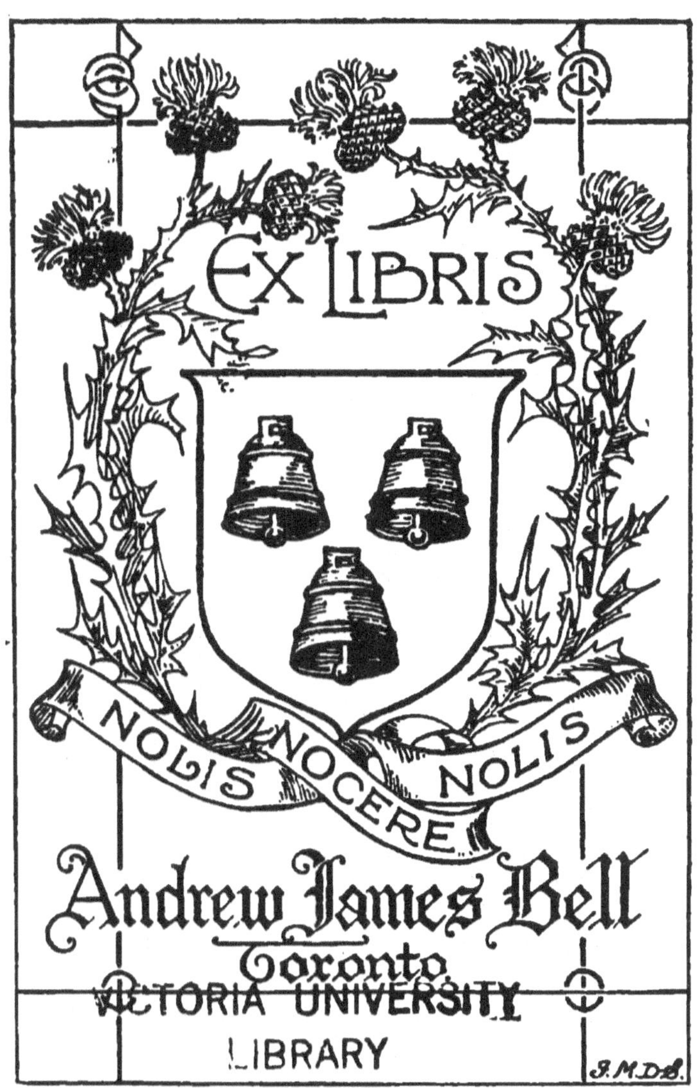
EX LIBRIS
NOLIS NOCERE NOLIS
Andrew James Bell
Toronto
VICTORIA UNIVERSITY
LIBRARY

The Muses' Library.

The Muses' Library.

POEMS

OF

WILLIAM BROWNE

VOL. II.

THE POEMS OF
WILLIAM BROWNE

OF TAVISTOCK:

EDITED BY GORDON GOODWIN,

WITH AN INTRODUCTION

BY A. H. BULLEN.

VOL. II.

LONDON:

LAWRENCE & BULLEN,

16 HENRIETTA STREET, W.C.

1894.

NEW YORK:

CHARLES SCRIBNERS' SONS,

743 & 745 BROADWAY.

1894.

LONDON:
PRINTED BY WOODFALL AND KINDER,
70 TO 76, LONG ACRE, W.C.

CONTENTS.

x CONTENTS.

VIII.—*Paraphrases, &c.*

IX.—*Miscellaneous Pieces.*

CONTENTS. xi

BRITANNIA'S PASTORALS

BOOK III

Book III. of *Britannia's Pastorals* was printed for the first time in 1852 by the Percy Society, under the editorship of Mr. T. Crofton Croker, from the MS. in the library of Salisbury Cathedral. The following MS. Commendatory Poems were printed by Beloe in *Anecdotes of Literature*, vi. 58–85. He found them inserted in a copy of the 1625 edition of the *Pastorals*.

Euterpe to her dearest Darling W. B.

THY lines, thy worth, thy wit to praise,
Were mine own honour to upraise,
And those same gifts commend in thee
Which thou received hast of me ;
Yet may I boast that by mine aid
All ears to thee are captive made,
And thy amazed countrymen
Admire, extol thy golden pen.
Hearing such madrigals as these
Astonish'd is Philisides,[a]
And vanquish'd by thy sweeter lays
Forswears / Resigns his pipe ; yields thee the bays:
And Colin Clout[b] his oaten reed,
Which did to us such pleasure breed,
Resigns to thee ; griev'd because his
Mulla[c] by Tavy vanquish'd is

[a] *Philisides*, Sir Philip Sidney.
[b] *Colin Clout*, Spenser.
[c] *Mulla*, a poetical name given by Spenser to the river Awbey, which flowed by his residence at Kilcolman Castle, co. Cork.

Marina feigns though in her need
The storm did help ; yet she indeed
Was ravish'd, but ('tis her excuse)
'Twas only with thy sweet-tongu'd Muse ;
That though the Robin Redbreast fed
Her body, yet sh' had suffered
Death, hadst not thou with lines refin'd,
As with ambrosia, fed her mind.
Doridon weeps, although for who
He trows not, if 't be not for you ;
Since thee to write he could not move
One canto more on his true love.
See how each swain that should this day
Before Dame Thetis sing his lay,
Sighing gives back, for he doth fear
Willy, their Captain, won't be there.
All say thou art the elm (they know)
Whereby the Muses' vine doth grow,
And that if Cælia merit death,
All they must with her lose their breath,
That fairer boughs have pull'd from thee
Than e'er grew on Pan's golden tree.
Lastly, thy Aletheia says,
That future times shall sing thy praise,
And th' after ages strive in vain,
As thou hast done, to do again.

PHIL. PAPILLON, è Coll. Exon.

Carmina amo, mihi, Wille, placet tua fistula : felix !
En resonant laudes illa, vel illa tuas.

BUT stop, my Muse, listen to Willy's lays,
Hark whiles the Echo doth resound his praise ;
Let others speak, forbid not, but let me
Thou charming sweetly, listen unto thee.

P. S., Coll. Ex.

On the Author of Britannia's Peerless Pastorals.

I'LL take thy judgment, golden Midas, now,
Nor will of Phœbus harmony allow,
Since Pan hath such a shepherd, whose sweet lays
May claim deservedly the Delphic bays.
Thrice happy Syrinx, only great in this,
Thou kissest him in metamorphosis.
Flock hither, satyrs, learn a roundelay
Of him to grace Sylvanus' holiday.
Come hither, shepherds, let your bleating flocks
Of bearded goats browse on the mossy rocks.
Come from Arcadia, banish'd shepherds, come ;
Let flourishing Britannia be your home,
Crown'd with your anadems and chaplets trim ;
And invocate no other Pan but him.
'Tis he can keep you safe from all your flocks,
From greedy wolf, or oft-beguiling fox.
Let him but tune his notes, and you shall see
The wolf abandon his rapacity,
And innocently trip and frisk among
Your wanton lambkins at his swanlike song.
Yea, had the Thracian sung but half so well,
He had not left Eurydice in hell.
Then rally, swain, astonish human eyes,
And let thy Tavy high as Tiber rise.

On the Same.

AN ODE.

FEAR not, Willy, but go on
With thy song of Doridon,
Which will ne'er surpassed be
By the best pipe in Arcady.
What though Roger of the plains,
Hobinoll and other swains,

Join'd with Colin of the glen,
Perigot and other men,
Warble sweetly, thou when they
Sung on Pan's last holiday,
Won'st the chaplet which was made
Hard by Tavy in a glade.
Walla, Marine, Fida too,
Do thy lasting favour woo ;
The fountain's god will rising be
From his waters to hear thee ;
Hung'ring for thee makes us rave,
All shut up in Limos' cave ;
O be thou the Redbreast, cherish
Those who but for thee would perish,
Or be Triton who alone
May'st remove the mighty stone.
Then in thine honour every shepherd shall
Keep the day stricter than Pan's festival.

EDW. HALL, è Coll. Exon.

On the Author of Britannia's Peerless Pastorals.

CEASE, skilful Orpheus, whose mellifluous strains
Have erst made stones and trees skip o'er the plains ;
A sweeter harmony invites our ears
Than e'er was sent from the celestial spheres.
Clear Tavy now his silver head may raise,
A shepherd of his own can sing his praise.
Sweet-tongu'd Arion, strive not with such odds,
Thy song mov'd but the dolphins : his the gods.
O hadst thou deign'd to move thy sweeter tongue,
The wolf had stay'd to hearken to thy song ;
Had Pan's ears suck'd the nectar of thy breath,
For thy sake Cælia had been free from death,
But that the Fates denied, as who should say
By Willy's pen her fame shall live for aye.

Walla a garland will compose no more
To crown her Tavy's temples as before ;
But as to them that best deserve the praise,
She'll give to thee the garland and the bays ;
And if a verse thy glory may confine,
Thou sing'st Britannia's praise, Britannia thine.

Jo. Dynham, è Coll. Exon.

Upon the Occasion of Reading this complete Poem.

TO THE AUTHOR W. BROWNE.

αὐτοχεδιαστικον :

1.

Cease, cease Pierian dames,
   Be henceforth mute ;
Leave of[a] your wanton games ;
   Apollo's lute
Hath crack'd a string : it grates my ears,
'Tis harsh, as are the heavenly spheres :
List ! Willie sings and tunes his oaten reed,
To whom all hearts, all ears do yield themselves as meed.

2.

Hark, hark, the jolly lad
   So sweetly sings,
The vales as proud, as glad
   The murmuring springs,
Both join to tell the neighbour hills
That there's no music like to Will's.
Echo enamour'd on the piping swain
Recovers (silly wretch !) her voice, repeats each strain.

[a] *Leave of,* desist from.

3.

The bucksome[a] shepherdess—
    Hark ! ha ! no more ?
Ah ! what unhappiness
    Was 't left us poor,
Bereft by thy neglected songs
Of life, of joy ! tell, tell what wrongs,
What sad disaster (Willie) is betide,
That we thy lays (not yet half done) should be denied ?

4.

What has some satyr rude,
    Wode[b] to those groves
His wily snares bestrew'd
    To catch your loves ?
To tempt a cred'lous shepherdess,
Who, crying out in her distress,
Has made you break or fling your pipe away,
Oh no ! your charms would erst have made the monster stay.

5.

Or is your pipe ybroke,
    And 'twill not sound ?
Go, go unto the oak
    By yonder mound :
Take Colin's[c] pipe (there 't hangs) in hand,
Or if not that you may command,
The whilom jolly swain's, Philisides.
But ah ! your broken pipe will sound as well as these.

6.

Has subtle Reynard caught
    A frisking lamb,
Or the fierce wolf distraught
    · The bleating dam

---

[a] *Bucksome*, blithe.   [b] *Wode*, went, or rather gone.
        [c] *Colin*, Spenser.

And you by rifling of their folds,
Which to regain your sport withholds?
Or has your lagging ewe a lambkin yean'd,[a]
Which makes you cease your notes, and midwif'ry attend?

7.

Or did some shepherd's boy
    (Thy lays are good,)
Nod 's head or pause and coy,
    He understood,
Not that it which he did so taunt
(If there were such), dull ignorant,
Or else despairing e'er to rise so high,
Would work thee, swain, from thy deserv'd supremacy.

8.

Did the round[b] yesterday,
    Which thou began'st
So merrily to play,
    Thou them entranc'st?
O[r] did they raise thy worth so high,
And made thee blush for modesty?
Did they with garlands girt thy curled locks,
Call'd thee fine piper, while thou look'st all grief, for mocks?

9.

And would th' had woo'd thee too,
    A second part,
'Cause from their promis'd vow
    They 'gan to start :
In which th' hadst bound their seely swain,
Nor to commend nor praise thy vein,
Yet when they did begin (and who could spare?)
Thou cruel tor'st thy chaplets, and wouldst willow wear.

  [a] *Yeaned,* brought forth.   [b] *Round,* dance.

10.

See, cruel fair, see, see
  Each shepherd's brow,
That wont to smile with glee,
  Is tear-swoll'n now;
And pris'ning up their pearly wealth,
The straggling drops get out by stealth;
Yet could they hope to win thee for their prize,
To finish up thy song they'd bankrupt all their eyes.

11.

The pretty birds were mute
  To hear thee sing;
And see the shepherd youth
  All wantoning,
When having ceas'd thy notes all fitty,[a]
They all reserv'd their mournful ditty.
Philomel, fearing 'tis her fate denies
Thy sweeter accents, falls into thy breast and dies.

12.

The winds, that erst were whist,[b]
  Begin to roar;
Each tree, your songs being miss'd,
  Skreeks[c] as before;
Each sprouting pansy in the mead
For grief begins to hang a head;
The weeping brook in grumbling tones glide[s] down,
Dimples its once sleek cheeks, and thanks you with a frown

13.

Come, come, let's hear your skill;
  Ne'er say you can't.
  What, are you angry still?
  By Pan, you sha'n't.

[a] *Fitty,* apt, clever.   [b] *Whist,* silent.   [c] *Skreeks,* creaks.

Ne'er let your modesty deprive
Y' of what will keep your name alive,
Whilst o'er the curl'd-hair'd-Tavy's flowery side
There does on[e] shepherd lodge or seely sheep abide.

14.

Oh let not nice conceit,
   You are too young,
That there are iands more feat[a]
   I' th' shepherds' throng,
Who better able are to distil
Their soul in sonnets at their will.
If still to me you be obdurate, then
Let sheep, birds, trees, winds, flowers, brooks, teach thee
   melt again.

          SAM. HARDINGE, è Coll. Exon.

To the now unparalleled Sidney of his time, W. B.,
the ingenuous Author of Britannia's Pastorals.

PLAY on thy pipe new lessons; Willy, strike
More such as these which may each shepherd like;
And if it chance Thetis do once again
Visit our coasts, be thou the elected swain
To greet her with thy lays; let her admire
The varying accents of thy matchless lyre,
And so affect thee for thy poems' sake,
Adopt thee hers, and thee her usher make.
But leave us not, blithe swain; let Tavy's stream
Leave of to murmur list'ning to thy theme,
Lest thy sweet lays so great effect obtain,
As here on land, so there upon the main,
As lasses here admir'd thy matchless verse,

[a] *Feat*, clever.

So there the sea-nymphs still thy praise rehearse,
"Twixt both a great contention it will breed,
Who hath most interest in thine oaten reed,
Which harder will appeased be than theirs
Who strove to be esteem'd the blind bard's heirs.
Those claim thee theirs in that thou dost forsake
Thy native cotes,[a] and there thy mansion make ;
The lambkins here did frisk to hear thee play,
Less nourish'd by their grass than with thy lay ;
So would the dolphins then attend thy song,
And none left Triton whom to ride upon,
Which might incense him seeing one the fry,
And vaster shoals pressing to come most nigh,
To hear thy melody, and to refuse
His trumpet's sounds, to which they still did use
Before to throng, to pray thee do not come,
But sweetly pipen at thy native home.
Continue still with us, and let our vales
Reverberate in echo thy sweet tales.

CHR. GEWEN, è Coll. Exon.

An Ode entreating him to proceed in the continuation of his Brittaunia's Pastorals.

WILLY, see but how the swains
Mourn thy silence on the plains,
And do sadly pace along,
'Cause they cannot hear thy song ;
Roget[b] grieves : these notes would hear
Fain which ravish'd erst his ear,
And to hear thy song alway
In his prison would he stay

[a] *Cotes*, cottages.

[b] *Roget*, George Wither, who was imprisoned in the Marshalsea for his satire *Abuses Stript and Whipt* (1613).

With most willingness than be
Depriv'd thereof, though set free.
He and Cuddy,[a] that blithe swain,
Whose flocks feed on yonder plain,
Would be glad their skill to try
At your opportunity,
And though sent to be one tome,
They would undergo thy doom,
And be glad to yield to thee,
To whom is due all victory.
'Tis their wish each place could tell
Thy conquests like Saint Dunstan's well,
And that thy pipe would sound so well,
As 't whilom did in thick[b] same dell.
Doridon mourns 'cause his sweet
Guided is not by thy feet
To her haven of wish'd joy,
But is left to all annoy
By thy cruelty ; he fears
Lest by this she's drown'd in tears.
Old swains would die, could they have
Thee but write upon their grave
Sith afford thou wilt not all
Once to hear thy pastoral.
Each shepherdess doth lament,
'Cause thou art their discontent,
And had it been another lad
Which their wakes[c] thus hinder'd had
They'd revenge it, and with speed
Discard his silent oaten reed,
But thy former lays have got
Thee praises ne'er to be forgot,

[a] *Cuddy*, Christopher Brooke.
[b] *Thick*, this.
[c] *Wakes*, village festivals, properly on the dedication day
of the church.

Therefore they forbear to spoil
Thy pipe which hath given the foil
To opposers ; nor would be
Cruel to thy pipe or thee.
All the swains are yonder set
On the hillock, and are met
To celebrate Pan's festival
With some pleasing madrigal ;
But they're dumb, and so will be,
'Less that thou augment their glee ;
For their custom 's at this feast,
Here 'mongst shepherds that the best
Must begin, and then each one
Follows till they all have done.
Why dost then thy music linger,
And suppress theirs ? they would finger
Willingly their pipes ; they stay
But till thou thy lesson play.
Hie thee, Willy, hie apace,
With all speed to the place
Where the shepherds are set round,
Waiting there till thy pipe sound
At thy tuning ; when thy lay
Thou hast ended, they will play ;
For which art brave Thetis shall
Crown with praise thy madrigal,
And Pan himself shall always be
A patron to thy Muse and thee,
When that he knows in this her matchless lay
Thy Muse keeps his, not her own holiday.

B. N.

To the Author, W. B.

R IVERS, be silent ; peace, you Muses nine ;
O rpheus, be dumb, for now no praise is thine ;
B end all your ears unto Britannia's peer,
E ver be praising, ne'er to praise him fear.

R ight as the painters garnish with their sable[a]
'l' heir brighter colours in a curious table,[b]
T ime so will place thee in the shield of fame,
A s chief of men t' immortalize thy name.
Y et why should I with rude rhymes seek to raise thee ?
L et every sonnet in thy Pastorals praise thee.
O dasht[c] Apollo, hide thy face for shame,
R ender to shepherds henceforth all the fame.

è Coll. Exon.

On the Author, W. B.

SHALL I implore the Muses nine,
To grace with sweets my ruder line,
When all the arts the Muses can
Are sweetly sung within this span?
Or shall I invocate great Pan
To tune the song thy pipe best can ?
Pan swore to me the other day
He broke his pipe, and ran to hear thy lay.
Apollo, lend thy sacred quill,
That I may chant a note more shrill.
Alas ! Apollo's drown'd in tears,
To see a god o'errule his spheres.
Let's see what golden Spenser can ;
He's dead, and thou the living man.
The god, I see, can wear no bays
But what is pluck'd from thy bright lays.
If Pan a song more smoother sings,
'Tis 'cause 'twas dipp'd in Tavy's springs.

RO. TAYLER, Exon. Coll.

[a] *Sable*, dark.   [b] *Table*, picture.   [c] *Dasht*, abashed.

To the unparalleled Author of the sequent Poems,
W. B.

HAIL, Albion's swain, whose worthy brow those bays,
G'en to the victor in Pan's pastoral plays,
Ere since thy pipe's first birth have bound, whose tongue
Our loves on once lov'd Syrinx freely sung.
When mountains' heads and storm-wrong'd shrubs did cast
Their long shades westward, and when shepherds haste
To 'nbed their pended[a] flocks, how oft among
The various sonnets of a neighbouring throng
Hast thou enchanted with a strong desire
To learn thy accents great Sylvanus' quire,
Who, like young infants willing to obtain
Their nurses' dialect and perfect strain,
Labour'd a repetition ; here the thrush
Strove with his whistle ; in next bord'ring bush,
Shrouded about, was the small redbreast set,
With list'ning ears, and unwilling to let
Nought pass, turn'd echo to thy tunes ; above,
The soaring lark did meditating move
Her gutling[b] tongue ; but each in vain ; at last,
Though out of tune, proud Philomel's distaste
To hear a rival did dispose the choice
Of nat'ral notes into an artlike voice.
Thy heavenly harmony sounding below,
Among the vales, the river gods did draw
Above their streams, shaking their silver hair ;
Then lifted up, the anthems seem'd more rare ;
Rap'd[c] with such music their cold monarchy
Abandon'd straight, they mounted up on high,

[a] *Pended*, penned, or enclosed in a sheep-pen.
[b] *Gutling*, greedy, eager : here used as an adjective.
[c] *Rap'd*, ravished.

There stood attentive all, as if upon
Parnassus' top, Apollo's station,
He harping lay, and with smooth Mercury
Had shar'd the spheres by better melody.
Thus long in admiration of both lays,
They gave the sentence, thou obtain'st the praise,
And with insinuation did entreat
That Tavy's banks might be thy frequent seat :
They had their will, thou yield'st a loath consent,
Thy winds must calm their swelling element,
And hear the water-nymphs e'er since that time.
We hinds, remembering thy mellifluous rhyme,
Covet to drive our cherelie[a] flocks along
That crystal lake to hear thy wonted song,
That song which metamorphos'd raping[b] bears,
And train'd the crafty fox into her snares.
The happier Fates had favour'd fair Marine,
Had thy lips woo'd for her her Celandine ;
If Remond could persuade as thou canst move,
Had chang'd to hate that beauty's disdain'd love ;
Nor had the labour of a deity
Needed to quicken her mortality,
Thy charming voice had done 't ; for thy song's sake
Charon had wherried from the Stygian lake
Again her ghost ; nor hath thy peerless verse
Done less, thou must immortalize thy herse.
Thou'st quite forsook Pan's sports, the more the grief,
His joy the more, thou absent, he's the chief ;
We've lost thy fellowship, not lost thy fame,
We'll teach our children to adore thy name.
When as our Cornish or Devonian swains
Still sport among their lambkins on the plains,
Or celebrate their festivals, we'll raise
Our old reed once to Pan's, twice to thy praise ;

    [a] *Cherelie*, cheerful.
    [b] *Raping*, ravening.

And when great Jove thy soul angelical
Shall summon us to sing thy madrigal,
Our . . . . shall want their tallow, but we'll burn
Continual candles on thy lasting urn.

NICH. DOWNEY, Coll. Exon.

Idem ad Eundem.

AN ODE.

I HEARD the mountain gods complain,
Sweet Willy, thou neglects thy strain,
And that thou wouldst not bless again
        Thy fellow swain.

The sisters did bewail,
That he whose notes did oft assail
Apollo's skill, yea, did prevail,
        Their art disdains.

What if some forward stub-chinn'd boy
Takes up a reed, and does employ
His artless lips, can this annoy
        Thy sweeter song ?

Could thy exactness brook a foil,
Without disparagement ; their soil
Commends thy tongue more smooth than oil,
        Our sports among.

Great Pan e'er since thou went'st away
Has miss'd the glories of his day ;
No shepherd dares begin a lay
        To honour him.

Behold how all our joys do turn
To sadness, see hot sighs which burn
Our breasts, look how our swoll'n eyes mourn
      And weep till dry.

Our crooks are trail'd along the ground,
Our pipes grow dumb, or sadly sound ;
No flow'ry chaplets e'er hath crown'd
      Since thine a brow.

Each shepherdess, as in despair,
Mean more to be proclaimed fair,
Th' fit time to trim her fluent hair
      Doth scarce allow.

Our lambs do leave to skip about,
And ape their dams' sad pace throughout
The hills with woes, as if they doubt
      Security.

Now thou art absent, whose smooth reed
Did in the wolves and tigers breed
A nature tame, and thus them freed
      From cruelty.

Each Muse, god, sheep, and shepherds all,
Join in the art thy madrigal ;
For Pan's sake at thy festival
      Renew thy strains.

Why should that spright which soar'd so high
Above the ken of emulous eye,
Ere Doridon be finish'd, die,
      And shun our plains?

                N. D. Ex. Coll.

On the Author of Britannia's Matchless (though unfinish'd) Pastorals.

1.

Look how the dying swan on Tagus' shore,
  Singing a lullably to her last sleep,
Ties to her golden tongue the leaping ore,
  And binds th' ashamed water-nymphs to keep
    Eternal silence, whilst the dumb waves stay,
    And dare not with their murmuring pebbles play,
Or through the whistling rushes take their wonted way :

2.

Look how the gentle breath of southern gales,
  Buzzing their tunes amongst the querulous reeds,
Or whispering music to the sounding vales,
  In all the aëry nation envy breeds,
    And into sleep the lazy grooms[a] doth rock,
    Or calls th' amazed shepherd from his flock,
And prompts the straining echo of the neighbouring rock :

3.

So sat our noble Willy, happy swain,
  With peerless songs encroaching sorrow drowning,
And Tavy's curled locks (who danc'd amain
  Unto his pipe) with bays immortal crowning ;
    The whilst the woods their leafy heads inclin'd,
    In list'ning wise, and mix'd their envious wind
With those more heavenly airs which in his voice they find.

4.

Once when the jolly lad began a lay
  Of his Marina's fate, the wond'ring rout[b]
Of neighbouring swains, leaving their wonted play,
  Ran to encircle their new Pan about,
    Where grown forgetful of their former care,
    Although they fed on nought but his sweet air,
Vow'd that the quintessence of nectar was their fare.

a *Grooms*, servants.   b *Rout*, company.

5.

And as their captive souls were chain'd unto
  The charming pipe ; when they it least suspected,
The smiles and winks which forth did steal, would show
  How much that loved sound they all respected,
    And all amaz'd in a deep ecstasy
    Would swear he was some chorister of the sky,
Or (though their eyes said no) Phœbus' own deity.

Each peerless nymph that bathes her dewy curls
  In too too happy Tavy's crystal waves,
Into the singing, echoing champion hurls,
  And there our Willy's head with flow'rs embraves,*
    Robs her own banks, and decks a coronet
    With blushing roses and the violet,
Which on the head of her admired swain is set.

7.

The merry emulous songsters of the wood
  In silence listen'd to his better song,
And the soft murmurs of the bubbling flood
  (Which seem'd to laugh as he did ride along)
    Presum'd to bear the burthen of his lay,
    The whilst the jocund satyrs all would say
They were not half so blest even on Pan's holiday.

8.

But midst these thankful shouts and signs of joy,
  Whilst all expect to see a happy close,
Upon the sudden starts the peevish boy,
  And runs away in haste as from his foes :
    Nor can our speaking sighs, and begging tears,
    Nor all our prayers and plaints he daily hears,
Or melt his stubborn heart, or banish his vain fears.

* *Embraves*, adorns.

9.

So, when as Philomel her hapless fate
  Unto the tell-tale echo doth bemoan,
The whilst some envious bough presents in hate
  A dagger to her breast, and there is none
    That praises not her music's heavenly grace,
    The bashful bird with leaves doth veil her face,
Or to her shroud and tomb, some thicket, flies apace.

10.

And now he haunts the woods and silent groves,
  (Poor lad) and teaches silence to the winds ;
H' has now forgot our sports and harmless loves.
  Ah ! can such deeds agree with heavenly minds ?
    Great flakes of moss, bred in some silent cave,
    Stop his pipe's mouth, and now his spirit leave,
Now a dead soul entomb'd within a living grave.

11.

But, Willy boy, let not eternal sleep
  Captive thy sprightly Muse ; so shall we all
Rejoice at her new life, and henceforth keep
  Unto thy name a yearly festival ;
    May she but imp[a] her wings with thy blest pen,
    And take her wonted flight, heaven says Amen,
The music of the spheres shall ne'er be heard again.

12.

So may a sunshine day smile on our sports,
  So may the pretty lambs live free from harm,
So may the tender lass that here resorts
  Ne'er feel the clownish winds' cold boist'rous arm.
    As we do love thee, Willy, as we all
    Do wistly[b] for thy peerless music call,
And as we plait for thee a matchless coronal.

PERIGOT.

[a] *Imp*, in hawking, to insert a new feather in the place of
a broken one ; often used metaphorically.
[b] *Wistly*, wistfully.

BRITANNIA'S PASTORALS.

THE THIRD BOOK.

THE FIRST SONG.

The Argument is wanting.

THRICE had the pale-fac'd Cynthia fill'd her horns,
And through the circling zodiac, which adorns
Heaven's goodly frame, the horses of the sun
A fourth part of their race had fiercely run,
Since fair Marina left her gentle flock ;   5
Whose too untimely loss the watchful cock
No oft'ner gave a summons to the day,
Then some kind shepherd on the fertile ley

8.—*Ley*, lea, meadow.

Took a sad seat, and, with a drowned eye,
Bemoan'd in heart far more than elegy.   10

Here sits a shepherd whose mellifluous tongue
On shaded banks of rivers whilom sung
Many sweet lays to her harmonious ear;
Recounting former joys, when she liv'd there,
With present woes, and every pleasure gone   15
Tells with a hundred tears, and, those drops done,
A thousand sighs ensue, and gives not o'er
Until he faints, and so can sigh no more.
    Yonder, another, on some swelling hill,
Records her sweet praise to a gentle rill   20
Which, in requital, takes no little pain
To roll her silver sands up to the swain ;
And almost wept that time would not permit
That beauteous maid to bathe herself in it ;
Whose touch made streams, and men, and plants
        more proud   25
Than he that clasp'd the Juno-seeming cloud.
    Amongst the rest (that ere the sun did shine
Sought the thick groves) neglectful Celadyne
Was come abroad ; and underneath a tree
Dead as his joys, and from all moisture free   30
As were the fountains of his lovely eyes,
With lavish weeping, discontented lies.

26.—*Juno-seeming cloud*, an allusion to the fable of Ixion
Ovid, *Met.* iv. 465, x. 42).
28.—*Celadyne*, called "Celandine " in the First Book.

Now, like a prodigal, he minds in vain
What he hath lost, and cannot lose again.
Now thinks he on her eyes, like some sad wight,   35
Which new struck blind bemoans the want of light.
Her cheeks, her lips, to mind he doth recall,
As one in exile clean bereav'd of all.
Her modest graces, her affection more,
That wounds him most which only can restore.   40
And lastly to his pipe (which woods nor plains
Acquainted not, but with the saddest strains,
Yet he more sad than song or places can)
Varied his plaints, and thus anew began :—

    Marina's gone, and now sit I,   45
      As Philomela (on a thorn,
    Turn'd out of nature's livery),
      Mirthless, alone, and all forlorn:
    Only she sings not, while my sorrows can
    Breathe forth such notes as fit a dying swan. 50

    So shuts the marigold her leaves
      At the departure of the sun ;
    So from the honeysuckle sheaves
      The bee goes when the day is done ;
    So sits the turtle when she is but one,   55
    And so all woe, as I, since she is gone.

    To some few birds, kind Nature hath
      Made all the summer as one day ;

Which once enjoy'd, cold winter's wrath,
   As night, they sleeping pass away.   60
Those happy creatures are, that know not yet
The pain to be depriv'd or to forget.

I oft have heard men say there be
   Some, that with confidence profess
The helpful Art of Memory ;   65
   But could they teach forgetfulness,
I'd learn, and try what further art could do,
To make me love her and forget her too.

Sad melancholy, that persuades
   Men from themselves, to think they be   70
Headless, or other bodies' shades,
   Hath long and bootless dwelt with me ;
For could I think she some idea were,
I still might love, forget, and have her here.

But such she is not : nor would I,   75
   For twice as many torments more,
As her bereavèd company
   Hath brought to those I felt before,
For then no future time might hap to know
That she deserv'd, or I did love her so.   80

Ye hours, then, but as minutes be !
(Though so I shall be sooner old)

> Till I those lovely graces see,
>   Which, but in her, can none behold ;
> Then be an age ! that we may never try   85
> More grief in parting, but grow old and die.

Here ceas'd the shepherd's song, but not his woe ;
Grief never ends itself.   And he doth know
Nothing but time or wisdom to allay it ;
Time could not then ; the other should not stày it. 90

Thus sits the hapless swain : now sighs, now sings :
Sings, sighs, and weeps at once.   Then from the
    springs
Of pity begs his pardon.   Then his eye,
Wronging his oraisons, some place hard by
Informs his intellect, where he hath seen .   95
His mistress feed her flock, or on the green
Dance to the merry pipe : this drives him thence
As one, distracted with the violence
Of some hot fever, casts his clothes away,
Longs for the thing he loath'd but yesterday,   100
And fondly thinking 'twill his fits appease,
Changeth his bed, but keeps still the disease.
Quitting the plains to seek the gloomy springs,
He, like a swan that on Meander sings,
Takes congey of his mates with ling'ring haste, 105
To find some stream where he may sing his last.

105.—*Congey*, farewell.

So have I left my Tavy's flow'ry shore,
Far-flowing Thamesis, and many more
Attractive pleasures which sweet England yields,
Her peopled cities and her fertile fields,   110
For Amphitrite's plains; those hath mine eye
Chang'd for our whilom fields of Normandy;
For Seine those have I left; for Loire, the Seine:
And for the Thoüé changed Loire again;
Where to the nymphs of Poitou now I sing   115
A stranger note (yet such as ev'ry spring
Rolls smiling to attend): for none of those
Yet have I lessen'd or exchang'd my woes.
Dear, dearest isle, from thee I pass'd away
But as a shadow, when the eye of day   120
Shines otherwhere; for she whose I have been,
By her declining makes me live unseen.
Nor do I hope that any other light
Can make me her's; the pallid queen of night
And Venus, or some err, may with their rays   125
Force an observing shade; but none of these,
Meteors to my set sun, can ever have
That power thou hadst.   Sweet soul, thy silent
     grave
I give my best verse, if a shepherd's wit
Can make a dead hand capable of it.   130
Chaste were our loves, as mutual; nor did we
Hardly dream otherwise; our secrecy
Such as I think the world hath never known
I had a mistress, till that I had none.

Poor Celadyne and I (but happier he)   135
Only in dreams meet our felicity ;
Our joys but shadows are ; our constant woes
The day shows real ; O, unhappy those,
Thrice, thrice unhappy, who are ever taking   [140
Their joys in sleep, but are most wretched waking !

Seated at last near Tavy's silver stream,
Sleep seiz'd our shepherd ; and in sleep a dream
Show'd him Marina all bedew'd with tears :
Pale as the lily of the field appears,   [145
When the unkiss'd morn from the mountains' tops
Sees the sweet flow'rs distil their silver drops.
She seem'd to take him by the hand and say :
O Celadyne, this, this is not the way
To recompense the wrong which thou hast done
And I have pardon'd, since it was begun   150
To exercise my virtue ; I am thine
More than I wish'd, or thou canst now divine.
Seek out the aged Lama, by whose skill
Thou may'st our fortunes know, and what the
     will
Of fate is in thy future.   This she spoke,   155
And seem'd to kiss him, wherewith he awoke,—
And missing what (in thought) his sleep had
     gain'd,
He mus'd, sigh'd, wept, and lastly thus complain'd :
     Vain dreams, forbear ! ye but deceivers be,
For as in flatt'ring glasses women see   160

More beauty than possess'd : so I in you
Have all I can desire, but nothing true.
  Who would be rich, to be so but an hour,
Eats a sweet fruit to relish more the sour.
If but to lose again we things possess,   165
Ne'er to be happy is a happiness.
  Men walking in the pitchy shades of night
Can keep their certain way ; but if a light
O'ertake and leave them, they are blinded more,
And doubtful go that went secure before.   170
For this (though hardly) I have oft forborne
To see her face, fair as the rosy morn ;
Yet mine own thoughts in night such traitors be,
That they betray me to that misery.
Then think no more of her—as soon I may   175
Command the sun to rob us of a day,
Or with a net repel a liquid stream,
As lose such thoughts, or hinder but a dream.
  The lightsome air as eas'ly hinder can
A glass to take the form of any man   180
That stands before it, as or time or place
Can draw a veil between me and her face.
  Yet, by such thoughts my torments hourly thrive ;
For (as a pris'ner by his perspective)
By them I am inform'd of what I want ;   185
I envy now none but the ignorant.
He that ne'er saw her (O, too happy wight !)
Is one born blind that knows no want of light ;
He that ne'er kiss'd her lips, yet sees her eyes,

Lives, while he lives so, still in paradise ;   190
But if he taste those sweets as hapless I,
He knows his want, and meets his misery.
   An Indian rude that never heard one sing
A heav'nly sonnet to a silver string,
Nor other sounds, but what confused herds   195.
In pathless deserts make, or brooks or birds,
Should he hear one the sweet pandora touch,
And lose his hearing straight ; he would as much
Lament his knowledge as do I my chance,
And wish he still had liv'd in ignorance.   200
   I am that Indian ; and my soothing dreams
In thirst have brought me but to painted streams,
Which not allay, but more increase desire :
A man, near frozen with December's ire,
Hath, from a heap of glowworms, as much ease 205
As I can ever have by dreams as these.
   O leave me then ! and strongest memory
Keep still with those that promise-breakers be.
Go, bid the debtor mind his payment day,
Or help the ignorant devout to say   210
Prayers they understand not ; lead the blind,
And bid ingrateful wretches call to mind
Their benefactors ; and if Virtue be
(As still she is) trod on by misery,

197.—*Pandora*, or pandore, a stringed instrument of the
cither kind, invented in England, and popular at the beginning
of the seventeenth century.

Show her the rich, that they may free her want,   215
And leave to nurse the fawning sycophant ;
Or, if thou see fair honour careless lie,
Without a tomb for after memory,
Dwell by the grave, and teach all those that pass
To imitate, by showing who it was.   220
   This way, Remembrance, thou may'st do some
       good,
And have due thanks ; but he that understood
The throes thou bring'st on me, would say I miss
The sleep of him that did the pale moon kiss,
And that it were a blessing thrown on me,   225
Sometimes to have the hated lethargy.
   Then, dark Forgetfulness, that only art
The friend of lunatics, seize on that part
Of memory which hourly shows her me !
Or suffer still her waking fantasy,   230
Even at the instant when I dream of her,
To dream the like of me ! so shall we err
In pleasure's endless maze without offence,
And both connex as souls in innocence.

   His sorrow this way yet had further gone,   235
For now his soul, all in confusion,
Discharg'd her passions on all things she met,
And, rather than on none, on counterfeit.
For in her suff'rings she will sooner frame
Subjects fantastical, forms without name,   240

234.—*Connex*, join together.

Deceive itself against her own conceit,
Then want to work on somewhat thought of weight.
Hence comes it, those affections which are tied
To an enforced bed, a worthless bride,
(Wanting a lawful hold) our loving part   245
To subjects of less worth doth soon convert
Her exercise, which should be nobly free,
Rather on dogs, or dice, than idle be.
    Thus on his memory, poor soul, he cast
His exclamations ; and the day had pass'd   250
With him as sadly as his sighs were true,
And on this subject.   When (as if he flew)
Leap'd from a near grove (as he thought) a man,
And to th' adjoining wood as quickly ran ;   [255
This stay'd his thoughts.   And, whilst the other
        fled,
He rose, scarce knowing why, and followed.
    It was a gentle swain, on whose sweet youth
Fortune had thrown her worst, and all men's ruth ;
Who, like a satyr now, from men's abode
The uncouth paths of gloomy deserts trod ;   260
Deep, sullen vales, that never mercy won,
To have a kind look from the pow'rful sun ;
But mantled up in shades as fearful night,
Could merry hearts with awful terror smite.
Sad nooks and dreadful clefts of mighty rocks   265
That knew no guest within their careless locks,

266.—*Locks*, cavities.

But baneful serpents, hated beasts of prey,
And fatal fowl, that from the blessed day
Hid their abhorred heads ; these, only these,
Were his companions and his cottages.   270
    Wayfaring man, for aftertimes y-bore,
Whoe'er thou be, that on the pleasant shore
Of my dear Tavy hap'st to tread along,
When Willy sings no more his rural song,
But long dissolv'd to dust, shall hardly have   275
A tear or verse bestow'd upon his grave—
Think on that hapless lad, for all his meed,
Who first this lay tun'd to an oaten reed ;
Then ask the swains who, in the valleys deep,
Sing lays of love and feed their harmless sheep, 280
Ask them for Ramsham (late a gallant wood
Whose gaudy nymphs, tripping beside the flood,
Allur'd the sea-gods from their brackish strands
To court the beauties of the upper lands) ;
And near to it, halfway, a high-brow'd hill,   285
Whose maiden sides ne'er felt a coulter's ill,
Thou may'st behold, and (if thou list) admire
An arched cave cut in a rock entire,
Deep, hollow, hideous, overgrown with grass,
With thorns and briars, and sad mandragoras :   290
Poppy and henbane thereby grew so thick,

The Description of the Den of Oblivion.

281.—*Ramsham*, near Tavistock on the Tavy, not far from
Shilla Mill, in Crowndale.
    286.—*Coulter*, ploughshare.
    290.—*Mandragoras*, mandrakes.

That had the earth been thrice as lunatic
As learn'd Copernicus in sport would frame her,
We there had sleepy simples found to tame her.
    The entrance to it was of brick and stone, 295
Brought from the ruin'd tower of Babylon.
On either side the door a pillar stood,
Whereon of yore, before the general flood,
Industrious Seth in characters did score
The mathematics' soul-enticing lore. 300
    Cheek-swoll'n Lyæus near one pillar stood,
And from each hand a bunch, full with the blood
Of the care-killing vine, he crushed out,
Like to an artificial water-spout;
But of what kind it was, the writers vary: 305
Some say 'twas claret, others swear canary.
On th' other side, a statue strangely fram'd,
And never till Columbus' voyage nam'd,
The Genius of America blew forth
A fume that hath bewitched all the north. 310
    A noise of ballad-makers, rhymers, drinkers,
Like a mad crew of uncontrolled tinkers,
Lay there, and drunk, and sung, and suck'd, and
       writ
Verse without measure, volumes without wit;
Complaints and sonnets, vows to young Cupido, 315
May be in such a manner as now I do.
    He that in some fair day of summer sees
A little commonwealth of thrifty bees
Send out a pretty colony, to thrive

Another where, from their too-peopled hive, 320
And marks the young adventurers with pain
Fly off and on, and forth, and back again,
May well conceive with how much labour these
Drunk, writ, and wrong'd the learn'd Pierides ;
Yet time, as soon as e'er their works were
        done, 325
Threw them and it into oblivion.
   Into this cave the forlorn shepherd enters,
And Celadyne pursues ; yet ere he venters
On such an obscure place, knowing the danger
Which oft betided there the careless stranger, 330
Moly or such preservative he takes,
And thus assur'd, breaks through the tangling brakes ;
Searcheth each nook to find the hapless swain,
And calls him oft, yet seeks and calls in vain.
   At last, by glimm'ring of some glowworms
        there, 335
He finds a dark hole and a winding stair ;
Uncouth and hideous the descent appears,
Yet, unappall'd with future chance or fears,
Essays the first step, and goes boldly on ;
Pieces of rotten wood on each side shone, 340
Which, rather than to guide his vent'rous pace,
With a more dreadful horror fill'd the place.
Still he descends, and many a step doth make,

324.—*Pierides*, Muses.
328.—*Venters*, ventures.
331.—*Moly*, a fabulous herb of magic power.

As one whose naked foot treads on a snake :
The stairs so worn, he feareth in a trice   345
To meet some deep and deadly precipice.
   Thus came he down into a narrow vault,
Whose rocky sides (free from the smallest fault,
Enforc'd by age or weather) and the roof
Stood firmly strong and almost thunder-proof.   350
'Twas long ; and at the far-off further end
A little lamp he spies, as he had kenn'd
One of the fixed stars ; the light was small,
And distance made it almost nought at all.   [355
'Tow'rds it he came, and, from the swain which fled,
These verses fall'n took up, went near and read :

   Listen ! ye gentle winds, to my sad moan ;
And, mutt'ring brooks, attend my heavy plaints.
Ye melodists, which in the low groves sing,
Strive with your fellows for sweet skill no more, 360
But wail with me ! and if my song ye pass
For dreary notes, match with the nightingale.
Henceforward with the rueful nightingale
No other but sad groves shall hear my moan,
And night bear witness of my doleful plaints.   365
Sweet songs of love let others quaintly sing,
For fate decrees I shall be known no more
But by my woes.   All pleasures from me pass,
As gliding torrents to the ocean pass,
Ne'er to come back.   The all-voice nightingale 370
Comforts her fellows, and makes dear her moan ;

But (where I would) regardless are my plaints,
And but for echo should unanswer'd sing ;
Can there in others be affection more
Than is in me, yet be neglected more ?   375
Then such neglect and love shall no man pass.
For voice she well may mate the nightingale,
And from her syren's song I learn'd to moan ;
Yet she, as most imperfect deems my plaints,
Though too too long I them have us'd to sing,   380
Yet to no happier key she lets me sing.
Shall I then change ? O, there are others more
(As I hear shepherds wailing, when I pass
In deserts wild to hear the nightingale)
Whose ears receive no sound of any moan,   385
But hear their praises rather than our plaints.
Then since to flint I still address my plaints,
And my sad numbers to a deaf ear sing,
My cries shall beat the subtile air no more,
But all my woes imprison ; and so pass   390
The poor rest of my days.   No nightingale
Shall be disturb'd in forests with my moan.
And when through inpent moan I hide my plaints,
And what I should sing makes me live no more,
Tell her my woes did pass the nightingale.   395

    Sad swain, quoth Celadyne, whoe'er thou be,
I grieve not at my pains to follow thee ;
Thou art a fit companion for my woe,
Which hearts sunk into misery should know.

O, if thou hear me, speak : take to thy home !   400
Receive into this dismal living tomb
A sorrow-laden wretch ! one that would die
And tread the gloomy shades of destiny
Only to meet a soul that could relate
A story true as his and passionate !   405
  By this a sad and heavy sound began
To fill the cave ; and by degrees he wan
So near, he heard a well-accorded lute,
Touch'd by a hand had struck the Thracian mute.
  Had it been heard when sweet Amphion's tones
Gave motion to the dull and senseless stones ;   [410
When, at the notes his skilful fingers warble,
The pebble took the flint, the flint the marble ;
And rolling from the quarry justly fall,
And masonless built Cadmus' town* a wall.   415 * Thebes.
Each one each other to this labour woo,
And were the workmen and materials too.
Had this man play'd when t' other touch'd his
    lyre,
Those stones had from the wall been seen retire ;
Or stopp'd half-way to hear him striking thus,   420
Though each had been a stone of Sisyphus.
Nay, the musician had his skill approv'd,
And been as ravish'd as the rocks he mov'd.
  Celadyne listen'd ; and the arched skies
Might wish themselves as many ears as eyes,   425
That they might teach the star-bestudded spheres
A music new, and more divine than theirs.

To these sad-sweet strings, as e'er woe befriended,
This verse was married :—

  Yet one day's rest for all my cries !   430
   One hour amongst so many !
  Springs have their sabbaths ; my poor eyes
   Yet never met with any.

  He that doth but one woe miss,
   O Death, to make him thine ;   435
  I would to God that I had his,
   Or else that he had mine !

  By this sad wish we two should have
   A fortune and a wife ;
  For I should wed a peaceful grave, 440
   And he a happy life.

  Yet let that man whose fortunes swim
   So high by my sad woe,
  Forbear to tread a step on him
   That died to make them so.   445

  Only to acquit my foes,
   Write this where I am lain :
  Here lies the man whom others' woes
   And those he lov'd have slain.

—— —— Here the music ended.   450
But Celadyne leaves not his pious quest ;
For, as an artist curiously address'd

To some conclusion, having haply found
A small encouragement on his first ground,
Goes cheerful on ; nor from it can be won,   455
Till he have perfected what he begun :
So he pursues, and labours all he can,
Since he had heard the voice, to find the man.
  A little door, at last, he in the side
Of the long-stretched entry had descried,   460
And coming to it with the lamp, he spies
These lines upon a table writ :—

   Love ! when I met her first whose slave I am,
   To make her mine,. why had I not thy flame ?
     Or else thy blindness not to see that day ?   465
   Or if I needs must look on her rare parts,
   Love ! why to wound her had I not thy darts,
     Since I had not thy wings to fly away ?

   Winter was gone ; and by the lovely spring
     Each pleasant grove a merry quire became, 470
   Where day and night the careless birds did sing,
     Love, when I met her first whose slave I am.

   She sat and listen'd (for she lov'd his strain)
     To one whose songs could make a tiger tame ;
   Which made me sigh, and cry, O happy swain ! 475
     To make her mine, why had I not thy flame ?

   I vainly sought my passion to control :
     And therefore (since she loves the learned lay),

Homer, I should have brought with me thy soul,
　　Or else thy blindness, not to see that day !   480

Yet would I not (mine eyes) my days outrun
　　In gazing (could I help it, or the arts),
Like him that died with looking on the sun ;
　　Or if I needs must, look on her rare parts !

Those, seen of one who every herb would try, 485
　　And what the blood of elephants imparts
To cool his flame, yet would he (forced) cry,
　　Love ! why to wound her had I not thy darts ?

O Dædalus ! the lab'rinth fram'd by thee
　　Was not so intricate as where I stray ;　　　490
There have I lost my dearest liberty,
　　Since I had not thy wings to fly away.

————His eyes,
And still attentive ears, do now discover
Sufficient cause to think some hapless lover　　495
Inhabited this dark and sullen cell,
Where none but shame or dismal grief would dwell.
　　As I have seen a fowler, by the floods
In winter time, or by the fleeced woods,
Steal softly, and his steps full often vary,　　500
As here and there flutters the wished quarry ;
Now with his heel, now with his toe he treads,
Fearing the crackling of the frozen meads ;
Avoids each rotten stick near to his foot,

And creeps, and labours thus to get a shoot :   505
So Celadyne approaches near the door,
Where sighs amaz'd him as the lute before ;
Sighs fetch'd so deep, they seem'd of pow'r to carry
A soul fit for eternity to marry.
   Had Dido stood upon her cliffs and seen   510
Ilium's Æneas stealing from a queen,
And spent her sighs as pow'rful as were these,
She had enforc'd the fair Nereides
To answer hers ; those had the Naiads won,
To drive his winged pine round with the sun,   515
And long ere Drake (without a fearful wrack)
Girdled the world, and brought the wand'rer back.
   Celadyne gently somewhat oped the door,
And by a glimm'ring lamp upon the floor
Descried a pretty curious rocky cell ;   520
A spout of water in one corner fell
Out of the rock upon a little wheel,
Which speedy as it could the water feel
Did, by the help of other engines lent,
Set soon on work a curious instrument,   525
Whose sound was like the hollow, heavy flute,
Join'd with a deep, sad, sullen cornemute.
This had the unknown shepherd set to play

505.—*Shoot*, shot.
517.—*Girdled*, circumnavigated ; *cf.* Shakespeare,—
      " I'll put a girdle round about the earth
       In forty minutes."
Midsummer's Night's Dream, Act II. Sc. i.
527.—*Cornemute*, a rustic instrument, blown like a bagpipe.

Such a soul-thrilling note, that if that day
Celadyne had not seen this uncouth youth   530
Descend the cave, he would have sworn for truth
That great Apollo, slid down from his sphere,
Did use to practise all his lessons there.
    Upon a couch the music's master lay;
And whilst the handless instrument did play   535
Sad heavy accents to his woes as deep,
To woo him to an everlasting sleep,
Stretch'd carelessly upon his little bed,
His eyes fix'd on the floor, his careful head
Leaning upon his palm, his voice but faint,   540
Thus to the sullen cave made his complaint :

    Fate ! yet at last be merciful.   Have done !
Thou canst ask nothing but confusion :
Take then thy fill ! strike till thine edge be dull !
Thy cruelty will so be pitiful.   545
He that at once hath lost his hopes and fears
Lives not, but only tarries for more years !
Much like an aged tree which moisture lacks,
And only standeth to attend the axe.
So have, and so do I : I truly know   550
How men are born, and whither they shall go ;
I know that like to silkworms of one year,
Or like a kind and wronged lover's tear,
Or on the pathless waves a rudder's dint,
Or like the little sparkles of a flint,   555
Or like to thin round cakes with cost perfum'd,

Or fireworks only made to be consum'd ;
I know that such is man, and all that trust
In that weak piece of animated dust.
The silkworm droops, the lover's tears soon shed, 560
The ship's way quickly lost, the sparkle dead ;
The cake burns out in haste, the firework's done,
And man as soon as these as quickly gone.

Day hath her night ; millions of years shall be
Bounded at last by long eternity.   565
The roses have their spring, they have their fall,
So have the trees, beasts, fowl, and so have all ;
The rivers run and end : stars rise and set ;
There is a heat, a cold, a dry, a wet ;
There is a heaven, a hell, an earth, a sky ;   570
Or teach me something new, or let me die !
Dear fate, be merciful by prayers won,
Teach me once what Death is, and all is done !

Thou may'st object ; there's somewhat else to learn ;
O do not bring me back unto the quern   575
To grind for honours, when I cannot tell
What will be said in the next chronicle !
Let my unblemish'd name meet with a tomb
Deservedly unspurn'd at, and at home !

I know there are possessions to inherit ;   580
But since the gate is stopp'd up to all merit,
Some hapless souls, as I, do well observe it,
The way to lose a place is to deserve it. .

575.—*Quern*, mill.

I am not ignorant besides of this,
Each man the workman of his fortune is ;   585
But to apply and temper well his tools,
He follow must th' advice of babes and fools ;
Though virtue and reward be the extremes
Of fortune's line, yet there are other beams,
Some sprigs of bribery imp'd in the line ;   590
Pand'rism or flatt'ry from the Florentine,
Which whoso catches, comes home crown'd with bay,
Ere he that runs the right line runs half way.
What love and beauty is (thou know'st, O Fate !)
I have read over ; and, alas ! but late ;   595
Their wounds yet bleed, and yet no help is nigh ;
Then teach me something new, or let me die !

Honours and places, riches, pleasures be
Beyond my star, and not ordain'd for me ;
Or sure the way is lost, and those we hold   600
For true, are counterfeits to those of old.
How sprout they else so soon, like osier tops,
Which one spring breeds and which next autumn lops?
Why are they else so fading : so possess'd
With guilt and fear, they dare not stand the test ? 605
Had virtue and true merit been the basis,
Whereon were rais'd their honours and high places,
They had been stronger seated, and had stood
To after ages, as our ancient blood,

590.—*Imp'd*, engrafted.   591.—*The Florentine*, Machiavelli.

Whose very names, and courages well steel'd,   610
Made up an army, and could crown a field.
  Open the way to merit and to love !
That we may teach a Cato and a dove
To heart a cause and weigh affection dear,
And I will think we live, not tarry here.   615

  Further his plaint had gone (if needed more),
But Celadyne, now widing more the door,
Made a small noise, which startling up the man,
He straight descried him, and anew began :
What sorrow, or what curiosity,   620
Say (if thou be a man), conducted thee
Into these dark and unfrequented cells,
Where nought but I and dreadful horror dwells?
Or if thou be a ghost, for pity say   [625
What pow'r, what chance, hath led thee to this way?
If so thou be a man, there can nought come
From them to me, unless it be a tomb,
And that I hold already.   See ! I have
Sufficient too to lend a king a grave,
A bless'd one too, within these hollow vaults ;   630
Earth hides but bodies, but oblivion, faults.
Or if thou be a ghost sent from above,
Say, is not blessed virtue and fair love,
Faith and just gratitude, rewarded there ?
Alas ! I know they be : I know they wear   635
Crowns of such glory, that their smallest ray
Can make us lend th' Antipodes a day :

Nay, change our sphere, and need no more the sun
Than those that have that light whence all begun.
  Stay further inquisition, quoth the swain,   640
And know I am a man, and of that train
Which near the western rivers feed their flocks.
I need not make me known ; for if the rocks
Can hold a sculpture, or the pow'r of verse
Preserve a name, the last-born may rehearse   645
Me and my fortunes.   Curiosity
Led me not hither : chance, in seeing thee,
Gave me the thread, and by it I am come
To find a living man within a tomb.
Thy plaints I have o'erheard ; and let it be   650
No wrong to them that they were heard of me.
May be that Heaven's great providence hath led
Me to these horrid caves of night and dread,
That, as in physic by some signature
Nature herself doth point us out a cure :   655
The liverwort is by industrious art
Known physical and sovereign for that part
Which it resembles ; and if we apply
The eye-bright by the like unto the eye,
Why may'st not thou (disconsolate) as well   660
From me receive a cure, since in me dwell
All those sad wrongs the world hath thrown on thee ;
Which wrought so much on my proclivity,
That I have entertain'd them, and th' are grown
And so incorporated, and mine own,   665
That grief, elixir-like, hath turn'd me all

Into itself; and therefore physical?
For if in herbs there lie this mystery,
Say, why in other bodies may not we   [670
Promise ourselves the like? why shouldst not thou
Expect the like from me this instant now?
And more, since Heaven hath made me for thy cure
Both the physician and the signature.

   Ah! Celadyne, quoth he, and think 't not strange
I call thee by thy name; though times' now change
Makes thee forget what mine is, with my voice [675
I have recorded thine: and if the choice
Of all our swains, which by the western rills
Feed their white flocks and tune their oaten quills,
Were with me now, thou only art the man   680
Whom I would choose for my physician.
The others I would thank and wish away.
There needs but one sun to bring in the day,
Nor but one Celadyne to clear my night
Of discontent, if any human wight   685
Can reach that possibility: but know
My griefs admit no parallax; they go,
Like to the fixed stars, in such a sphere,
So high from meaner woes and common care
That thou canst never any distance take   690
'Twixt mine and others' woes; and till thou make
And know a diff'rence in my saddest fate,
The cause, the station and the ling'ring date,
From other men which are in grief o'ergone
(Since it is best read by comparison),   695

Thou never canst attain the least degree
Of hope to work a remedy on me.
  I know to whom I speak. On Isis' banks,
And melancholy Cherwell, near the ranks
Of shading willows, often have we lain   700
And heard the Muses and Apollo's strain
In heavenly raptures, as the pow'rs on high
Had there been lecturers of poesy,
And nature's searcher, deep philosophy;
Yet neither these, nor any other art   705
Can yield a means to cure my wounded heart.
Stay then from losing longer time on me,
And in these deep caves of obscurity
Spend some few hours to see what is not known
Above; but on the wings of rumour blown.   710
Here is the fairies' court, if so they be.
With that he rose. Come near, and thou shalt see
Who are my neighbours. And with that he led
(With such a pace as lovers use to tread
Near sleeping parents) by the hand the swain   715
Unto a pretty seat, near which these twain
By a round little hole had soon descried
A trim feat room, about a fathom wide,
As much in height, and twice as much in length,
Out of the main rock cut by artful strength.   720
The two-leav'd door was of the mother pearl,
Hinged and nail'd with gold. Full many a girl,

718.—*Feat*, neat.

Of the sweet fairy ligne, wrought in the loom
That fitted those rich hangings clad the room.
In them was wrought the love of their great
    king,   725
His triumphs, dances, sports, and revelling :
And learned Spenser, on a little hill
Curiously wrought, lay, as he tun'd his quill ;
The floor could of respect complain no loss,
But neatly cover'd with discolour'd moss,   730
Woven into stories, might for such a piece
Vie with the richest carpets brought from Greece.
  A little mushroom (that was now grown thinner,
By being one time shaven for the dinner
Of one of Spain's grave grandees, and that day   735
Out of his greatness' larder stol'n away
By a more nimble elf than are their wits,
Who practise truth as seldom as their spits)—
This mushroom (on a frame of wax y-pight,
Wherein was wrought the strange and cruel fight 740
Betwixt the troublous commonwealth of flies,
And the sly spider with industrious thighs)
Serv'd for a table ; then a little elf
(If possible, far lesser than itself),
Brought in the covering made of white   rose
    leaves,   745
And (wrought together with the spinner's sleaves)

723.—*Ligne*, lineage.   739.—*Y-pight*, fixed.
746.—*Sleaves*, soft floss or unspun silk.

Met in the table's middle in right angles ;
The trenchers were of little silver spangles :
The salt the small bone of a fish's back,
Whereon in little was express'd the wrack 750
Of that deplored mouse, from whence hath sprung
That furious battle Homer whilom sung
Betwixt the frogs and mice : so neatly wrought
Yet could not work it lesser in a thought.
Then on the table, for their bread, was put 755
The milk-white kernels of the hazel nut ;
The cupboard, suitable to all the rest,
Was as the table with like cov'ring dress'd.
The ewer and bason were, as fitting well,
A periwinkle and a cockle-shell : 760
The glasses pure, and thinner than we can
See from the sea-betroth'd Venetian,
Were all of ice not made to overlast
One supper, and betwixt two cowslips cast :
A prettier fashion hath not yet been told, 765
So neat the glass was, and so feat the mould.
 A little spruce elf then (just of the set
Of the French dancer or such marionette)
Clad in a suit of rush, woven like a mat,
A monkshood flow'r then serving for a hat ; 770
Under a cloak made of the spider's loom :
This fairy (with them held a lusty groom)
Brought in his bottles ; neater were there none,
And every bottle was a cherrystone.
To each a seed pearl served for a screw, 775

And most of them were fill'd with early dew.
Some choicer ones, as for the king most meet,
Held mel-dew and the honeysuckle's sweet.
    All things thus fitted ; straightways follow'd in
A case of small musicians, with a din   780
Of little hautboys, whereon each one strives
To show his skill ; they all were made of seives,
Excepting one, which puff'd the player's face,
And was a chibole, serving for the bass.
    Then came the service. The first dishes were 785
In white broth boil'd a crammed grasshopper ;
A pismire roasted whole ; five crayfish eggs ;
The udder of a mouse ; two hornets' legs ;
Instead of olives, cleanly pickl'd sloes ;
Then of a bat were serv'd the pettitoes ;   790
Three fleas in souse, a cricket from the brine ;
And of a dormouse, last, a lusty chine.
    Tell me, thou grandee, Spain's magnifico,
Couldst thou e'er entertain a monarch foe,
Without exhausting most thy rents and fees,   795
Told by a hundred thousand marvedis,
That bragging poor account ? If we should hear
Some one relate his incomes every year

    778.—*Mel-dew*, honey-dew, a sweet gum which exudes from
the leaves or bark of certain trees.
    780.—*Case*, a pair.
    782.—*Seives*, or seaves, dwarf rushes.
    784.—*Chibole*, properly chipple, a small green onion.
    796.—*Marvedis*, very small Spanish coins, thirty-four to a
sixpence.

To be five hundred thousand farthings told,
Could ye refrain from laughter ? could ye hold ?   800
Or see a miser sitting down to dine
On some poor sprat new squeezed from the brine,
Take out his spectacles, and with them eat,
To make his dish seem larger and more great ;
Or else to make his gold its worth surpass,   805
Would see it through a multiplying glass :
Such are their audits ; such their high esteems ;
A Spaniard is still less than what he seems :
Less wise, less potent ; rich, but glorious ;
Prouder than any and more treacherous.   810
But let us leave the braggadocio here,
And turn to better company and cheer.
·   The first course thus serv'd in, next follow'd on
The fairy nobles, ushering Oberon,
Their mighty king, a prince of subtle pow'r,   815
Clad in a suit of speckled gilliflow'r.
His hat by some choice master in the trade
Was (like a helmet) of a lily made.
His ruff a daisy was, so neatly trim,
As if of purpose it had grown for him.   820
His points were of the lady-grass, in streaks,
And all were tagg'd, as fit, with titmouse beaks.
His girdle, not three times as broad as thin,

809.—*Glorious*, vain-glorious.
819.—*Ruff*, frill.
821. –*Points*, tagged laces used for tying any part of the
dress.

Was of a little trout's self-spangled skin.
His boots, for he was booted at that tide,   825
Were fitly made of half a squirrel's hide.
His cloak was of the velvet flow'rs, and lin'd
With flow'r-de-luces of the choicest kind.
   Down sat the king ; his nobles did attend ;
And after some repast he 'gan commend   830
Their hawks and sport.   This in a brave place flew :
That bird too soon was taken from the mew :
This came well through the fowl, and quick again
Made a brave point straight up upon her train.
Another for a driver none came nigh ;   835
And such a hawk truss'd well the butterfly.
That was the quarry which their pastime crown'd ;
Their hawks were wagtails, most of them mew'd
         round.
   Then of their coursers' speed, sure-footing pace,
Their next discourse was; as that famous race,   840
Engender'd by the wind, could not compare
With theirs, no more than could a Flemish mare
With those fleet steeds that are so quickly hurl'd,
And make but one day's journey round the world.
Nay, in their praises, some one durst to run   845
So far to say, that if the glorious sun
Should lame a horse, he must come from the spheres
And furnish up his team with one of theirs.
Those that did hear them vaunt their excellence

832.—*Mew*, cage for moulting hawks.   838.—*Mew'd*, caged.

Beyond all value with such confidence,   850
Stood wond'ring how so little elfs as these
Durst venture on so great hyperboles ;
But more upon such horses.   But it ceas'd
(I mean the wonder) when each nam'd his beast.
My nimble squirrel, quoth the king, and then   855
Pinching his hat, is but a minute's ken.
The earth ran speedy from him, and I dare
Say, if it have a motion circular,
I could have run it round ere she had done
The half of her circumvolution.   860
Her motion, lik'd with mine, should almost be
As Saturn's, mine the primum mobile.
Then, looking on the fairies most accounted,
I grant, quoth he, some others were well mounted,
And praise your choice ; I do acknowledge that 865
Your weasel ran well too ; so did your rat ;
And were his tail cut shorter to the fashion,
You in his speed would find an alteration.
Another's stoat had pass'd the swiftest tegs,
If somewhat sooner he had found his legs ;   870
His hare was winded well ; so had indeed
Another's rabbit tolerable speed.
Your cat (quoth he) would many a courser baffle ;
But sure he reins not half well in a snaffle.
I know her well ; 'twas Tybert that begat her,   875
But she is flew, and never will be fatter :

869.— *Tegs*, young sheep or deer.
876.—*Flew*, weak, or tender.

The vare was lastly prais'd, and all the kind,
But on their pasterns they went weak behind.
   What brave discourse was this ! now tell me, you
That talk of kings and states, and what they do ; 880
Or gravely silent with a Cato's face,
Chew ignorance until the later grace ;
Or such, who (with discretion then at jar)
Dare check brave Grenville and such sons of war,
With whom they durst as soon have measur'd swords,
                              [885
(Howe'er their pens fight or wine-prompted words)
As not have left him all with blood besmear'd,
Or ta'en an angry lion by the beard.
Forbear that honour'd name ! you, that in spite
Take pains to censure, more than he to fight,   890
Trample not on the dead ! those wrongly lay
The not-success, who soonest ran away.
Kill not again whom Spain would have repriev'd !
Had ten of you been Grenvilles, he had liv'd.
   Were it not better that you did apply   895
Your meat, unlaugh'd at of the standers-by ?
Or (like the fairy king) talk of your horse,
Or such as you, for want of something worse.
   Let that dear name for ever sacred be :
Cæsar had enemies, and so had he ;   900

877.—*Vare*, vair, a kind of weasel.
878.—*Pasterns*, hind quarters.
884.—*Grenville*, Sir Richard Grenville.

But Grenville did that Roman's fate transcend,
And fought an enemy into a friend.
   Thus with small things I do compose the great.
Now comes the king of fairies' second meat ;
The first dish was a small spawn'd fish and fried, 905
Had it been lesser, it had not been spied ;
The next, a dozen larded mites ; the third,
A goodly pie fill'd with a lady-bird.
Two roasted flies, then of a dace the poll,
And of a miller's thumb a mighty joll ;   910
A butterfly which they had kill'd that day,
A brace of fern-webs pickled the last May.
A well-fed hornet taken from the souse,
A lark's tongue dried, to make him to carouse.
   As when a lusty sawyer, well prepar'd,   915
His breakfast eaten, and his timber squar'd,
About to raise up as he thinketh fit
A good sound tree above his sawing pit,
His neighbours call'd ; each one a lusty heaver,
Some steer the roller, others ply the lever ;   920
Heave here, says one ; another calls, shove thither ;
Heave, roll, and shove ! cry all, and altogether ;
Look to your foot, sir, and take better heed,
Cries a by-stander, no more haste than need ;
Lift up that end there ; bring it gently on ;   925
And now thrust all at once, or all is gone,
Hold there a little ; soft ; now use your strength,

903.— *Compose*, compare.   912.—*Fern-web*, a small beetle.

And with this stir, the tree lies fit at length :
Just such a noise was heard when came the last [930
Of Oberon's second mess.   One cried, hold fast ;
Put five more of the guard to 't, of the best ;
Look to your footing ; stop awhile and rest ;
One would have thought, with so much strength and
        din,
They surely would have brought Behemoth in,
That mighty ox which (as the Rabbins say)   935
Shall feast the Jews upon the latter day.
But at the last, with all this noise and cry,
Ten of the guard brought in a minnow-pie.
   The mountain labour'd and brought forth a mouse,
And why not in this mighty prince's house   940
As any others?   Well, the pie was placed,
And then the music struck, and all things graced.
   It was a concert of the choicest set
That never stood to tune, or right a fret ;
For Nature to this king such music sent,   945
Most were both players and the instrument.
   No famous sensualist, whate'er he be,
Who in the brazen leaves of history
Hath his name register'd, for vast expense
In striving how to please his hearing sense,   950
Had ever harmony chose for his ear
So fit as for this king; and these they were.

   944.—*Fret*, the point at which a string is to be stopped in
such an instrument as the lute or guitar.

The treble was a three-mouth'd grasshopper,
Well tutor'd by a skilful quirister :
An ancient master, that did use to play   955
The friskings which the lambs do dance in May,
And long time was the chiefest call'd to sing,
When on the plains the fairies made a ring ;
Then a field-cricket, with a note full clean,
Sweet and unforc'd and softly sung the mean,   960
To whose accord, and with no mickle labour,
A pretty fairy play'd upon a tabor :
The case was of a hazel-nut, the heads
A bat's-wing dress'd, the snares were silver threads ;
A little stiffen'd lamprey's skin did suit   965
All the rest well, and serv'd them for a flute ;
And to all these a deep well-breasted gnat,
That had good sides, knew well his sharp and
          flat,
Sung a good compass, making no wry face,—
Was there as fittest for a chamber bass.   970
    These choice musicians to their merry king
Gave all the pleasure which their art could bring.
At last he ask'd a song ; but ere I fall
To sing it over in my Pastoral,
Give me some respite : now the day grows old,   975
And 'tis full time that I had pitch'd my fold.
When next sweet morning calls us from our beds,
With harmless thoughts and with untroubled heads,

964.—*Snares*, strings.

Meet we in Rowden meadows, where the flood
Kisses the banks, and courts the shady wood ;   980
A wood wherein some of these lays were dress'd,
And often sung by Willy of the west :
Upon whose trees the name of Licea stands,
Licea more fleeting than my Tavy's sands.
Grow old, ye rinds ! and shed away that name ; 985
But oh ! what hand shall wipe away her shame ?
    There let us meet.   And if my younger quill
Bring not such raptures from the sacred hill
With others, to whom Heaven infused breath
When reign'd our glorious dear Elizabeth,   990
(The nurse of learning and the blessed arts,
The centre of Spain's envy and our hearts),
If that the Muses fail me not, I shall
Perfect the little fairies' festival,
And charm your ears so with that prince's song, 995
That those fair nymphs which daily tread along
The western rivers and survey the fountains,
And those which haunt the woods, and sky-kiss'd
       mountains,
Shall learn and sing it to ensuing times
When I am dust.   And, Tavy, in my rhymes   1000
Challenge a due ; let it thy glory be,
That famous Drake and I were born by thee !

THE END OF THE FIRST SONG OF THE THIRD
BOOK.

979.—*Rowden meadows,* on the Okehampton road, about a
mile N.E. of Tavistock.

THE SECOND SONG.

THE ARGUMENT.

Good day to all, ye merry western swains,
And ev'ry gentle shepherdess that deigns
A kind attentive ear to what I sing.
Come, sit you round about me in a ring :
My reed is fitted, and I mean to play
The fairies' song I promis'd yesterday ;
And though for length I have it over-run,
This was the matter, thus the elf begun :

OF royal parents in a country rich
  Were born three daughters, with all beauties
     crown'd
That could the eyes of men or gods bewitch,
  Or poets' sacred verse did ever sound ;
But Nature's favour flew a higher pitch,   5
  When with the youngest she enrich'd this round,
Though her first work for praise much right might
     hold,
Her last outwent it, and she broke the mould.

From countries far remote, wing'd with desire,
  Strangers pass'd gladly o'er a tedious way   10
To see if fame would now be found a liar,
  Who said another sun brought in the day ;
Poor men ! ye come too near to such a fire,
  And for a look your lives at hazard lay.
Stay, stay at home, read of her beauty there,   15
And make not those sweet eyes your murderer.

The curious statuaries, painters quaint,
  From their great monarchs come, from ev'ry land,
That what the chisel could or pencil paint,
  Might in her portrait have the skilfull'st hand ;   20
But, seely men, they meet a sad restraint,
  And they themselves as turn'd to statues stand :
So many graces in her feature lurk,
They turn all eye and have no hands to work.

The altars of the gods stood now forlorn ;   25
  Their myrrh and frankincense was kept away,
And fairest Cytherea (that was born
  Out of the white froth of the working sea)
Wanted her votaries ; nay, some in scorn
  Durst vaunt, while they the sacrifice delay,   30
This was a deity, indeed, for whom
The gods themselves might be a hecatomb.

Divers believ'd, who, ravish'd with the sight,
  Stood gazing, as amaz'd, at her fair eyes,

That Nature had produc'd another light,   35
  New kind of star, and in a newer guise ;
And from the earth, not from the sea, should rise
  A Venus worthier to unlength the night ;
And though the first be for a goddess plac'd,
This was more heavenly fair, more truly chaste.   40

Hence came it Paphos and Cythera now,
  Gnidus and Amathus, could see no more
The ships the parent of their goddess plough,
  Nor pilgrims land on their forsaken shore.
No man a gift could to her shrine allow,   45
  Nor rose nor myrtle crown her image wore ;
The beds contemn'd, hearth fireless and unfit,
And men's devotions were as cold as it.

Anger and rage possess'd the queen of love
  To see a fairer queen of love than she ;   50
And that a mortal with the powers above
  Came in divine rites to a like degree ;
Nay, that the ravish'd people always strove
  That this none other could than Venus be ;
Impatient ought on earth deserv'd her name,   55
Thus murmur'd she, and scorn still fed the flame.

Have I, quoth she, the most confus'd abyss,
  The chaos rude unwound, the vault of heaven
Compos'd, and settled all that order is ?
  The name of nursing mother to me given,   60

And all regardless? must I, after this,
    Be from my temples and mine altars driven?
And she that is the source of human things
Pay, as a vassal, tribute to her springs?

No ; 'tis a competition too-too low,   65
    To stand with one compos'd of elements
Which their original to me do owe ;
    Shall fading creatures prosecute intents
With us that all eternity do know?
    And the like victims have and sacred scents?   70
Or share with me in any rites of mine,
And mingle mortal honours with divine?

What boots it then that men me rightly call
    The daughter of the mighty thunderer?
And that I can ascend up to my stall   75
    Along the milky way by many a star?
And where I come, the powers celestial
    Rise more to me than any goddess far?
And all those countries by bright Phœbus seen
Do homage and acknowledge me their queen.   80

Shall I then leave the prize I whilom won
    On stately Ida (for my beauty's charms),
Given me by Paris, Priam's fatal son,
    From stately Juno and the Maid of Arms,
By which old Simois long with blood did run?   85
    If such ambition her proud bosom warms,

I must descend : she fly to heaven, and there
Sit in my glorious orb, and guide my sphere.   .

No ! this usurping maid shall feel the pow'r
   Of an incensed deity, and see   90
Those cheeks of red and white, that living flow'r,
   And those her limbs of truest symmetry,
Want winning eloquence to 'scape the show'r
   Of due revenge must fall on her from me.
She shall repent those beauties, and confess   95
She had been happier in deformedness.

She said no more : but full of ire ascends
   Her chariot drawn by white enamour'd doves ;
Her passion to their speed more swiftness lends.
   And now to search her son (that various loves   100
Worketh each where) she studiously intends :
   She sought him long among th' Elysian groves,
But missing him, to earthward bent her reins,
And with a shepherd found him on the plains.

It was a shepherd that was born by-west,   105
   And well of Tityrus had learn'd to sing ;
Little knew he, poor lad, of love's unrest,
   But by his fellow-shepherds' sonneting ;
A speculative knowledge with the best
   He had, but never felt the golden sting ;   110

106.—*Tityrus*, Chaucer.

And to comply with those his fellow-swains,
He sung of love and never felt the pains.

The little Cupid lov'd him for his verse,
   Though low and tuned to an oaten reed ;
And that he might the fitter have commerce   115
   With those that sung of love and lovers' deed,
Struck (O but had Death struck her to a herse)
   Those wounds had not been ope which freshly
       bleed—
Struck a fair maid and made her love this lad,
From whence his sorrows their beginnings had.   120

Long time she lov'd : and Cupid did so dear
   Affect the shepherd, that he would not try
A golden dart to wound him (out of fear
   That they might not be stricken equally),
But turned orator, and coming there   125
   Where this young pastor did his flocks apply,
He wooes him for the lass sick of his hand,
And begs, who might imperiously command :

Shall that sweet paradise neglected lie
   ('Twas so, and had a serpent in it too),   130
Shall those sweet lips, that pity-begging eye
   Beget no flame, when common beauties do ?
Those breasts of snow, beds of felicity,
   Made to enforce a man of ice to woo,

Make nought for her, in whose soul-melting flashes
A salamander might consume to ashes?   [135

Pity her sighs, fond swain ! believe her tears ;
    What heart of marble would not rend to see her
Languish for love ? poor soul, her tender years
        Have flame to feed her fire, not words to free
            her.   140
Bad orators are younger loves and fears.
    Thus Cupid wooes, and could a mortal flee her ?
But Venus coming, Cupid threw a dart
To make all sure, and left it in his heart.

Thus to the winged archer Venus came,   145
    Who, though by Nature quick enough inclin'd
To all requests made by the Cyprian dame,
    She left no grace of look or word behind
That might raise up that fire which none can tame :
    Revenge, that sweet betrayer of the mind,   150
That cunning, turbulent, impatient guest,
Which sleeps in blood, and but in death hath rest.

Into her chariot she him quickly takes,
    And swift as time, cutting the yielding air,
Her discontent she tells him, as she makes   155
    Towards Psyche's sweet abode a sad repair.
Psyche the lady hight, that now awakes
    Fair Venus' fury ; look, quoth she, and there
Behold my grief ; O Cupid, shut thine eyne,
Or that which now is hers will soon be thine.   160

See yonder girl, quoth she, for whom my shrine
   Is left neglected and of all forlorn ;
Hark how the poets court the sacred Nine
   To give them raptures full and highly born
That may befit a beauty so divine,   165
   And from the threshold of the rosy morn
To Phœbus' western inn, fill by their lays
All hearts with love of her, all tongues with praise.

By that maternal rightful pow'r, my son,
   Which I have with thee, and may justly
      claim :   [170
By those gold darts which I for thee have won,
   By those sweet wounds they make without a
      maim :
By thy kind fire which hath such wonders done,
   And all fair eyes from whence thou takest aim :
By these and by this kiss, this and this other,   175
Right a wrong'd goddess and revenge thy mother.

And this way do it : make that glorious maid
   Slave in affection to a wretch as rude
As ever yet deformity array'd
   Or all the vices of the multitude.   180
Let him love money ! and a friend betray'd
   Proclaim with how much wit he is endued ;
Let not sweet sleep but sickness make his bed !
And to the grave bring home her maidenhead.

When   the   bless'd   day   calls   others   from   their
      sleep,   185
  And birds' sweet lays rejoice all creatures waking,
Let her lame husband's groans and sighing deep
  Affright her from that rest which she is taking !
And (spite of all her care) when she doth weep,
  Let him mistrust her tears and faith's forsaking !
In brief, let her affect (thus I importune)   [190
One wrong'd as much as Nature could or Fortune.

Thus spoke she, and a winning kiss she gave,
  A long one with a free and yielding lip,
Unto the god ; and on the brackish wave   195
  (Leaving her son ashore) doth nimbly trip.
Two dolphins with a chariot richly brave
  Waited, and with her unto Cyprus strip ;
The little Cupid she had left behind,
And gave him sight then when he should be blind. 200

Cupid, to work his wiles that can apply
  Himself, like Proteus, to what form he list,
Fierce as a lion, nimble as an eye,
  As glorious as the sun, dark as a mist,
Hiding himself within a lady's eye,   205
  Or in a silken hair's ensnaring twist ;
And those within whose breasts he oft doth fall,
And feel him most, do know him least of all.

198. —*Strip*, move rapidly.

The god now us'd his pow'r, and him address'd
   Unto a fitting stand, where he might see   210
All that kind Nature ever yet express'd
   Of colour, feature, or due symmetry ;
It seem'd heaven was come down to make earth
      bless'd.
   No wonder then if there this god should be ;
No ; wonder more which way he can be driven, 215
To leave this sight for those he knew in heaven.

Her cheeks the wonder of what eye beheld,
   Begot betwixt a lily and a rose,
In gentle rising plains divinely swell'd,
   Where all the graces and the loves repose.   220
Nature in this piece all her works excell'd,
   Yet show'd herself imperfect in the close,
For she forgot (when she so fair did raise her)
To give the world a wit might duly praise her.

Her sweet and ruddy lips, full of the fire   225
   Which once Prometheus stole away from heaven,
Could by their kisses raise a like desire
   To that by which Alcides once was driven
To fifty beds, and in one night entire
   To fifty maids the name of mother given ;   230
But had he met this dame first, all the other
Had rested maids : she fifty times a mother !

When that she spoke, as at a voice from heaven
   On her sweet words all ears and hearts attended ;

When that she sung, they thought the planets
        seven   235
   By her sweet voice might well their tunes have
        mended ;
When she did sigh, all were of joy bereaven ;
   And when she smil'd, heaven had them all
        befriended.
If that her voice, sighs, smiles, so many thrill'd,
O, had she kiss'd, how many had she kill'd !   240

Her hair was flaxen, small, and full and long,
   Wherewith the soft enamour'd air did play,
And here and there with pearls was quaintly strung ;
   When they were spread (like to Apollo's ray)
They made the breasts of the Olympic throng   245
   To feel their flames, as we the flame of day ;
And to eternize what they saw so fair,
They made a constellation of her hair.

Her slender fingers (neat and worthy made
   To be the servants to so much perfection)   250
Join'd to a palm, whose touch would straight invade
   And bring a sturdy heart to low subjection.
Her slender wrists two diamond bracelets lade,
   Made richer by so sweet a soul's election.
O happy bracelets ! but more happy he   255
To whom those arms shall as a bracelet be !

241.—*Small*, fine.

Nature, when she made women's breasts, was then
  In doubt of what to make them, or how stain'd ;
If that she made them soft, she knew that men
  Would seek for rest there, where none could be
      gain'd :   260
If that she made them snow-like, they again
  Would seek for cold where love's hot flamings
      reign'd ;
She made them both, and men deceived so,
Find wakefulness in down, and fire in snow.

Such were fair Psyche's lillied beds of love,   265
  Or rather two new worlds where men would fain
Discover wonders by her stars above,
  If any guide could bring them back again.
But who shall on those azure riverets move,
  Is lost, and wanders in an endless main ;   270
So many graces, pleasures, there apply them,
That man should need the world's age to descry
      them.

As when a woodman on the greeny lawns,
  Where daily chants the sad-sweet nightingale,
Would count his herd, more bucks, more prickets,
      fawns   275
  Rush from the copse and put him from his tale ;
Or some wayfaring man, when morning dawns,
  Would tell the sweet notes in a joysome vale,

275.—*Prickets*, bucks in their second year.

At ev'ry foot a new bird lights and sings,
And makes him leave to count their sonnetings :   280

So when my willing Muse would gladly dress
　Her several graces in immortal lines,
Plenty impoors her ; ev'ry golden tress,
　Each little dimple, every glance that shines
As radiant as Apollo, I confess   285
　My skill too weak for so admir'd designs ;
For whilst one beauty I am close about,
Millions do newly rise and put me out.

Never was maid to various nature bound
　In greater bonds of thankfulness than she,   290
As all eyes judg'd ; nor on the massy round
　For all perfections could another be
Upon whose any limn was to be found
　Ought, that on hers could vant of mastery ;
Yet though all eyes had been a wishful feast,   295
Who saw nought but her body saw her least.

Blest was the womb that bore so fair a birth ;
　Blest was the birth for blessing of the womb ;
Blest was the hand that took her to the earth ;
　Blest ev'ry shady arbour, every room ;   300
Blest were the deserts rough where zephyr stirr'th ;
　Blest ev'ry craggy rock and rushy coombe :

280.—*Leave*, cease.　　283.—*Impoors*, impoverishes.
291.—*Massy round*, globe.　　294.—*Vant*, vaunt.

All things that held, touch'd, saw her, still confess'd
To time's last period they were ever bless'd.

My fairest Cælia, when thine eyes shall view   305
   These, and all other lines ere writ by me,
Wherein all beauties are describ'd, and true,
   Think your devoted shepherd's fantasy,
Rapt by those heavenly graces are in you,
   Had thence all matter fit for elogy.   310
Your blest endowments are my verses' mothers,
For by your sweetness I describe all others.

THE SHEPHEARDS PIPE.

LONDON,
Printed by *N. O.* for *George Nor-*
ton, and are to be fold at his Shop
without Temple-barre.. 1614.

TO

The truly Virtuous, and worthy of all Honour,
the Right Honourable

EDWARD,

LORD ZOUCH, ST. MAUR AND CANTELUPE,

and one of His Majesty's Most Honourable
Privy Council.

BE pleas'd, great Lord, when underneath the shades
Of your delightful Bramshill, where the spring
Her flowers for gentle blasts with Zephyr trades,
Once more to hear a silly[a] shepherd sing.
Yours be the pleasure, mine the sonneting :
Ev'n that hath his delight ; nor shall I need
To seek applause amongst the common store.[b]
It is enough if this mine oaten reed

[a] *Silly,* simple.　　　　[b] *Store,* multitude.

Please but the ear it should ; I ask no more :
Nor shall those rural notes[a] which heretofore
Your true attention grac'd and wing'd for fame
Imperfect lie ; oblivion shall not gain
Ought on your worth, but sung shall be your name
So long as England yields or song or swain.
 Free are my lines, though dress'd in lowly state,
 And scorn to flatter but the men I hate.

Your Honour's

W. BROWNE.

[a] *Those rural notes*, i.e., *Britannia's Pastorals*, of which the first book only had appeared.

Of his Friend

MASTER WILLIAM BROWNE.

A POET'S born, not made : no wonder then
Though Spenser, Sidney (miracles of men,
Sole English makers,[a] whose ev'n names so high
Express by implication poesy)
Were long unparallel'd : for Nature, bold
In their creation, spent that precious mould,
That nobly better earth, that purer spirit
Which poets, as their birthrights, claim t' inherit :
And in their great production prodigal,
Careless of futures, well-nigh spent her all.
Viewing her work, conscious sh' had suffer'd wrack,[b]
Hath caus'd our countrymen e'er since to lack
That better earth and form : long thrifty grown,
Who truly might bear poets, brought forth none :

[a] *Makers, i.e.,* of verse, a literal rendering of the Greek word ποιητής.

[b] *Wrack,* loss.

Till now of late, seeing her stocks new full
(By time and thrift) of matter beautiful,
And quintessence of forms, what several
Our elder poets graces had, those all
She now determin'd to unite in one,
So to surpass herself, and call'd him Browne.
That beggar'd by his birth, she's now so poor
That of true maker[s] she can make no more.
Hereof accus'd, answer'd, she meant that he
A species should, no individuum,[a] be.
That, Phœnix-like, he in himself should find
Of poesy contain'd each several kind ;
And from this Phœnix's urn thought she could take
Whereof all following-poets well to make.
    For of some former she had now made known
    They were her errors whilst sh' intended Browne.

In libellum inscriptionemque.

Not Æglogues your, but Eclogues : to compare :
Virgil's selected, yours elected are.
He imitates, you make : and this your creature
Expresseth well your name, and theirs, their nature.

E. JOHNSON,
Int. Temp.

[a] *Individuum*, an atom, indivisible particle.

To his better beloved than known Friend,

MR. BROWNE.

SUCH is the fate of some (write) nowadays
Thinking to win and wear, they break the bays.
As a slow footman striving near to come
A swifter that before him far doth run,
Puff'd with the hope of Honour's goal to win,
Runs out of breath yet furthest off from him :
So do our most of poets whose Muse flies
About for honour, catch poor butterflies.
But thou, fair friend, not rank'd shall be 'mongst
     those
That make a mountain where a molehill grows ;
Thou whose sweet-singing pen such lays hath writ
That in an old way teacheth us new wit ;
Thou that wert born and bred to be the man
To turn Apollo's glory into Pan,
And when thou lists of shepherds leave to write,
To great Apollo add again his light.

G 2

For never yet like shepherds forth have come
Whose pipes so sweetly play as thine have done.
Fair Muse of Browne, whose beauty is as pure
As women brown that fair and long'st endure,
Still may'st thou as thou dost a lover move,
And as thou dost each mover may thee love,
Whilst I myself in love with thee must fall,
Browne's Muse the fair brown woman still will call.

JOHN ONLEY,

Int. Temp.

THE SHEPHERD'S PIPE.

THE FIRST ECLOGUE.

THE ARGUMENT.

Roget[a] and Willie[b] both ymet
  Upon a greeny ley,
With roundelays and tales are set
  To spend the length of day.

WILLIE.   ROGET.

Willie.

ROGET, droop not, see the spring
Is the earth enamelling,
And the birds on every tree
Greet this morn with melody:
Hark, how yonder thrustle chants it,   5
And her mate as proudly vants it;

[a] *Roget*, George Wither.   [b] *Willie*, William Browne.
5.—*Thrustle*, thrush.

See how every stream is dress'd
By her margin with the best
Of Flora's gifts ; she seems glad
For such brooks such flow'rs she had.   10
All the trees are quaintly tired
With green buds, of all desired ;
And the hawthorn every day
Spreads some little show of May :
See the primrose sweetly set   15
By the much-lov'd violet,
All the banks do sweetly cover,
As they would invite a lover
With his lass to see their dressing
And to grace them by their pressing :   20
Yet in all this merry tide
When all cares are laid aside,
Roget sits as if his blood
Had not felt the quick'ning good
Of the sun nor cares to play,   25
Or with songs to pass the day
As he wont : fie, Roget, fie,
Raise thy head, and merrily
Tune us somewhat to thy reed :
See our flocks do freely feed,   30
Here we may together sit,
And for music very fit
Is this place ; from yonder wood
Comes an echo shrill and good,
Twice full perfectly it will   35

Answer to thine oaten quill.
Roget, droop not then, but sing
Some kind welcome to the spring.

Roget.

All Willie, Willie, why should I
Sound my notes of jollity?   40
Since no sooner can I play
Any pleasing roundelay,
But some one or other still
'Gins to descant on my quill ;
And will say, by this he me   45
Meaneth in his minstrelsy.
If I chance to name an ass
In my song, it comes to pass,
One or other sure will take it
As his proper name, and make it   50
Fit to tell his nature too,
Thus whate'er I chance to do
Happens to my loss, and brings
To my name the venom'd stings
Of ill report : how should I   55
Sound then notes of jollity?

Willie.

'Tis true indeed, we say all,
Rub a gall'd horse on the gall,
Kick he will, storm and bite ;
But the horse of sounder plight   60

Gently feels his master's hand.
In the water thrust a brand
Kindled in the fire, 'twill hiss ;
When a stick that taken is
From the hedge, in water thrust,   65
Never rokes as would the first,
But endures the water's touch :
Roget, so it fares with such
Whose own guilt hath them inflam'd,
Rage whene'er their vice is blam'd.   70
But who in himself is free
From all spots, as lilies be,
Never stirs, do what thou can.
If thou slander such a man,
Yet he's quiet, for he knows   75
With him no such vices close.
Only he that is indeed
Spotted with the lep'rous seed
·Of corrupted thoughts, and hath
An ulcerous soul in the path   80
Of reproof, he straight will brawl
If you rub him on the gall.

Roget.

But in vain then shall I keep
These my harmless flock of sheep ;
And though all the day I tend them,   85
And from wolves and foxes shend them,

66.— *Rokes*, hisses.   86.—*Shend*, defend, guard.

Wicked swains that bear me spite,
In the gloomy veil of night,
Of my fold will draw the pegs,
Or else break my lambkins' legs,   90
Or unhang my wether's bell,
Or bring briars from the dell,
And them in my fold by pieces
Cast, to tangle all their fleeces.
Well-a-day ! such churlish swains   95
Now and then lurk on our plains :
That I fear a time ere long,
Shall not hear a shepherd's song,
Nor a swain shall take in task
Any wrong, nor once unmask   100
Such as do with vices rife
Soil the shepherd's happy life :
Except he means his sheep shall be
A prey to all their injury.
This causeth me I do no more   105
Chant so as I wont of yore :
Since in vain then should I keep
These my harmless flock of sheep.

Willie.

YET if such thou wilt not sing,
Make the woods and valleys ring   110
With some other kind of lore :
Roget hath enough in store.
Sing of love, or tell some tale,

Praise the flowers, the hills, the vale :
Let us not here idle be ;   115
Next day I will sing to thee.
Hark, on knap of yonder hill
Some sweet shepherd tunes his quill ;
And the maidens in a round
Sit to hear him on the ground ;   120
And if thou begin, shall we
Grac'd be with like company ;
And to gird thy temples bring
Garlands for such fingering.
Then raise thee, Roget——

Roget.

Gentle swain,   125
Whom I honour for thy strain,
Though it would beseem me more
To attend thee and thy lore,
Yet lest thou might'st find in me
A neglect of courtesy,   130
I will sing what I did lere
Long agone in Janivere
Of a skilful aged sire,
As we toasted by the fire.

Willie.

Sing it out, it needs must be   135
Very good what comes from thee.

117.—*Knap*, top.   131.—*Lere*, learn.

Roget.

WHILOM an Emperor, prudent and wise,
Reigned in Rome, and had sons three,
Which he had in great cherete and great price,
And when it shop so that th' infirmity   140
Of death, which no wight may eschew or flee,
 Him threw down in his bed, he let to call
 His sons, and before him they came all.

And to the first he said in this manneer :
All th'eritage which at the dying   145
Of my fadir, he me left, all in feere
Leave I thee : and all that of my buying
Was with my peny, all my purchasing,
 My second son, bequeath I to thee.
 And to the third son thus said he :   150

Unmoveable good right none withouten oath
Thee give I may ; but I to thee devise
Jewels three, a ring, a brooch and a cloth :
With which, and thou be guied as the wise,
Thou may'st get all that ought thee suffice.   155
 Whoso that the ring useth still to wear
 Of all folks the love he shall conquer.

137.—*An Emperor, i.e.* "Godfridus."
139.—*Cherete*, affection.   140 —*Shop*, befell.
146.—*Fadir*, father.   *In feere*, together.
148.—*Peny*, money.   154.—*Guied*, guided.

And whoso the brooch beareth on his breast,
It is eke of such virtue and such kind,
That think upon what thing him liketh best,   160
And he as blive shall it have and find.
My words, son, imprint well in mind.
   The cloth eke hath a marvellous nature,
   Which that shall be committed to thy cure.

Whoso sit on it, if he wish where   165
In all the world to been, he suddenly
Without more labour shall be there.
Son, those three jewels bequeath I
To thee, unto this effect certainly
   That to study of the university   170
   Thou go, and that I bid and charge thee.

When he had thus said, the vexation
Of death so hasted him, that his spirit
Anon forsook his habitation
In his body : death would no respite   175
Him yeve at all : he was of his life quit.
   And buried was with such solemnity,
   As fell to his imperial dignity.

Of the youngest son I tell shall,
And speak no more of his brethren two,   180

161.—*Blive*, immediately.   164.—*Cure*, care, keeping.
176.—*Yeve*, give.

For with them have I not to do at all.
Thus spake the mother Jonathas unto:
Sin God hath his will of thy father do,
    To thy father's will would I me conform,
    And truly all his testament perform.   185

He three jewels, as thou knowest well,
A ring, a brooch, and a cloth thee bequeath,
Whose virtues he thee told every deal,
Or that he pass'd hence and yalde up the breath.
O good God, his departing, his death   190
    Full grievously sticketh unto mine heart,
    But suffered mot been, all how sore it smart.

In that case women have such heaviness,
That it not lieth in my cunning aright
To tell of so great sorrow the excess :
But wise women can take it light,
And in short while put unto the flight
    All sorrow and woe, and catch again comfort :
    Now to my tale make I my resort.

Thy father's will, my son, as I said ere,   200
Will I perform ; have here the ring and go
To study anon, and when that thou art there,
    As thy father thee bade, do even so,
    And as thou wilt my blessing have also.

183.—*Sin*, since.   189.—*Or*, ere, before.   *Yalde*, yielded.

She unto him as-swythe took the ring   205
And bade him keep it well for anything.

He went unto the study general
Where he gat love enough, and acquaintance
Right good and friendly, the ring causing all ;
And on a day to him befell this chance   210
With a woman, a morsel of pleasance,
   By the streets of the university
   As he was in his walking, met he.

And right as blive he had with her a tale,
And therewithal sore in her love he brent ;   215
Gay, fresh and piked was she to the sale,
For to that end and to that intent
She thither came, and both forth they went,
   And he a pistle rowned in her ear,
   Nat wot I what, for I ne came nat there.   220

She was his paramour shortly to say.
This man to folkès all was so leefe,
That they him gave abundance of money ;
He feasted folk, and stood at high boncheefe ;
Of the lack of good he felt no grief   225
   All whiles the ring he with him had ;
   But failing it his friendship 'gan sad.

205.—*As-swythe*, quickly.   215.—*Brent*, burnt.
216.—*Piked*, picked.
219.—*Pistle*, epistle, tale.   *Rowned*, rounded, whispered.
222.—*Leefe*, agreeable.   224.—*Boncheefe*, prosperity.

His paramour, which that ycalled was
Fellicula, marvelled right greatly
Of the dispences of this Jonathas,   230
Sin she no peny at all with him sy ;
And on a night as there she lay him by
    In the bed, thus she to him spake and said,
    And this petition assoile him pray'd :

O reverent sir, unto whom, quoth she,   235
Obey I would aye with heart's humbleness,
Since that ye han had my virginity,
You I beseech of your high gentleness,
Telleth me whence com'th the good and richesse
    That ye with feasten folk, and han no store, 240
    By ought I see can, ne gold, ne tresore.

If I tell it, quoth he, paraventure
Thou wilt discover it, and out it publish ;
Such is woman's inconstant nature,
They cannot keep counsel worth a rish :   245
Better is my tongue keep than to wish
    That I had kept close that is gone at large,
    And repentance is thing that I mote charge.

229.—*Fellicula*, a name formed from the Latin word *fel*,
gall.   230.—*Dispences.* expenditure.
    231.—*Sy*, saw.   234.—*Assoile*, answer.
    237.—*Han*, have.   245.—*Rish*, rush.

Nay, good sir, quoth she, holdeth me not suspect,
Doubteth nothing, I can be right secree.   250
Well worthy were it me to been abject
From all good company, if I, quoth she,
Unto you should so mistake me.
   Be not adread your counsel me to show.
   Well, said he, thus it is at words few :   255

My father the ring, which that thou may'st see
On my finger, me at his dying day
Bequeath'd, which this virtue and property
Hath, that the love of men he shall have aye
That weareth it, and there shall be no nay   260
   Of what thing that him liketh ask and crave,
   But with good will he shall as blive it have.

Through the ring's virtuous excellence
Thus am I rich, and have ever ynow.
Now, sir, yet a word by your licence   265
Suff'reth me to say, and to speak now :
Is it wisdom, as that it seemeth you,
   Wear it on your finger continually?
   What wouldst thou mean, quoth he, thereby?

What peril thereof might there befall?   270
Right great, quoth she, as ye in company

250.—*Secree*, secret.   251.—*Abject*, rejected.
254.—*Adread*, afraid.   264.—*Ynow*, enough.

Walk often, from your finger might it fall,
Or plucked off been in a ragery
And so be lost, and that were folly :
   Take it me, let me been of it warden,   275
   For as my life keep it would I certain.

This Jonathas, this innocent young man,
Giving unto her words full credence,
As youth not avised best be can,
The ring her took of his insipience.   280
When this was done the heat and the fervence
   Of love which he beforn had purchased,
   Was quench'd, and love's knot was unlaced.

Men of their gifts to stint began.
Ah, thought he, for the ring I not ne bear,   285
Faileth my love ; fetch me, woman,
Said he, my ring : anon I will it wear.
She rose, and into chamber dresseth her,
   And when she therein had been a while,
   Alas, quoth she, out on falsehood and guile,   290

The chest is broken, and the ring take out.
And when he heard her complaint and cry,
He was astonied sore, and made a shout,
And said : Cursed be the day that I
Thee met first, or with mine eyne sy.   295

273.—*Ragery*, wantonness.   275.—*Take*, give.
280.—*Insipience*, folly.   288.—*Dresseth*, approacheth.
293.—*Astonied*, astounded.

She wept and showed outward chere of woe,
But in her heart was it nothing so.

The ring was safe enough, and in her chest
It was; all that she said was leasing,
As some woman other while at best   300
Can lie and weep when is her liking.
This man saw her woe, and said : Dearling,
  Weep no more, God's help is nigh.
  To him unwist how false she was and sly.

He twined thence, and home to his countree   305
Unto his mother the straight way he went ;
And when she saw thither comen was he,
My son, quoth she, what was thine intent
Thee fro the school now to absent ?
  What caused thee fro school hither to hie ?   310
  Mother, right this, said he, nat would I lie.

Forsooth, mother, my ring is agoe.
My paramour to keep I betook it,
And it is lost, for which I am full woe ;
Sorrowfully unto mine heart it sit.   315
Son, often have I warned thee, and yet
  For thy profit I warn thee, my son,
  Unhonest women thou hereafter shun.

296.—*Chere*, countenance.   299.—*Leasing*, lying.
304.—*Unwist*, unknown.   305.—*Twined*, departed.

Thy brooch anon right woll I to thee fet.
She brought it him, and charged him full deep 320
When he it took, and on his breast he it set,
Bet than his ring he should it keep,
Lest he the loss bewail should and weep.
   To the university, shortly to sain,
    In what he could, he hasted him again. 325

And when he comen was, his paramour
Him met anon, and unto her him took,
As that he did erst, this young revelour ;
Her company he nat a deal forsook,
Though he cause had, but as with the hook 330
   Of her sleight he beforn was caught and hent,
   Right so he was deceived oft and blent.

And as ihrough virtue of the ring before
Of good he had abundance and plentee,
While it was with him, or he had it lore : 335
Right so through virtue of the brooch had he
What good him list. She thought, How may this be ?
   Some privy thing now causeth this richesse,
   As did the ring herebefore, I guess.

Wond'ring hereon, she pray'd him, and besought 340
Busily night and day, that tell he would

319.—*Fet*, fetch.   322.—*Bet*, better.
331.—*Hent*, seized.   332.—*Blent*, blind
335.—*Lore*, lost.

H 2

The cause of this ; but he another thought :
He meant it close for him it kept be should,
And a long time it was or he it told.
    She wept aye too and too, and said : Alas,   345
    The time and hour that ever I born was !

Trust ye not on me, sir? she said,
Lever me were be slain in this place
By that good Lord that for us all died,
Than purpose again you any fallace ;   350
Unto you would I be my live's space
    As true as any woman in earth is
    Unto a man ; doubteth nothing of this.

Small may she do, that cannot well byheet,
Though not performed be such a promesse.   355
This Jonathas thought her words so sweet,
That he was drunk of the pleasant sweetness
Of them, and of his foolish tenderness
    Thus unto her he spake and said tho :
    Be of good comfort, why weepest thou so ?   360

And she thereto answered thus sobbing :
Sir, quoth she, my heaviness and dreed
Is this ; I am adread of the leesing
Of your brooch, as Almighty God forbeed
It happen so.   Now what, so God thee speed,   365

348.—*Lever*, rather.   350.—*Fallace*, deceit.
354.—*Byheet*, pledge, engage.   359.—*Tho*, then.
    363.—*Leesing*, losing.

Said he, wouldest thou in this case counsail ?
Quoth she, that I keep it might sans fail.

He said : I have a fear and dread algate,
If I so did thou wouldst it leese
As thou lostest my ring, now gone but late.
First God pray I, quoth she, that I not chese,   370
But that my heart as the cold frost may freeze,
   Or else be it brent with wild fire :
   Nay, surely it to keep is my desire.

To her words credence he gave pleneer,   375
And the brooch took her, and after anon,
Whereas he was beforn full leefe and cheer
To folk, and had good, all was gone.
Good and friendship him lacked, there was none.
   Woman, me fetch the brooch, quoth he ; swythee
   Into thy chamber for it go ; hie thee.   [380

She into chamber went, as then he bad,
But she not brought that he sent her for ;
She meant it nat ; but as she had be mad
Her clothes hath she all to rent and tore,   385
And cried, alas, the brooch away is bore,
   For which I wole anon right with my knife
   Myself slay : I am weary of my life.

368.—*Algate*, nevertheless.   371.—*Chese*, choose.
375.—*Pleneer*, full.   380.—*Swythee*, quickly.

This noise he heard, and blive he to her ran,
Weening she would han done as she spake,   390
And the knife in all haste that he can
From her took, and threw it behind his back,
And said : ne for the loss, ne for the lack
　　Of the brooch, sorrow not ; I forgive all ;
　　I trust in God, that yet us help he shall.   395

To th'emperess his mother this young man
Again him dresseth : he went her unto,
And when she saw him, she to wonder 'gan ;
She thought, now somewhat there is misdo,
And said, I dread thy jewels two   400
　　Been lost now, percase the brooch with the ring.
　　Mother, he said, yea, by heaven King.

Son, thou wotst well no jewel is left
Unto thee now, but the cloth precious
Which I thee take shall, thee charging eft   405
The company of women riotous
Thou flee, lest it be to thee so grievous
　　That thou it nat sustain shalt ne bear ;
　　Such company on my blessing forbear.

The cloth she fet, and it hath him take,   410
And of his lady his mother his leave

389.—*Blive*, quickly.　　　　393.—*Ne*, nor.
　　　　405.—*Eft*, again.

He took ; but first this forward 'gan he make :
Mother, said he, trusteth this weel and leeve,
That I shall seyn, for sooth ye shall it preeve,
   If I leese this cloth, never I your face   415
   Henceforth see wole, ne you pray of grace.

With God's help I shall do well ynow.
Her blessing he took, and to study is go ;
And as beforn told have I unto you,
His paramour, his privy mortal foe,   420
Was wont to meet him, right even so
   She did then, and made him pleasant cheer.
   They clip and kiss and walk homeward in feere.

When they were enter'd in the house, he sprad
This cloth upon the ground, and thereon sit,   425
And bade his paramour, this woman bad,
To sit also by him adown on it.
She doth as he commandeth and bit ;
   Had she this thought and virtue of the cloth
   Wist, to han set on it had she been loth.   430

She for a while was full sore affesed.
This Jonathas wish in his heart 'gan :
Would God that I might thus been eased,
That as on this cloth I and this woman
Sit here, as far were, as that never man   435

413.—*Leeve*, believe.   428.—*Bit*, biddeth.
431.—*Affesed*, frightened.

Or this came ; and unneth had he so thought,
But they with the cloth thither weren brought

Right to the world's end, as that it were.
When apperceived had she this, she cried,
As though she through girt had be with a spear. 440
Harrow ! alas ! that ever shop this tide !
How came we hither ?   Nay, he said, abide,
 Worse is coming ; here sole wole I thee leave,
 Wild beasts shallen thee devour or eve.

For thou my ring and brooch hast from me holden.
O reverent sir ! have upon me pitee,   [445
Quoth, she, if ye this grace do me wolden,
As bring me home again to the citee
Where as I this day was, but if that ye
 Them have again, of foul death do me die :   450
 Your bounty on me kythe, I mercy cry.

This Jonathas could nothing beware,
Ne take ensample of the deceits twain
That she did him beforn, but faith him bare,
And her he commanded on death's pain   455
Fro such offences thenceforth her restrain.
 She swore, and made thereto forward ;
 But heark'neth how she bore her afterward.

436.—*Or*, before.   *Unneth*, scarcely.
443.—*Sole*, alone.   447.—*Wolden*, will.
    451.—*Kythe*, bestow.

When she saw and knew that the wrath and ire
That he to her had borne was gone and past,   460
And all was well, she thought him eft to fire,
In her malice aye stood she stedfast,
And to inquire of him was not agast
   In so short time how that it might be
   That they came thither out of her countree.   465

Such virtue hath this cloth on which we sit,
Said he, that where in this world us be list
Suddenly with the thought shallen thither flit,
And how thither come unto us unwist,
As thing fro far unknown in the mist.   470
   And therewith to this woman fraudulent,
   To sleep, he said, have I good talent.

Let see, quoth he, stretch out anon thy lap,
In which wole I my head down lay and rest.
So was it done, and he anon 'gan nap.   475
Nap? nay, he slept right well at best.
What doth this woman, one the ficklest
   Of women all, but that cloth that lay
   Under him, she drew lyte and lyte away.

When she it had all : would God, quoth she,   480
I were as I was this day morning !

<hr>

463.—*Agast*, afraid.   472.—*Talent*, inclination.
479.—*Lyte and lyte*, by little and little.

And therewith this root of iniquitee
Had her wish, and sole left him there sleeping.
O Jonathas ! like to thy perishing
   Art thou, thy paramour made hath thy beard ; 485
   When thou wakest cause hast thou to be ferd.

But thou shalt do full well ; thou shalt obteen
Victory on her ; thou hast done some deed
Pleasant to thy mother, well can I ween,
For which our Lord quite shall thy meed,   490
And thee deliver out of thy woful dreed.
   The child whom that the mother useth bless,
   Full often sythe is eased in distress.

When he awoke, and neither he ne fond
Woman ne cloth, he wept bitterly,   495
And said, Alas ! now is there in no lond
Man worse I know begon than am I.
On every side his look he cast, and sy
   Nothing but birds in the air flying,
   And wild beasts about him renning.   500

Of whose sight he full sore was agrysed.
He thought, all this well deserved I have.
What ail'd me to be so evil avised,
That my counsel could I nat keep and save ?
Who can fool play ? who can mad and rave ?   505

    485.—*Made hath thy beard, i.e.*, undone thee.
    486.—*Ferd*, terrified.   493.—*Sythe*, time.
    500.—*Renning*, running.   501.—*Agrysed*, terrified.

But he that to a woman his secree
Discovereth : the smart cleaveth now on me.

He thus departeth as God would harmless,
And forth of adventure his way is went,
But whitherward he draw, he conceitless   510
Was ; he nat knew to what place he was bent.
He pass'd a water which was so fervent
   That flesh upon his feet left it him none,
   All clean was departed from the bone.

It shop so that he had a little glass,   515
Which with that water anon filled he,
And when he further in his way gone was,
Before him he beheld and saw a tree
That fair fruit bore, and in great plentee :   '
   He ate thereof, the taste him liked well,   520
   But he there-through became a foul mesel.

For which unto the ground for sorrow and woe
He fell, and said, cursed be that day
That I was born, and time and hour also
That my mother conceived me, for aye   525
Now am I lost ; alas and well away !
   And when some deal slaked his heaviness,
   He rose, and on his way he 'gan him dress.

Another water before him he sy,
Which sore to comen in he was adrad :   530

512.—Fervent, hot   521.— Mesel, leper.

But nathless, since thereby other way
Ne about it there could none be had,
He thought, so streitly am I bestad,
    That though it sore me affese or gast,
    Assoil it wole I ; and through it he pass'd.   535

And right as the first water his flesh
Departed from his feet, so the second
Restored it, and made all whole and fresh :
And glad was he, and joyful that stownd
When he felt his feet whole were and sound :   540
    A vial of the water of that brook
    He fill'd, and fruit of the tree with him took.

Forth his journey this Jonathas held,
And as he his look about him cast,
Another tree from afar he beheld,   545
To which he hasted, and him hied fast.
Hungry he was, and of the fruit he thrast
    Into his mouth, and ate of it sadly,
    And of the lepry he purged was thereby.

Of that fruit more he raught, and thence is gone ;
And a fair castle from afar saw he,   [550

531.—*Nathless*, none the less, never the less.
534.—*Gast*, terrify.   535.—*Assoil*, attempt.
539.—*Stownd*, moment.   547.—*Thrast*, thrust.
548.—*Sadly*, heavily, heartily. 549.—*Lepry*, leprosy.
                550.—*Raught*, plucked.

In compass of which heads many one
Of men there hung, as he might well see
But not for that he shun would or flee ;
   He thither him dresseth the straight way   555
   In that ever that he can or may.

Walking so, two men came him again,
And saiden thus : Dear friend, we you pray
What man be ye ? Sirs, quoth he, certain
A leech I am, and though myself it say,   560
Can for the health of sick folks well purvey.
   They said him : Of yonder castle the king
   A leper is, and can whole be for nothing.

With him there hath been many a sundry leech
That undertook him well to cure and heal   565
On pain of their heads, but all to seech
Their art was ; 'ware that thou not with him deal,
But if thou canst the charter of health enseal,
   Lest that thou leese thy head, as didden they ;
   But thou be wise : thou find it shall no play.   570

Sirs, said he, you thank I of your reed,
For gently ye han you to me quit :
But I nat dread to lose mine heed,
By God's help full safe keep I will it ;
God of his grace such cunning and wit   575

561.—*Purvey*, provide.   566.—*Seech*, seek.
571.—*Reed*, advice.   572.—*Quit*, acquitted.

Hath lent me, that I hope I shall him cure.
Full well dare I me put in aventure.

They to the king's presence han him lad,
And him of the fruit of the second tree
He gave to eat, and bade him to be glad,   580
And said : Anon your health han shall ye ;
Eke of the second water him gave he
   To drink, and when he those two had received,
   His lepry from him voided was and weived.

The king (as unto his high dignity   585
Convenient was) gave him largely,
And to him said : If that it like thee
Abiden here, I more abundantly
Thee give wole.   My Lord, sickerly,
   Quoth he, fain would I your pleasure fulfil,   590
   And in your high presence abide still.

But I no while may with you abide,
So mochill have I to done elsewhere.
Jonathas every day to the sea-side,
Which was nigh, went to look and enquere   595
If any ship drawing hither were
   Which him home to his country lead might,
   And on a day of ships had he sight

584.—*Weived*, departed.   589.—*Sickerly*, certainly.
593.—*Mochill*, much.

Well a thirty toward the castle draw,
And at time of evensong they all   600
Arriveden, of which he was full faw,
And to the shipmen cry he 'gan and call,
And said : If it so hap might and fall
   That some of you me home to my countree
   Me bring would, well quit should he be.   605

And told them whither that they shoulden go.
One of the shipmen forth start at last,
And to him said : My ship and no moe
Of them that here been doth shop and cast
Thither to wend ; let see, tell on fast,   610
   Quoth the shipman, that thou for my travail
   Me give wilt, if that I thither sail.

They were accorded.   Jonathas forth goeth
Unto the king to ask him license
To twine thence, to which the king was loth,   615
And nathless with his benevolence,
This Jonathas from his magnificence
   Departed is, and forth to the shipman
   His way he taketh, as-swythe as he can.

Into the ship he ent'reth, and as blive   620
As wind and weather good shop to be,

     601.—*Faw*, glad.   615.—*Twine*, depart.

Thither as he purposed him arrive
They sailed forth, and came to the citee
In which this serpentine woman was ; she
   That had him terned with false deceitis,   625
   But where no remedy followeth, streit is.

Turns been quit, all be they good or bad
Sometime, though they put been in delay.
But to my purpose.   She deemed he had
Been devoured with beasts many a day   630
Gone ; she thought he delivered was for aye.
   Folk of the city knew not Jonathas,
   So many a year was past that he there was.

Misliking and thought changed eke his face.
Abouten he go'th, and for his dwelling   635
In the city, he hired him a place,
And therein exercised his cunning
Of physic, to whom weren repairing
   Many a sick wight, and all were healed.
   Well was the sick man that with him dealed. 640

Now shop it thus that this Fellicula,
(The well of deceivable doubleness,
Follower of the steps of Dallida,)
Was then exalted unto high richesse,
But she was fallen into great sickness   645

625.—*Terned*, tricked.   643.—*Dallida*, Delilah.
644.—*Richesse*, wealth.

And heard sain, for not might it been hid,
How masterful a leech he had him kid.

Messages solemn to him she sent,
Praying him to do so mochill labour
As come and see her ; and he thither went.   650
When he her saw, that she his paramour
Had been he well knew, and for that debtour
    To her he was, her he thought to quite
    Or he went, and no longer it respite.

But what that he was, she ne wist nat.   655
He saw her urine, and eke felt her pous,
And said, The sooth is this plain and flat,
A sickness han ye strange and marvellous,
Which to avoid is wonder dangerous :
    To heal you there is no way but one.   660
    Leech in this world other can find none.

Aviseth you whether you list it take
Or not, for I told have you my wit.
Ah, sir, said she, for God's sake,
That way me show, and I shall follow it,   665
Whatever it be : for this sickness sit
    So nigh mine heart, that I wot not how
    Me to demean : tell on, I pray yow.

647.—*Kid*, known, or made known.   656.—*Pous*, pulse.
659.—*Wonder*, wonderful, extraordinarily.
662.—*Aviseth*, consider.   663.—*Wit*, opinion.

Lady, ye must openly you confess,
And if against good conscience and right   670
Any good han ye take more or less,
Beforn this hour, of any manner wight,
Yield it anon ; else not in the might
   Of man is it to give a medicine
   That you may heal of your sickness and pine. 675

If any such thing be, tell out thy rede,
And ye shall been all whole I you beheet ;
Else mine art is naught, withouten drede.
O Lord, she thought, health is a thing full sweet,
Therewith desire I sovereignly to meet :   680
   Since I it by confession may recover.
   A fool am I but I my guilt discover.

How falsely to the son of th' Emperor,
Jonathas, had she done, before them all
As ye han heard above, all that error   685
By knew she.   O Fellicula thee call
Well may I so, for of the bitter gall
   Thou takest the beginning of thy name,
   Thou root of malice and mirror of shame.

Then said Jonathas : Where are those three   690
Jewels, that thee fro the clerk withdrew?

676.--*Rede*, confession.   678.—*Drede*, doubt.
691.—*Clerk*, scholar.

Sir, in a coffer at my bed's feet ye
Shall find them ; open it, and so pray I you.
He thought not to make it queint and tow,
   And say nay, and strain courtesy,   695
   But with right good will thither he 'gan hie.

The coffer he opened, and them there fond.
Who was a glad man but Jonathas ? who
The ring upon a finger of his hond
He put, and the brooch on his breast also,   700
The cloth eke under his arm held he tho ;
   And to her him dresseth to done his cure,
   Cure mortal, way to her sepulture.

He thought rue she should, and fore-think
That she her had unto him misbore ;   705
And of that water her he gave to drink,
Which that his flesh from his bones before
Had twined, wherethrough he was almost lore,
   Nad he relieved been, as ye above
   Han heard, and this he did eke for her love.   710

Of the fruit of the tree he gave her eat,
Which that him made into the leper stert,
And as blive in her womb 'gan they fret

694.—*Make it queint and tow*, make an unnecessary fuss.
708.—*Twined*, twisted off, *i.e.*, stripped.
709.—*Nad*, ne had.
712.—*Stert*, leap.   713.—*Fret*, gripe.

And gnaw so, that change 'gan her hert
Now heark'neth how it her made smert :   715
   Her womb opened, and out fell each entrail
   That in her was, thus it is said, sans fail.

Thus wretchedly (lo) this guile-man died,
And Jonathas with jewels three
No longer there thought to abide,   720
But home to the empress his mother hasteth he,
Whereas in joy and in prosperitee
   His life led he to his dying day ;
   And so God us grant that we do may.

Willie.

   By my hook this is a tale   725
   Would befit our Whitsun-Ale :
   Better cannot be, I wist,
   Descant on it he that list.
   And full gladly give I wold
   The best cosset in my fold   730
   And a mazor for a fee,
   If this song thou'lt teachen me

718.—*Guile-man*, beguiler of men.

726.—*Whitsun-Ale*, a festival held at Whitsuntide (Brand, *Pop. Antiq.*, ed. Bohn, i. 276–84).

730.—*Cosset*, hand-reared lamb.

731.—*Mazor*, mazer, a bowl made of maple and richly ornamented.

'Tis so quaint and fine a lay,
That upon our revel day
If I sung it, I might chance   735
(For my pains) be took to dance
With our Lady of the May.

Roget.

Roget will not say thee nay,
If thou deem'st it worth thy pains.
'Tis a song not many swains   740
Singen can, and though it be
Not so deck'd with nicety
Of sweet words full neatly choosed
As are now by shepherds used :
Yet if well you sound the sense,   745
And the moral's excellence,
You shall find it quit the while,
And excuse the homely style.
Well I wot the man that first
Sung this lay did quench his thirst   750
Deeply as did ever one
In the Muses' Helicon.
Many times he hath been seen
With the fairies on the green,
And to them his pipe did sound,   755
Whilst they danced in a round.

747.—*Quit the while,* be worth while, requite the pains.

Mickle solace would they make him,
And at midnight often wake him,
And convey him from his room
To a field of yellow broom ;   760
Or into the meadows where
Mints perfume the gentle air,
And where Flora spends her treasure :
There they would begin their measure.
If it chanc'd night's sable shrouds   765
Muffled Cynthia up in clouds,
Safely home they then would see him,
And from brakes and quagmires free him.
There are few such swains as he
Nowadays for harmony.   770

Willie.

What was he thou praisest thus ?

Roget.

Scholar unto Tityrus :
Tityrus, the bravest swain
Ever lived on the plain,
Taught him how to feed his lambs,   775
How to cure them, and their dams :
How to pitch the fold, and then
How he should remove agen :

772.—*Tityrus*, a name given to Chaucer by Spenser and
others.

Taught him when the corn was ripe,
How to make an oaten pipe,   780
How to join them, how to cut them,
When to open, when to shut them,
And with all the skill he had
Did instruct this willing lad.

Willie.

Happy surely was that swain !   785
And he was not taught in vain :
Many a one that prouder is,
Han not such a song as this,
And have garlands for their meed,
That but jar as Skelton's reed.   790

Roget.

'Tis too true : but see the sun
Hath his journey fully run ;
And his horses, all in sweat,
In the ocean cool their heat ;
Sever we our sheep and fold them,   795
'Twill be night ere we have told them.

Thomas Occleeve, one of the Privy Seal, composed first this
tale, and was never till now imprinted. As this shall
please, I may be drawn to publish the rest of his works,
being all perfect in my hands. He wrote in Chaucer's
time.

THE SECOND ECLOGUE.

THE ARGUMENT.

Two shepherds here complain the wrong
Done by a swinish lout,
That brings his hogs their sheep among,
And spoils the plains throughout.

WILLIE.   JOCKIE.

Willie.

JOCKIE, say : what might he be
That sits on yonder hill ?
And tooteth out his notes of glee
So uncouth and so shrill ?

Jockie.

Notes of glee ? bad ones I trow :   5
I have not heard beforn
One so mistook as Willie now :
'Tis some sow-gelder's horn.

And well thou asken might'st if I
  Do know him, or from whence   10
He comes, that to his minstrelsy
  Requires such patience.
He is a swinward, but I think
  No swinward of the best.
For much he reketh of his swink,   15
  And carketh for his rest.

Willie.

Harm take the swine !   What makes he here ?
  What luckless planet's frowns
Have drawn him and his hogs in feere
  To root our daisied downs?   20
Ill mote he thrive ! and may his hogs,
  And all that e'er they breed,
Be ever worried by our dogs
  For so presumptuous deed.
Why kept he not among the fens,   25
  Or in the copses by,
Or in the woods and braky glens,
  Where haws and acorns lie ?
About the ditches of the town
  Or hedgerows he might bring them.   30

13.—*Swinward*, swineherd.
15.—*Reketh*, taketh heed.   *Swink*, work.
16.—*Carketh*, is careful.   19.—*In feere*, together.

Jockie.

But then some pence 'twould cost the clown
  To yoke and eke to ring them ;
And well I ween he loves no cost
  But what is for his back :
To go full gay him pleaseth most,   35
  And lets his belly lack.
Two suits he hath, the one of blue,
  The other home-spun grey :
And yet he means to make a new
  Against next revel day ;   40
And though our May-lord at the feast
  Seem'd very trimly clad,
In cloth by his own mother dress'd,
  Yet comes not near this lad.
His bonnet neatly on his head,   45
  With button on the top,
His shoes with strings of leather red,
  And stocking to his slop.
And yet for all it comes to pass,
  He not our gibing 'scapes :   50
Some like him to a trimmed ass,
  And some to Jackanapes.

Willie.

It seemeth then, by what is said,
  That Jockie knows the boor ;
I would my scrip and hook have laid   55
  Thou knew'st him not before.

Jockie.

Sike loathed chance by fortune fell
  (If fortune ought can do) :
Not kend him?   Yes, I ken him well,
  And sometime paid for't too.   60

Willie.

Would Jockie ever stoop so low,
  As conissance to take
Of sike a churl?   Full well I know,
  No nymph of spring or lake,
No herdess, nor no shepherd's girl,   65
  But fain would sit by thee,
And sea-nymphs offer shells of pearl
  For thy sweet melody.
The satyrs bring thee from the woods
  The strawberry for hire,   70
And all the first fruits of the buds
  To woo thee to their quire.
Silvanus' songsters learn thy strain,
  For by a neighbour spring
The nightingale records again   75
  What thou dost primely sing.
Nor canst thou tune a madrigal,
  Or any dreary moan,

57.—*Sike*, such.   62.—*Conissance*, recognition.
76.—*Primely*, in the first instance.

But nymphs, or swains, or birds, or all
   Permit thee not alone.   80
And yet (as though devoid of these)
   Canst thou so low decline,
As leave the lovely naiades
   For one that keepeth swine ?
But how befell it ?

Jockie.

       T' other day,   85
  As to the field I set me,
Near to the Maypole on the way
  This sluggish swinward met me.
And seeing Weptol with him there,
  Our fellow-swain and friend,   90
I bade good day, so on did fare
  To my proposed end.
But as back from my wint'ring ground
  I came the way before,
This rude groom all alone I found   95
  Stand by the ale-house door.
There was no nay, but I must in
  And taste a cup of ale ;
Where on his pot he did begin
  To stammer out a tale.   100
He told me how he much desir'd
  Th' acquaintance of us swains,

95.—*Groom*, fellow.

And from the forest was retir'd
  To graze upon our plains :
But for what cause I cannot tell,   105
  He can nor pipe nor sing,
Nor knows he how to dig a well,
  Nor neatly dress a spring :
Nor knows a trap nor snare to till,
  He sits as in a dream ;   110
Nor scarce hath so much whistling skill
  Will hearten-on a team.
Well, we so long together were,
  I 'gan to haste away ;
He licens'd me to leave him there,   115
  And gave me leave to pay.

Willie.

Done like a swinward ! may you all
  That close with such as he,
Be used so ! that gladly fall
  Into like company.   120
But if I fail not in mine art,
  I'll send him to his yard,
And make him from our plains depart
  With all his dirty herd.
I wonder he hath suffer'd been   125
  Upon our common here ;

108.– *Spring*, a young tree or wood.   109.—*Till*, set.
112.—*Hearten-on*, encourage.

His hogs do root our younger trees,
   And spoil the smelling breer.
Our purest wells they wallow in,
   All overspread with dirt,   130
Nor will they from our arbours lin,
   But all our pleasures hurt.
Our curious benches that we build
   Beneath a shady tree,
Shall be o'erthrown, or so defil'd   135
   As we would loath to see.
Then join we, Jockie ; for the rest
   Of all our fellow-swains,
I am assur'd, will do their best
   To rid him fro our plains.   140

Jockie.

What is in me shall never fail
   To forward such a deed.
And sure, I think, we might prevail
   By some satiric reed.

Willie.

If that will do, I know a lad   145
   Can hit the master-vein.
But let us home, the skies are sad,
   And clouds distil in rain.

128.—*Breer*, briar.   131.—*Lin*, desist, refrain.

THE THIRD ECLOGUE.

THE ARGUMENT.

Old Neddy's poverty they moan,
  Who whilom was a swain
That had more sheep himself alone,
  Than ten upon the plain.

PIERS.   THOMALIN.

Thomalin.

WHERE is every piping lad
That the fields are not yclad
      With their milk-white sheep?
Tell me : is it holiday,
Or if in the month of May   5
      Use they long to sleep?

Piers.

Thomalin, 'tis not too late,
For the turtle and her mate
      Sitten yet in nest :

And the thrustle hath not been   10
Gath'ring worms yet on the green,
    But attends her rest.
Not a bird hath taught her young,
Nor her morning's lesson sung
    In the shady grove :   15
But the nightingale in dark
Singing woke the mounting lark :
    She records her love.
Not the sun hath with his beams
Gilded yet our crystal streams ;   20
    Rising from the sea,
Mists do crown the mountains' tops,
And each pretty myrtle drops :
    'Tis but newly day.
Yet see, yonder (though unwist)   25
Some man cometh in the mist ;
    Hast thou him beheld ?
See he crosseth o'er the land
With a dog and staff in hand,
    Limping for his eld.   30

Thomalin.

Yes, I see him, and do know him,·
And we all do rev'rence owe him,
    'Tis the aged sire
Neddy, that was wont to make
Such great feasting at the wake,   35
    And the blessing-fire.*

* The Mid-
summer fires
are termed so
in the west
parts of Eng-
land.

36.—*Blessing-fire.* Cf. Brand, *Pop. Antiq.*, ed. Bohn, i. 306

Good old man ! see how he walks
Painful and among the balks,
    Picking locks of wool !
I have known the day when he	40
Had as much as any three,
    When their lofts were full.
Underneath yond hanging rocks
All the valley with his flocks
    Was whilom overspread :	45
He had milch-goats without peers,
Well-hung kine, and fatten'd steers
    Many hundred head.
Wilkin's cote his dairy was,
For a dwelling it may pass	50
    With the best in town.
Curds and cream with other cheer
Have I had there in the year
    For a greeny gown.
Lasses kept it, as again	55
Were not fitted on the plain
    For a lusty dance :
And at parting, home would take us,
Flawns or syllabubs to make us
    For our jouisance.	60
And though some in spite would tell,
Yet old Neddy took it well ;
    Bidding us again

59.—*Flawns*, custards.   60.—*Jouisance*, enjoyment.

Never at his cote be strange :
Unto him that wrought this change,   65
    Mickle be the pain !

    Piers.

What disaster, Thomalin,
This mischance hath cloth'd him in,
    Quickly tellen me.
Rue I do his state the more,   70
That he clipped heretofore
    Some felicity.
Han by night accursed thieves
Slain his lambs, or stol'n his beeves,
    Or consuming fire   75
Brent his shearing-house, or stall ;
Or a deluge drowned all,
    Tell me it entire?
Have the winters been so set
To rain and snow, they have wet   80
    All his driest lair :
By which means his sheep have got
Such a deadly, cureless rot,
    That none living are ?

    Thomalin.

Neither waves, nor thieves, nor fire,   85
Nor have rots impoor'd this sire ;
    Suretyship, nor yet

73.---*Han*, have.   74.—*Beeves*, oxen.
    86.—*Impoor'd*, impoverished.

Was the usurer helping on
With his damn'd extortion,
    Nor the chains of debt.   90
But deceit that ever lies
Strongest arm'd for treacheries
    In a bosom'd friend:
That (and only that) hath brought it:
Cursed be the head that wrought it,   95
    And the basest end!
Grooms he had, and he did send them
With his herds a-field, to tend them.
    Had they further been!
Sluggish, lazy, thriftless elves;   100
Sheep had better kept themselves
    From the foxes' teen.
Some would kill their sheep, and then
Bring their master home agen
    Nothing but the skin;   105
Telling him, how in the morn
In the fold they found them torn,
    And ne'er lying lin.
If they went unto the fair
With a score of fatten'd ware,   110
    And did chance to sell,
If old Neddy had again
Half his own, I dare well sain,
    That but seldom fell.

102.—*Teen*, violence.   108.—*Lin*, cease.

They at their return would say,   115
Such a man or such would pay,
    Well known of your hyne.
Alas, poor man ! that subtle knave
Undid him, and vaunts it brave,
    Though his master pine.   120
Of his master he would beg
Such a lamb that broke his leg;
    And if there were none,
To the fold by night he'd hie,
And them hurt full ruefully   125
    Or with staff or stone.
He would have petitions new,
And for desp'rate debts would sue
    Neddy had forgot :
He would grant : the other then   130
Tears from poor and aged men :
    Or in jails they rot.
Neddy, lately rich in store,
Giving much, deceived more,
    On a sudden fell ;   135
Then the steward lent him gold,
Yet no more than might be told
    Worth his master's cell.
That is gone, and all beside
(Well-a-day, alack the tide) !   140
    In a hollow den

17.—*Hyne*, hind, used in Devonshire and Cornwall for a
bailiff or upper farm-servant.

Underneath yond gloomy wood
Wons he now, and wails the brood
    Of ingrateful men.

Fiers.

But, alas! now he is old,   145
Bit with hunger, nipp'd with cold.
    What is left him,
Or to succour or relieve him,
Or from wants oft to reprieve him?

Thomalin.

    All's bereft him,   150
Save he hath a little crowd,
He in youth was of it proud,
    And a dog to dance:
With them he on holidays
In the farmers' houses plays   155
    For his sustenance.

Piers.

See; he's near, let's rise and meet him,
And with dues to old age greet him;
    It is fitting so.

Thomalin.

'Tis a motion good and sage.   160
Honour still is due to age:
    Up, and let us go.

143.—*Wons*, dwells.   151.—*Crowd*, fiddle.

THE FOURTH ECLOGUE.

THE ARGUMENT.

In this the Author bewails the death of one whom he shadoweth under the name of Philarete, compounded of the Greek words φίλος and ἀρετή, a lover of virtue, a name well befitting him to whose memory these lines are consecrated, being sometime his truly loved (and now as much lamented) friend Mr. Thomas Manwood, son to the worthy Sir Peter Manwood, knight.

UNDER an aged oak was Willie laid,
Willie, the lad who whilom made the rocks
To ring with joy, whilst on his pipe he play'd,
And from their masters woo'd the neighb'ring flocks:
    But now o'ercome with dolours deep   5
      That nigh his heart-strings rent,
    Ne car'd he for his silly sheep,
      Ne car'd for merriment.
    But chang'd his wonted walks
      For uncouth paths unknown,   10
Where none but trees might hear his plaints,
    And echo rue his moan.

Autumn it was when droop'd the sweetest flow'rs,
And rivers, swoll'n with pride, o'erlook'd the banks ;
Poor grew the day of summer's golden hours,   15
And void of sap stood Ida's cedar-ranks.
      The pleasant meadows sadly lay
        In chill and cooling sweats
      By rising fountains, or as they
        Fear'd winter's wastfull threats.   20
    Against the broad-spread oak,
      Each wind in fury bears ;
    Yet fell their leaves not half so fast
      As did the shepherd's tears.

As was his seat, so was his gentle heart,   25
Meek and dejected, but his thoughts as high
As those aye-wand'ring lights, who both impart
Their beams on us, and heaven still beautify.
      Sad was his look (O, heavy fate !
        That swain should be so sad,   30
      Whose merry notes the forlorn mate
        With greatest pleasure clad,)
    Broke was his tuneful pipe
      That charm'd the crystal floods,
    And thus his grief took airy wings   35
      And flew about the woods.

Day, thou art too officious in thy place,
And night too sparing of a wished stay.

20.— Wastfull, devastating.

Ye wand'ring lamps, O be ye fix'd a space !
Some other hemisphere grace with your ray.   40
    Great Phœbus ! Daphne is not here,
      Nor Hyacinthus fair ;
    Phœbe ! Endymion and thy dear
      Hath long since cleft the air.
  But ye have surely seen   45
    (Whom we in sorrow miss)
  A swain whom Phœbe thought her love,
    And Titan deemed his.

But he is gone ; then inwards turn your light,
Behold him there : here never shall you more ;   50
O'erhang this sad plain with eternal night ;
Or change the gaudy green she whilom wore
    To fenny black !   Hyperion great
      To ashy paleness turn her !
    Green well befits a lover's heat,   55
      But black beseems a mourner.
  Yet neither this thou canst,
    Nor see his second birth,
  His brightness blinds thine eye more now,
    Than thine did his on earth.   60

Let not a shepherd on our hapless plains
Tune notes of glee, as used were of yore !
For Philarete is dead.   Let mirthful strains
With Philarete cease for evermore !

And if a fellow-swain do live   65
  A niggard of his tears,
The shepherdesses all will give
  To store him part of theirs.
Or I would lend him some,
  But that the store I have   70
Will all be spent before I pay
  The debt I owe his grave.

O what is left can make me leave to moan,
Or what remains but doth increase it more ?
Look on his sheep : alas ! their master's gone.   75
Look on the place where we two heretofore
    With locked arms have vow'd our love,
    (Our love which time shall see
    In shepherds' songs for ever move,
    And grace their harmony,)   80
  It solitary seems.
    Behold our flow'ry beds ;
Their beauties fade, and violets
  For sorrow hang their heads.

'Tis not a cypress' bough, a count'nance sad,   85
A mourning garment, wailing elegy,
A standing hearse in sable vesture clad,
A tomb built to his name's eternity,
    Although the shepherds all should strive
    By yearly obsequies,   90

And vow to keep thy fame alive
In spite of destinies,
That can suppress my grief :
All these and more may be,
Yet all in vain to recompense   95
My greatest loss of thee.

Cypress may fade, the countenance be chang'd,
A garment rot, an elegy forgotten,
A hearse 'mongst irreligious rites be rang'd,   [100
A tomb pluck'd down, or else through age be rotten :
All things th' unpartial hand of Fate
Can raze out with a thought,
These have a sev'ral fixed date
Which ended, turn to nought.
Yet shall my truest cause   105
Of sorrow firmly stay,
When these effects the wings of Time
Shall fan and sweep away.

Look as a sweet rose fairly budding forth
Bewrays her beauties to th' enamour'd morn,   110
Until some keen blast from the envious North
Kills the sweet bud that was but newly born ;
Or else her rarest smells delighting
Make her herself betray,
Some white and curious hand inviting   115
To pluck her thence away :

So stands my mournful case,
  For had he been less good,
He yet (uncropp'd) had kept the stock
  Whereon he fairly stood.   120

Yet though so long he liv'd not as he might,
He had the time appointed to him given.
Who liveth but the space of one poor night,
His birth, his youth, his age is in that even.
    Who ever doth the period see   125
      Of days by Heaven forth plotted,
    Dies full of age, as well as he
      That had more years allotted.
  In sad tones then my verse
    Shall with incessant tears   130
  Bemoan my hapless loss of him,
    And not his want of years.

In deepest passions of my grief-swoll'n breast
(Sweet soul !) this only comfort seizeth me,
That so few years did make thee so much blest, 135
And gave such wings to reach eternity.
    Is this to die ? No : as a ship,
      Well built, with easy wind,
    A lazy hulk doth far outstrip,
      And soonest harbour find :   140
  So Philarete fled,
    Quick was his passage given,
When others must have longer time
    To make them fit for heaven.

Then not for thee these briny tears are spent,   145
But as the nightingale against the breer
'Tis for myself I moan, and do lament
Not that thou left'st the world, but left'st me here :
    Here, where without thee all delights
      Fail of their pleasing pow'r,   150
    All glorious days seem ugly nights ;
      Methinks no April show'r
  Embroider should the earth,
    But briny tears distil,
  Since Flora's beauties shall no more   155
    Be honour'd by thy quill.

And ye his sheep (in token of his lack),
Whilom the fairest flock on all the plain,
Yean never lamb, but be it cloth'd in black :
Ye shady sycamores, when any swain   160
    To carve his name upon your rind
      Doth come, where his doth stand,
    Shed drops, if he be so unkind
      To raze it with his hand.
  And thou, my loved Muse,   165
    No more shouldst numbers move,
  But that his name should ever live,
    And after death my love.

This said, he sigh'd, and with o'erdrowned eyes [170
Gaz'd on the heavens for what he miss'd on earth.

146.—*Breer*, briar.

Then from the ground full sadly 'gan arise
As far from future hope as present mirth ;
    Unto his cote with heavy pace
      As ever sorrow trod
      He went with mind no more to trace   175
       Where mirthful swains abode ;
  And as he spent the day,
    The night he pass'd alone.
Was never shepherd lov'd more dear,
    Nor made a truer moan.   180

TO

*The Virtuous and much lamenting Sisters of
my ever admired friend,*

MR. THOMAS MANWOOD.

To me more known than you is your sad chance.
Oh ! had I still enjoy'd such ignorance ;
Then I by these spent tears had not been known,
Nor left another's grief to sing mine own.
Yet since his fate hath wrought these throes,
Permit a Partner in your woes:
The cause doth yield, and still may do,
Enough for YOU, and others too.
But if such plaints for YOU are kept,
Yet may I grieve since you have wept.
For he more perfect grows to be,
That feels another's MISERY.
And though these drops which mourning run,
From several fountains first begun,
And some far off, some nearer fleet,
They will (at last) in one stream meet.
Mine shall with yours, yours mix with mine,
And make one Off'ring at his Shrine :
For whose ETERNITY on earth, my Muse
To build this ALTAR, did her best skill use ;
And that you, I, and all that held him dear,
Our tears and sighs might freely offer here.

THE FIFTH ECLOGUE.

To his Ingenious Friend
MR. CHRISTOPHER BROOKE.

THE ARGUMENT.

Willie incites his friend to write
Things of a higher fame
Than silly shepherds use indite,
Veil'd in a shepherd's name.

WILLIE[a] and CUTTIE.[b]

Morn had got the start of night ;
Lab'ring men were ready dight
With their shovels and their spades
For the field, and (as their trades)
Or at hedging wrought or ditching   5
For their food more than enriching ;
When the shepherds from the fold
All their bleating charges told,

[a] *Willie*, William Browne.   [b] *Cuttie*, Christopher Brooke.

And (full careful) search'd if one
Of all their flock were hurt or gone,   10
Or (if in the night-time cull'd)
Any had their fleeces pull'd ;
'Mongst the rest (not least in care)
Cuttie to his fold 'gan fare,
And young Willie (that had given   15
To his flock the latest even
Neighbourhood with Cuttie's sheep,)
Shaking off refreshing sleep,
Hied him to his charge that blet;
Where he (busied) Cuttie met.   20
Both their sheep told, and none miss'd
Of their number ; then they bliss'd
Pan and all the gods of plains
For respecting of their trains
Of silly sheep, and in a song   25
Praise gave to that holy throng.
Thus they drave their flocks to graze,
Whose white fleeces did amaze
All the lilies, as they pass
Where their usual feeding was.   30
Lilies angry that a creature
Of no more eye-pleasing feature
Than a sheep, by nature's duty
Should be crown'd with far more beauty
Than a lily, and the pow'r   35

11.—*Cull'd*, chosen, picked out.   19.—*Blet*, bleated.

Of white in sheep outgo a flow'r,
From the middle of their sprout
(Like a Fury's sting) thrust out
Dart-like forks in death to steep them ;
But great Pan did safely keep them,   40
And afforded kind repair
To their dry and wonted lair,
Where their masters (that did eye them)
Underneath a hawthorn by them,
On their pipes thus 'gan to play,   45
And with rhymes wear out the day.

Willie.

Cease, Cuttie, cease, to feed these simple flocks,
And for a trumpet change thine oaten-reeds ;
O'erlook the valleys as aspiring rocks,
And rather march in steel than shepherd's weeds. 50
Believe me, Cuttie, for heroic deeds
Thy verse is fit, not for the lives of swains,
(Though both thou canst do well) and none proceeds
To leave high pitches for the lowly plains :
    Take thou a harp in hand, strive with Apollo ; 55
    Thy Muse was made to lead, then scorn to follow.

Cuttie.

Willie, to follow sheep I ne'er shall scorn,
Much less to follow any deity ;
Who 'gainst the Sun (though weaken'd by the morn)
Would vie with looks, needeth an eagle's eye.   60

I dare not search the hidden mystery
Of tragic scenes ; nor in a buskin'd style
Through death and horror march, nor their height fly
Whose pens were fed with blood of this fair Isle.
    It shall content me on these happy downs   65
    To sing the strife for garlands, not for crowns.

Willie.

O who would not aspire, and by his wing
Keep stroke with fame, and of an earthly jar
Another lesson teach the spheres to sing ?
Who would a shepherd that might be a star ?   70
See, learned Cuttie, on yond mountains are
Clear springs arising, and the climbing goat,
That can get up, hath water clearer far -
Than when the streams do in the valleys float.
    What madman would a race by torchlight run   75
    That might his steps have usher'd by the sun ?

We shepherds tune our lays of shepherds' loves,
Or in the praise of shady groves or springs ;
We seldom hear of Cytherea's doves,
Except when some more learned shepherd sings ;   80
And equal meed have to our sonnetings :
A belt, a sheep-hook, or a wreath of flow'rs,
Is all we seek, and all our versing brings ;
And more deserts than these are seldom ours.
    But thou, whose Muse a falcon's pitch can soar,   85
    Must share the bays even with a conqueror.

Cuttie.

Why doth not Willie then produce such lines
Of men and arms as might accord with these?

Willie.

'Cause Cuttie's spirit not in Willie shines.
Pan cannot wield the club of Hercules,   90
Nor dare a merlin on a heron seize.
Scarce know I how to fit a shepherd's ear :
Far more unable shall I be to please
In ought, which none but semi-gods must hear.
   When by thy verse (more able) time shall see,   95
   Thou canst give more to kings than kings to thee.

Cuttie.

But, well-a-day, who loves the Muses now,
Or helps the climber of the sacred hill?
None lean to them, but strive to disallow
All heavenly dews the goddesses distil.   100

Willie.

Let earthly minds base muck for ever fill,
Whose music only is the chime of gold ;
Deaf be their ears to each harmonious quill !
As they of learning think, so of them hold.   [105
   And if there's none deserves what thou canst do,
   Be then the poet and the patron too.

L 2

I tell thee, Cuttie, had I all the sheep,
With thrice as many moe, as on these plains
Or shepherd or fair maiden sits to keep,
I would them all forego, so I thy strains   110
Could equalize.   O how our neatest swains
Do trim themselves, when on a holiday
They haste to hear thee sing, knowing the trains
Of fairest nymphs will come to learn thy lay.
    Well may they run and wish a parting never,   115
    So thy sweet tongue might charm their ears for ever.

Cuttie.

These attributes, my lad, are not for me ;
Bestow them where true merit hath assign'd—

Willie.

And do I not, bestowing them on thee ?
Believe me, Cuttie, I do bear this mind,   120
That whereso'er we true deserving find,
To give a silent praise is to detract.
Obscure thy verses (more than most refin'd)
From any one of dulness so compact ;
And rather sing to trees than to such men,   125
Who know not how to crown a poet's pen.

Cuttie.

Willie, by thy incitement I'll assay
To raise my subject higher than tofore,

And sing it to our swains next holiday,   [130
Which (as approv'd) shall fill them with the store
Of such rare accents ; if dislik'd, no more
Will I a higher strain than shepherds use,
But sing of woods and rivers, as before.

Willie.

Thou wilt be ever happy in thy Muse.
   But see, the radiant sun is gotten high ;   135
   Let's seek for shadow in the grove here by.

THE SIXTH ECLOGUE.

The Argument.

Philos of his dog doth brag
For having many feats ;
The while the cur undoes his bag,
And all his dinner eats.

WILLIE.   JOCKIE.   PHILOS.

Willie.

STAY, Jockie, let us rest here by this spring,
And Philos too, since we so well are met ;
This spreading oak will yield us shadowing
Till Phœbus' steeds be in the ocean wet.

Jockie.

Gladly, kind swain, I yield, so thou wilt play,   5
And make us merry with a roundelay.

Philos.

No, Jockie, rather wend we to the wood ;
The time is fit, and filberds waxen ripe.

Let's go and fray the squirrel from his food ;
We will another time hear Willie pipe.   10

Willie.

But who shall keep our flocks when we are gone ?
I dare not go, and let them feed alone.

Jockie.

Nor I : since but the other day it fell,
Leaving my sheep to graze on yonder plain,
I went to fill my bottle at the well,   15
And ere I could return two lambs were slain.

Philos.

Then was thy dog ill taught, or else asleep ;
Such curs as those shall never watch my sheep.

Willie.

Yet Philos hath a dog not of the best :
He seems too lazy, and will take no pains ;   20
More fit to lie at home and take his rest,
Than catch a wand'ring sheep upon the plains.

Jockie.

'Tis true indeed : and Philos, wot ye what ?
I think he plays the fox, he grows so fat !

Philos.

Yet hath not Jockie nor yet Willie seen   25
A dog more nimble than is this of mine,

Nor any of the fox more heedful been,
When in the shade I slept, or list to dine.
And though I say't, hath better tricks in store
Than both of yours, or twenty couple more.   30

How often have the maidens strove to take him,
When he hath cross'd the plain to bark at crows?
How many lasses have I known to make him
Garlands to gird his neck, with which he goes
   Vaunting along the lands so wondrous trim,   35
   That not a dog of yours durst bark at him.

And when I list, as oftentimes I use,
To tune a hornpipe or a morris-dance,
The dog, as he by nature could not choose,
Seeming asleep before, will leap and dance.   40

Willie.

Belike your dog came of a pedlar's brood,
Or Philos' music is exceeding good.

Philos.

I boast not of his kin, nor of my reed,
Though of my reed and him I well may boast;
Yet if you will adventure that some meed   45
Shall be to him that is in action most,
   As for a collar of shrill-sounding bells,
   My dog shall strive with yours, or any's else.

Jockie.

Philos, in truth I must confess your Wag
(For so you call him) hath of tricks good store.   50
To steal the victuals from his master's bag
More cunningly I ne'er saw dog before.
  See, Willie, see ! I prithee, Philos, note
  How fast thy bread and cheese goes down his
    throat.

Willie.

Now, Philos, see how mannerly your cur,   55
Your well-taught dog, that hath so many tricks,
Devours your dinner.

Philos.

    I wish 'twere a bur
To choke the mongrel !

Jockie.

    See how clean he licks
Your butter-box ; by Pan, I do not meanly
Love Philos' dog that loves to be so cleanly.   60

Philos.

Well flouted, Jockie.

Willie.

    Philos ! run amain,
For in your scrip he now hath thrust his head
So far, he cannot get it forth again ;
See how he blindfold strags along the mead,

64.—*Strags,* stumbles.

And at your scrip your bottle hangs, I think.   65
He loves your meat, but cares not for your drink.

Jockie.

Ay, so it seems : and Philos now may go
Unto the wood or home for other cheer.

Philos.

'Twere better he had never serv'd me so :
Sweet meat, sour sauce, he shall aby it dear.   70
    What, must he be aforehand with his master ?

Willie.

Only in kindness he would be your taster.

Philos.

Well, Willie, you may laugh, and urge my spleen ;
But by my hook I swear he shall it rue,
And had far'd better had he fasting been.   75
But I must home for my allowance new.
So farewell, lads.   Look to my fleeced train
Till my return.

Jockie.

We will.

Willi

Make haste again.

65.—*Scrip*, bag.   70.—*Aby*, pay for, expiate.

THE SEVENTH ECLOGUE.

———

THE ARGUMENT.

Palinode entreats his friend
To leave a wanton lass ;
Yet he pursues her to his end,
And lets all counsel pass.

———

### PALINODE.	HOBBINOLL.

WHITHER wends Hobbinoll so early day?
What, be thy lambkins broken from the fold,
And on the plains all night have run astray?
Or are thy sheep and sheep-walks both ysold ?	[5
What mister-chance hath brought thee to the field
Without thy sheep? thou were not wont to yield
To idle sport,
But didst resort

5.—*Mister-chance,* manner of chance.

As early to thy charge from drowsy bed
As any shepherd that his flock hath fed   10
                Upon these downs.

                Hobbinoll.
                Such heavy frowns
Fortune for others keeps ; but bends on me
Smiles would befit the seat of majesty.
                        Hath Palinode   15
                        Made his abode
Upon our plains, or in some uncouth cell,
That hears not what to Hobbinoll befell ?
Phillis the fair, and fairer is there none,
To-morrow must be link'd in marriage bands.   20
'Tis I that must undo her virgin zone :
Behold the man, behold the happy hands.

                Palinode.
Behold the man ?   Nay, then the woman too :
Though both of them are very small beholding
To any power that set them on to woo.   25
Ah, Hobbinoll ! it is not worth unfolding
What shepherds say of her; thou canst not choose
But hear what language all of Phillis use ;
                Yet, than such tongues,
                To her belongs   30
More men to sate her lust !   Unhappy elf !
That wilt be bound to her to lose thyself :
                Forsake her first.

        31.—Ed. 1620, More then to sate, &c.

Hobbinoll.

Thou most accurs'd !

Durst thou to slander thus the innocent,   35
The graces' pattern, virtue's president?
She in whose eye
Shines modesty:

Upon whose brow lust never looks with hope?
Venus rul'd not in Phillis' horoscope.   40
'Tis not the vapour of a hemlock stem
Can spoil the perfume of sweet cinnamon;
Nor vile aspersions, or by thee or them
Cast on her name, can stay my going on.

Palinode.

On may'st thou go, but not with such a one,   45
Whom, I dare swear, thou know'st is not a maid.
Remember, when I met her last alone,
As we to yonder grove for filberds stray'd,
Like to a new-struck doe from out the bushes
Lacing herself, and red with gamesome blushes,   50
Made towards the green,
Loath to be seen :

And after in the grove the goatherd met.
What saidst thou then?   If this prevail not, yet
I'll tell thee moe.   55
Not long ago

36.—*Presi.'cnt*, precedent, model.

Too long I lov'd her, and as thou dost now,
Would swear Diana was less chaste than she,
That Jupiter would court her, knew he how
To find a shape might tempt such chastity :   60
And that her thoughts were pure as new-fall'n snow,
Or silver swans that trace the banks of Po,
   And free within
   From spot of sin :
Yet like the flint her lust-swoll'n breast conceal'd 65
A hidden fire ; and thus it was reveal'd :
   Cladon, the lad
   Who whilom had
The garland given for throwing best the bar,
I know not by what chance or lucky star,   70
   Was chosen late
   To be the mate
Unto our Lady of the gleesome May,
And was the first that danc'd each holiday.
None would he take but Phillis forth to dance,   75
Nor any could with Phillis dance but he.
On Palinode she thenceforth not a glance
Bestows, but hates him and his poverty.
Cladon had sheep and limbs for stronger load
Than e'er she saw in simple Palinode ;   80
   He was the man
   Must clip her then ;
For him she wreaths of flowers and chaplets
   made,
To strawberries invites him in the shade

In shearing time: 85
And in the prime
Would help to clip his sheep and guard his lambs,
And at a need lend him her choicest rams ;
And on each stock
Work such a clock   90
With twisted colour'd thread, as not a swain
On all these downs could show the like again.
But, as it seems, the well grew dry at last,
Her fire unquench'd ; and she hath Cladon left.
Nor was I sorry ; nor do wish to taste   95
The flesh whereto so many flies have cleft.
Oh, Hobbinoll ! canst thou imagine she
That hath so oft been tried, so oft misdone,
Can from all other men be true to thee ?   [100
Thou know'st with me, with Cladon, she hath gone
Beyond the limits that a maiden may,
And can the name of wife those rovings stay?
She hath not ought
That's hid, unsought :
These eyes, these hands, so much know of that
  woman   105
As more thou canst not ; can that please that's
  common ?
No : should I wed,
My marriage bed
And all that it contains should as my heart

86.—*Prime*, spring.

Be known but to myself ; if we impart   110
        What golden rings
        The fairy brings,
We lose the gem : nor will they give us more.
Wives lose their value, if once known before.
Behold this violet that cropped lies,   115
I know not by what hand, first from the stem,
With what I pluck myself shall I it prize ?
I scorn the offals of a diadem.
A virgin's bed hath millions of delights,
If then good parents please she know no more : 120
Nor hath her servants nor her favourites
That wait her husband's issuing at door.
She that is free both from the act and eye
Only deserves the due of chastity.
        But Phillis is   125
        As far from this,
As are the poles in distance from each other :
She well beseems the daughter of her mother.
        Is there a brake
        By hill or lake   130
In all our plains that hath not guilty been
In keeping close her stealths ; the Paphian Queen
        Ne'er used her skill
        To win her will
Of young Adonis with more heart than she   135
Hath her allurements spent to work on me.

      121.—*Servants*, paramours.

Leave, leave her, Hobbinoll; she is so ill
That any one is good that's nought of her,
Though she be fair, the ground which oft we till
Grows with his burden old and barrener.   140

Hobbinoll.

With much ado, and with no little pain
Have I out-heard thy railing 'gainst my love :
But it is common what we cannot gain
We oft disvalue ; sooner shalt thou move
Yond lofty mountain from the place it stands,   145
Or count the meadow's flowers, or Isis' sands,
Than stir one thought
In me, that ought
Can be in Phillis which Diana fair
And all the goddesses would not·wish their.   150
Fond man, then cease
To cross that peace
Which Phillis' virtue and this heart of mine
Have well begun ; and for those words of thine
I do forgive,   155
If thou wilt live
Hereafter free from such reproaches moe,
Since goodness never was without her foe.

Palinode.

Believe me, Hobbinoll, what I have said
Was more in love to thee than hate to her :   160

Think on thy liberty; let that be weigh'd;
Great good may oft betide, if we defer,
And use some short delays ere marriage rites;
Wedlock hath days of toil as joysome nights.
                    Canst thou be free   165
                    From jealousy?
Oh no : that plague will so infect thy brain
That only death must work thy peace again.
                    Thou canst not dwell
                    One minute well   170
From whence thou leav'st her; lock on her thy
        gate,
Yet will her mind be still adulterate.
                    Not Argus' eyes,
                    Nor ten such spies,
Can make her only thine ; for she will do   175
With those that shall make thee mistrust them too.

Hobbinoll.

Wilt thou not leave to taint a virgin's name ?

Palinode.

A virgin ? yes : as sure as is her mother.
Dost thou not hear her good report by fame?

Hobbinoll.

Fame is a liar, and was never other.   180

Palinode.

Nay, if she ever spoke true, now she did :
And thou wilt once confess what I foretold :
The fire will be disc [l] os'd that now lies hid,
Nor will thy thought of her thus long time hold.
Yet may she (if that possible can fall)   185
Be true to thee, that hath been false to all.

Hobbinoll.

So pierce the rocks
A redbreast's knocks
As the belief of ought thou tell'st me now.
Yet be my guest to-morrow.

Palinode.

Speed your plough.   190
I fear ere long
You'll sing a song
Like that was sung hereby not long ago :
Where there is carrion never wants a crow.

Hobbinoll.

Ill-tutor'd swain,   195
If on the plain
Thy sheep henceforward come where mine do feed,
They shall be sure to smart for thy misdeed.

182.—*Once*, at some time, by-and-by.

190.—*Speed your plough, i.e.*, God prosper you—a shepherd's
benediction.

Palinode.

Such are the thanks a friend's forewarning brings.
Now by the love I ever bore thee, stay!   200
Meet not mishaps ! themselves have speedy wings.

Hobbinoll.

It is in vain.   Farewell.   I must away.

FINIS.   W. B.

THE
INNER TEMPLE
MASQUE.

Presented by the gentlemen there.   Jan. 13, 1614.

WRITTEN BY W. BROWNE.

OVID. AD PISONEM.
———— *Non semper Gnosius arcu*
Destinat, exempto sed laxat cornua nervo.

Gentlemen,—

I give you but your own. If you refuse to foster it, I know not who will. By your means it may live. If it degenerate in kind from those other our Society hath produced, blame yourselves for not seeking to a happier Muse. I know it is not without faults, yet such as your loves, or at least Poetica Licentia (the common salve) will make tolerable. What is good in it, that is yours; what bad, mine; what indifferent, both; and that will suffice, since it was done to please ourselves in private by him that is

All yours,

W. Browne.

THE

INNER TEMPLE MASQUE.

The Description of

THE FIRST SCENE.

*On one side the hall towards the lower end was dis-
covered a cliff of the sea done over in part white
according to that of Virgil, lib. 5.*

Jamque adeo scopulos sirenum advecta subibat,
Difficiles quondam multorumque ossibus albos.

Upon it were seated two sirens as they are described by
Hyginus *and* Servius, *with their upper parts like*

* The *Inner Temple Masque* was printed for the first time
in 1772, from the MS. in the Library of Emmanuel College,
Cambridge, by Thomas Davies, the bookseller, in his edition
of Browne's works.

women to the navel and the rest like a hen.   One of these at the first discovery of the scene (a sea being done in perspective on one side the cliff) began to sing this Song, being as lascivious proper to them and beginning as that of theirs in Hom. *lib.* μ. Οδ.   Δεῖρ' ἄγ' ἰὼν πολύαιν' 'Οδυσεῦ, μέγα κῦδος 'Αχαιῶν.

STEER hither, steer, your winged pines,
    All beaten mariners,
Here lie Love's undiscover'd mines,
    A prey to passengers ;
Perfumes far sweeter than the best   5
Which make the Phœnix' urn and nest.
    Fear not your ships,
Nor any to oppose you save our lips,
    But come on shore,
Where no joy dies till love hath gotten more. 10

The last two lines were repeated as from a grove near by a full Chorus, and the siren about to sing again, Triton (*in all parts as* Apollonius, *lib.* 4. *Argonautic. shows him*) *was seen interrupting her thus :*

TRITON.

Leave, leave, alluring siren, with thy song
To hasten what the Fates would fain prolong :

Your sweetest tunes but groans of mandrakes be ;
He his own traitor is that heareth thee.
Tethys commands, nor is it fit that you   15
Should ever glory you did him subdue
By wiles whose policies were never spread
Till flaming Troy gave light to have them read.
Ulysses now furrows the liquid plain
Doubtful of seeing Ithaca again.   20
For in his way more stops are thrust by time,
Than in the path where virtue comes to climb :
She that with silver springs for ever fills
The shady groves, sweet meadows, and the hills,
From whose continual store such pools are fed   25
As in the land for seas are famoused.
'Tis she whose favour to this Grecian tends,
And to remove his ruin Triton sends.

Siren.

But 'tis not Tethys, nor a greater power,
Cynthia, that rules the waves ; scarce he (each
          hour)   30
That wields the thunderbolts, can things begun
By mighty Circe, daughter to the Sun,
Check or control ; she that by charms can make
The scaled fish to leave the briny lake,
And on the seas walk as on land she were ;   35
She that can pull the pale moon from her sphere,
And at mid-day the world's all-glorious eye
Muffle with clouds in long obscurity ;

She that can cold December set on fire,
And from the grave bodies with life inspire ;   40
She that can cleave the centre, and with ease
A prospect make to our Antipodes ;
Whose mystic spells have fearful thunders made,
And forc'd brave rivers to run retrograde.
She without storms that sturdy oaks can tear   45
And turn their roots where late their curl'd tops were.
She that can with the winter solstice bring
All Flora's dainties, Circe, bids me sing ;
And till some greater power her hand can stay,
Whoe'er commands, I none but her obey.   50

TRITON.

* Hom:
'Αλλά ἐ
Νηοηὶς
θυγάτηρ, &c

Then Nereus' daughter* thus you'll have me tell.

SIREN.

You may.

TRITON.

Think on her wrath.

SIREN.

I shall.   Triton ! farewell.

SIREN.

Vain was thy message, vain her hest, for I
Must tune again my wanton melody.

53.—*Hest*, behest, command.

Here she went on with her Song thus:

For swelling waves our panting breasts,   55
   Where never storms arise,
Exchange ; and be awhile our guests :
   For stars gaze on our eyes.
The compass love shall hourly sing,
And as he goes about the ring,   60
   We will not miss
To tell each point he nameth with a kiss.

CHORUS.

Then come on shore,
Where no joy dies till love hath gotten more.

At the end of this song Circe *was seen upon the rock,
quaintly attired, her hair loose about her shoulders,
an anadem of flowers on her head, with a wand
in her hand ; and then, making towards the
sirens, called them thence with this speech :*

Sirens, enough ; cease ; Circe hath prevail'd ;   65
The Greeks which on the dancing billows sail'd,
About whose ships a hundred dolphins clung
Rapt with the music of Ulysses' tongue,
Have with their guide by pow'rful Circe's hand
Cast their hook'd anchors on Æœa's strand.   70
Yond stands a hill crown'd with high waving trees,
Whose gallant tops each neighb'ring country sees,

Under whose shade an hundred silvans play,
With gaudy nymphs far fairer than the day;
Where everlasting spring with silver showers   75
Sweet roses doth increase to grace our bowers;
Where lavish Flora, prodigal in pride,
Spends what might well enrich all earth beside,
And to adorn this place she loves so dear,
Stays in some climates scarcely half the year.   8o
When would she to the world indifferent be,
They should continual April have as we.
Midway the wood and from the levell'd lands
A spacious yet a curious arbour stands,
Wherein should Phœbus once to pry begin,   85
I would benight him ere he get his inn,
Or turn his steeds awry, so draw him on
To burn all lands but this like Phaeton.
Ulysses near his mates by my strong charms
Lies there till my return in sleep's soft arms: 90
Then, sirens, quickly wend we to the bower
To fit their welcome, and show Circe's power.

SIREN.

What all the elements do owe to thee
In their obedience is perform'd in me.

CIRCE.

Circe drinks not of Lethe: then away   95
To help the nymphs who now begin their lay.

73.—*Silvans*, fauns.   74.—*Gaudy*, gay.

THE SECOND SCENE.

While Circe *was speaking her first speech, and at these words, "*Yond stands a hill, &c.,*" a traverse*[a] *was drawn at the lower end of the hall, and gave way for the discovery of an artificial wood so near imitating nature that I think, had there been a grove like it in the open plain, birds would have been faster drawn to that than to Zeuxis' grapes. The trees stood at the climbing of an hill, and left at their feet a little plain, which they circled like a crescent. In this space upon hillocks were seen eight musicians in crimson taffety*[b] *robes, with chaplets of laurel on their heads, their lutes by them, which being by them touched as a warning to the nymphs of the wood, from among the trees was heard this Song . . . .*

THE SONG IN THE WOOD.

WHAT sing the sweet birds in each grove ?
Nought but love.
What sound our echoes day and night ?
All delight.   100
What doth each wind breathe as it fleets ?
Endless sweets.

[a] *Traverse,* curtain.
[b] *Taffety,* taffeta, a kind of thin silk.

CHORUS.

Is there a place on earth this Isle excels,
Or any nymphs more happy live than we?
When all our songs, our sounds, and breathings
    be,   105
That here all love, delight, and sweetness dwells.

By this time Circe *and the sirens being come into the
    wood,* Ulysses *was seen lying as asleep, under the
    covert of a fair tree, towards whom* Circe *coming
    bespake thus:—*

CIRCE.

Yet holds soft sleep his course.   Now, Ithacus,
Ajax would offer hecatombs to us,
And Ilium's ravish'd wives, and childless sires,
With incense dim the bright ethereal fires,   110
To have thee bound in chains of sleep as here ;
 But that thou may'st behold, and know how dear
Thou art to Circe, with my magic deep
And powerful verses thus I banish sleep.

THE CHARM.

    Son of Erebus and Night,   115
    Hie away ; and aim thy flight
    Where consort none other fowl
    Than the bat and sullen owl ;

107.—*Ithacus,* Ulysses.

Where upon the limber grass
Poppy and mandragoras   120
With like simples not a few
Hang for ever drops of dew.
Where flows Lethe without coil
Softly like a stream of oil.
Hie thee thither, gentle Sleep :   125
With this Greek no longer keep.
Thrice I charge thee by my wand ;
Thrice with moly from my hand
Do I touch Ulysses' eyes,
And with the jaspis : Then arise,   130
Sagest Greek. . . . .

Ulysses (*as by the power of* Circe) *awaking thus
began :*

ULYSSES.

. . . . . Thou more than mortal maid,
Who when thou lists canst make, as if afraid,
The mountains tremble and with terror shake
The seat of Dis ; and from Avernus' lake

119.—*Limber*, easily bent.
120.—*Mandragoras*, mandrakes.
123.—*Coil*, tumult.
128.—*Moly*, a fabulous plant supposed to be endowed with magic power.
130.—*Jaspis*, jasper, the precious stone believed by the ancients to have the virtue of breaking a charm or spell.

Grim Hecate with all the Furies bring 135
To work revenge, or to thy questioning
Disclose the secrets of th' infernal shades,
Or raise the ghosts that walk the under-glades !
To thee, whom all obey, Ulysses bends.
But may I ask, great Circe, whereto tends 140
Thy never-failing hand ?   Shall we be free?
Or must thine anger crush my mates and me ?

CIRCE.

Neither, Laertes' son : with wings of love
To thee, and none but thee, my actions move.   [145
My art went with thee and thou me may'st thank
In winning Rhesus' horses ere they drank
Of Xanthus' stream ; and when with human gore
Clear Hebrus' channel was all stained o'er ;
When some brave Greeks, companions then with
        thee,
Forgot their country through the lotus-tree ; 150
I tyn'd the firebrand that (beside thy flight)
Left Polyphemus in eternal night ;
And lastly to Æœa brought thee on,
Safe from the man-devouring Læstrigon.
This for Ulysses' love hath Circe done, 155
And if to live with me thou shalt be won

151.—*Tyn'd*, kindled.

Aurora's hand shall never draw away
The sable veil that hides the gladsome day,
But we new pleasures will begin to taste,
And, better still, those we enjoyed last.   160
To instance what I can : Music, thy voice,
And of all those have felt our wrath the choice
Appear ; and in a dance 'gin that delight
Which with the minutes shall grow infinite.

*Here one attired like a woodman in all points came
    forth of the wood and going towards the stage sung
    this song to call away the first Antimasque.*

SONG.

COME ye whose horns the cuckold wears,   165
The witol too with asses' ears ;
        Let the wolf leave howling,
        The baboon his scowling,
        And Grillus hie
        Out of his sty.   170
Though grunting, though barking, though braying,
        ye come,
We'll make ye dance quiet and so send ye home.
        No gin shall snare you,
        Nor mastive scare you,

166.—*Witol*, a contented cuckold.
169.—*Grillus*, Greek γρύλλος, a hog.

Nor learn the baboon's tricks, 175
Nor Grillus scoff
From the hog trough,
But turn again unto the thicks.
Here's none ('tis hop'd) so foolish scorns
That any else should wear the horns ; 180
Here's no cur with howling,
Nor an ape with scowling,
Shall mock or moe
At what you show.
In jumping, in skipping, in turning, or ought 185
You shall do to please us, how well or how nought.
If there be any
Among this many,
Whom such an humour steers,
May he still lie 190
In Grillus' sty,
Or wear for ever the asses' ears.

*While the first staff of this song was singing out of
the thickets on either side the boscage*[a] *came rush-
ing the Antimasque, being such as by* Circe *were
supposed to have been transformed (having the
minds of men still) into these shapes following :*

178.—*Thicks*, thickets.
183.—*Moe*, mow, make mouths.
189.—*Steers*, disturbs, frightens.
[a] *Boscage*, wood.

2. With parts, heads and bodies as Actæon is pictur'd.

2. Like Midas with asses' ears.

2. Like wolves as Lycaon is drawn.

2. Like baboons.

Grillus (of whom Plutarch writes in his Morals) in the shape of a hog.

The music was composed of treble violins with all the inward parts, a bass viol, bass lute, sagbut,* cornamute, and a tabor and pipe.

These together dancing an antic measure towards the latter end of it missed Grillus, who was newly slipped away, and whilst they were at a stand, wondering what was become of him, the woodman stepped forth and sung this song:

SONG.

GRILLUS is gone ; belike he hath heard
The dairy-maid knock at the trough in the yard :
 Through thick and thin he wallows,   195
 And weighs nor depths nor shallows.
Hark how he whines !
Run all ere he dines ;
  Then serve him a trick
  For being so quick,   200
And let him for all his pains
  Behold you turn clean off
    His trough,
And spill all his wash and his grains,

---

 * *Sagbut*, sackbut.

*With this the triplex[a] of their tune was played twice
    or thrice over, and by turns brought them from
    the stage; when the woodman sung this other
    staff of the last song, and then ran after them :*

And now 'tis wish'd that all such as he   205
Were rooting with him at the trough or the tree.
            Fly, fly, from our pure fountains,
            To the dark vales or the mountains.
List, some one whines
With voice like a swine's,   210
            As angry that none
            With Grillus is gone,
Or that he is left behind.
            O let there be no stay
                    In his way,   215
To hinder the boar from his kind.

                    CIRCE.

How likes Ulysses this ?

                    ULYSSES.

                    . . . . Much like to one
Who in a shipwreck being cast upon
The frothy shores, and safe beholds his mates
Equally cross'd by Neptune and the Fates.   220
You might as well have ask'd how I would like
A strain, whose equal Orpheus could not strike,

            * *Triplex*, triple time.

Upon a harp whose strings none other be
Than of the heart of chaste Penelope.
O let it be enough that thou in these   225
Hast made most wretched Laertiades :
Let not the sad chance of distressed Greeks
With other tears than Sorrow's dew your cheeks !
Most abject baseness hath enthrall'd that breast
Which laughs at men by misery oppress'd.   230

CIRCE.

In this, as lilies, or the new-fall'n snow,
Is Circe spotless yet.   What though the bow,
Which Iris bends, appearing to each sight
In various hues and colours infinite,
The learned know that in itself is free,   235
And light and shade make that variety?
Things far off seen seem not the same they are ;
Fame is not ever truth's discoverer ;
For still where envy meeteth a report   [240
Ill she makes worse, and what is good come short.
In whatsoe'er this land hath passive been,
Or she that here o'er other reigneth queen,
Let wise Ulysses judge.   Some, I confess,
That tow'rds this Isle not long since did address
Their stretched oars, no sooner landed were,   245
But, careless of themselves, they here and there

226.—*Laertiades*, the son of Laertes, *i.e.*, Ulysses himself.
232.—*The bow*, rainbow, of which Iris was the goddess.

Fed on strange fruits, envenoming their bloods,
And now like monsters range about the woods.
If those thy mates were, yet is Circe free :
For their misfortunes have not birth from me.   250
Who in th' apothecary's shop hath ta'en,
Whilst he is wanting, that which breeds his bane,
Should never blame the man who there had plac'd it,
But his own folly urging him to taste it.

ULYSSES.

Æœa's Queen and great Hyperion's pride,   255
Pardon misdoubts ; and we are satisfied.

CIRCE.

Swifter the lightning comes not from above,
Than do our grants borne on the wings of love.
And since what's past doth not Ulysses please,
Call to a dance the fair nereides,   260
With other nymphs which do in every creek,
In woods, on plains, on mountains, simples seek
For powerful Circe, and let in a song
Echoes be aiding, that they may prolong
My now command to each place where they be, 265
To bring them hither all more speedily.

Presently in the wood was heard a full music of lutes,
which descending to the stage had to them sung

252.—*Wanting*, absent.

*this following song, the Echoes being placed in
several parts of the boscage :*

SONG.

CIRCE bids you come away.
    Echo : Come away, come away.
From the rivers, from the sea.
    Echo : From the sea, from the sea.   270
From the green woods every one.
    Echo : Every one, every one.
Of her maids be missing none.
    Echo : Missing none, missing none.
No longer stay, except it be to bring   275
    A med'cine for love's sting.
That would excuse you and be held more dear
Than wit or magic, for both they are here.
    Echo : They are here, they are here.

*The Echo had no sooner answered to the last line of
the song,* They are here, *but the second Anti-
masque came in, being seven nymphs, and were
thus attired :*

Four { *in white taffeta robes, long tresses, and chaplets
of flowers, herbs and weeds on their heads, with
little wicker baskets in their hands, neatly
painted. These were supposed to be maids
attending upon* Circe, *and used in gathering
simples for their mistress's enchantments.—*
(Pausanias in prioribus Eliacis.)

Horat. lib. 3. carmin.

Three { *in sea-green robes, greenish hair hanging loose, with leaves of coral and shells intermixed upon it.   These are by* Ovid *affirmed to help the nymphs of* Circe *in their collections by these.*

Ovid. lib. 14. Metam.

Nereides nymphæque simul quæ vellera motis
Nulla trahunt digitis, nec fila sequentia ducunt,
Gramina disponunt ; sparsosque sine ordine flores
Secernunt calathis, variisque coloribus herbas.
Ipsa, quod hæ faciunt, opus exigit—

These having danced a most curious measure to a softer tune than the first Antimasque (as most fitting) returned as they came ; the nereides towards the cliffs and the other maids of Circe towards the woods and plains, after which Ulysses, *thus :*

ULYSSES.

Fame adds not to thy joys, I see in this,   280
But like a high and stately pyramis
Grows least at farthest.   Now, fair Circe, grant,
Although the fair-hair'd Greeks do never vaunt,
That they in measur'd paces ought have done,
But where the god of battles led them on ;   285
Give leave that (freed from sleep) the small remain
Of my companions on the under plain
May in a dance strive how to pleasure thee
Either with skill or with variety.

CIRCE.

Circe is pleas'd.   Ulysses, take my wand   290
And from their eyes each child of sleep command ;
Whilst my choice maids with their harmonious voices,
Whereat each bird and dancing spring rejoices,
Charming the winds when they contrary meet,
Shall make their spirits as nimble as their feet.   295

THE THIRD SCENE'S

Description.

Circe *with this speech delivering her wand to* Ulysses
  *rests on the lower part of the hill, while he going
  up the hill and striking the trees with his wand,
  suddenly two great gates flew open, making as it
  were a large glade through the wood, and along
  the glade a fair walk ; two seeming brick walls
  on either side, over which the trees wantonly
  hung : a great light (as the sun's sudden un-
  masking) being seen upon this discovery.   At the
  further end was descried an arbour, very curiously
  done, having one entrance under an architrave
  borne up by two pillars with their chapters and
  bases gilt ; the top of the entrance beautified
  with postures of satyrs, wood-nymphs, and other
  antick work ; as also the sides and corners :
  the covering archwise interwove with boughs, the
  back of it girt round with a vine, and artificially
  done up in knots towards the top ; beyond it was*

a wood seen in perspective, the fore part of it opening at Ulysses *his approach; the maskers were discovered in several seats leaning as asleep.*

THEIR ATTIRE.

Doublets of green taffeta, cut like oaken leaves, as upon cloth of silver; their skirts and wings cut into leaves, deep round hose of the same, both laid with sprig lace spangled; long white silk stockings; green pumps, and roses done over with silver leaves; hats of the same stuff, cut narrow-brimmed, and rising smaller compass at the crown, white wreath hatbands, white plumes, egrettes[a] with a green fall,[b] ruff, bands and cuffs.

Ulysses *severally came and touched every one of them with the wand while this was sung:*

SONG.

SHAKE off sleep, ye worthy knights,
Though ye dream of all delights;
Show that Venus doth resort
To the camp as well as court

---

[a] *Egrettes*, French aigrette, a tuft of feathers, diamonds, etc.: an ornament of ribbons.

[b] *Fall*, falling-band or vandyke: it fell flat upon the dress from the neck, and was at one time worn with the ruff.

By some well-timed measure,   300
And on your gestures and your paces
Let the well-composed Graces,
Looking like, and part with pleasure.

By this the knights being all risen from their seats
were by Ulysses *(the loud music sounding) brought*
to the stage ; and then to the violins danced their
first measure ; after which this song brought them
to the second.

SONG.

ON and imitate the Sun,
Stay not to breathe till you have done :   305
     Earth doth think as other where
     Do some women she doth bear :
Those wives whose husbands only threaten
Are not lov'd like those are beaten.   [310
     Then with your feet to suff'ring move her,
     For whilst you beat earth thus, you love her.

Here they danced their second measure, and then this
song was sung, during which time they take out
the ladies :

SONG.
CHOOSE now among this fairest number,
Upon whose breasts love would for ever slumber :

Choose not amiss since you may where you will,
　Or blame yourselves for choosing ill.　　　315
Then do not leave, though oft the music closes,
Till lilies in their cheeks be turn'd to roses.

CHORUS.

And if it lay in Circe's power,
　Your bliss might so persever,
That those you choose but for an hour　320
　You should enjoy for ever.

*The knights with the ladies dance here the old measures,
galliards, corantoes, the brawls, &c., and then
(having led them again to their places) danced
their last measure; after which this song called
them away:*

SONG.

WHO but Time so hasty were
To fly away and leave you here?
　Here where delight
　Might well allure　　　　　325
A very Stoic from this night
　To turn an Epicure.

But since he calls away; and Time will soon repent,
He stay'd not longer here, but ran to be more idly
　spent.

Τέλος.　　　FINIS.　　　THE END.

MISCELLANEOUS POEMS

FROM LANSDOWNE MS. 777

AND OTHER SOURCES.

MISCELLANEOUS POEMS.

I. LOVE POEMS

I.

LOVE who will, for I'll love none,
   There's fools enough beside me :
Yet if each woman have not one,
   Come to me where I hide me,
And if she can the place attain,
For once I'll be her fool again.

It is an easy place to find,
   And women sure should know it ;
Yet thither serves not every wind,
   Nor many men can show it :
It is the storehouse, where doth lie
All women's truth and constancy.

If the journey be so long,
  No woman will adventer ;
But dreading her weak vessel's wrong,
  The voyage will not enter :
Then may she sigh and lie alone,
In love with all, yet lov'd of none.

II.

ON A FAIR LADY'S YELLOW HAIR, POWDERED WITH WHITE.

WRITTEN IN THE DISSOLVING OF A SNOW.

SAY, why on your hair yet stays
  That snow resembling white ;
Since the sun's less powerful rays
  Thaw'd that which fell last night ?

Sure to hinder those extremes
  Of love they might bestow ;
Art hath hid your golden beams
  Within a fleece of snow.

Yet as on a cloth of gold,
  With silver flowers wrought o'er,
We do now and then behold
  A radiant wire or more :

So sometimes the amorous air
  Doth with your fair locks play,
And unclouds a golden hair;
  And then breaks forth the day.

On your cheeks the rosy morn
  We plainly then descry;
And a thousand Cupids born,
  And playing in each eye.

Now we all are at a stay,
  And know not where to turn us;
If we wish that snow away,
  Those glorious beams would burn us.

If it should not fall amain,
  And cloud your loveful eyes,
Each gentle heart would soon be slain,
  And made their sacrifice.

III.

Not long agone a youthful swain,
Much wronged by a maid's disdain,
Before Love's altar came and did implore
That he might like her less, or she love more.
The god him heard, and she began
To dote on him; he, foolish man,
Cloy'd with much sweets, thus chang'd his note
    before,
"O let her love me less, or I like more."

IV.

SHALL I love again, and try
  If I still must love to lose,
And make weak mortality
  Give new birth unto my woes?
No, let me ever live from Love's enclosing,
Rather than love to live in fear of losing.

One whom hasty Nature gives
  To the world without his sight,
Not so discontented lives,
  As a man depriv'd of light :
'Tis knowledge that gives vigour to our woe,
And not the want, but loss that pains us so.

With the Arabian bird then be
  Both the lover and belov'd ;
Be thy lines thy progeny
  By some gracious fair approv'd ;
So may'st thou live, and be belov'd of many,
Without the fear of loss, or want of any.

V.

DEEP are the wounds which strike a virtuous name,
Sharp are the darts Revenge still sets on wing :
Consuming Jealousy's abhorred flame !
Deadly the frowns of an enraged king.

Yet all these to Disdain's heart-searching string,
Deep, sharp, consuming, deadly, nothing be,
Whose darts, wounds, flames, and frowns, meet all
    in me.

VI.

POOR silly fool ! thou striv'st in vain to know,
If I enjoy, or love whom thou lov'st so ;
Since my affection ever secret tried
Blooms like the fern, and seeds still unespied.

And as the subtle flames of Heaven, that wound
The inward part, yet leave the outward sound :
My love wars on my heart, kills that within,
When merry are my looks, and fresh my skin.

Of yellow jaundice lovers as you be,
Whose faces straight proclaim their malady,
Think not to find me one ; who know full well,
That none but French and fools love now and tell.

His griefs are sweet, his joys (O) heavenly move,
Who from the world conceals his honest love ;
Nay, lets his mistress know his passion's source
Rather by reason than by his discourse.

This is my way, and in this language new
Showing my merit, it demands my due ;
And hold this maxim, spite of all dispute,
He asks enough that serves well and is mute.

VII.

WELCOME, welcome, do I sing,
Far more welcome than the spring ;
He that parteth from you never
Shall enjoy a spring for ever.

He that to the voice is near
   Breaking from your iv'ry pale,
Need not walk abroad to hear
   The delightful nightingale.

Welcome, welcome, then I sing,
Far more welcome than the spring ;
He that parteth from you never
Shall enjoy a spring for ever

He that looks still on your eyes,
   Though the winter have begun
To benumb our arteries,
   Shall not want the summer's sun.
      Welcome, welcome, then I sing, &c.

He that still may see your cheeks,
   Where all rareness still reposes,
Is a fool, if e'er he seeks
   Other lilies, other roses.
      Welcome, welcome, &c.

He to whom your soft lip yields,
   And perceives your breath in kissing,

All the odours of the fields
  Never, never shall be missing.
      Welcome, welcome, &c.

He that question would anew
  What fair Eden was of old,
Let him rightly study you,
  And a brief of that behold.
      Welcome, welcome, then I, &c.

VIII.

Ye merry birds, leave of to sing,
  And lend your ears awhile to me ;
Or if you needs will court the spring
  With your enticing harmony,
    Fly from this grove, leave me alone ;
    Your mirth cannot befit my moan.

But if that any be inclin'd
  To sing as sad a song as I,
Let that sad bird be now so kind
  As stay and bear me company :
    And we will strive which shall outgo,
    Her heavy strains or my sad woe.

Ye nymphs of Thames, if any swan
  Be ready now her last to sing,
O bring her hither, if ye can,
  And sitting by us in a ring,

Spend each a sigh, while she and I
Together sing, together die.

Alas ! how much I err to call
  More sorrow, where there is such store ;
Ye gentle birds, come not at all,
  And Isis' nymphs forbear the shore.
    My sighs as groans of mandrakes be,
    And would kill any one but me.

To me my griefs none other are
  Than poison is to one that long
Had fed on it without impair
  Unto his health, or Nature's wrong ;
    What others' lives would quickly spill,
    I take, but cannot take to kill.

Then, sorrow, since thou wert ordain'd
  To be the inmate of my heart,
Thrive there so long, till thou hast gain'd
  In it than life a greater part :
    And if thou wilt not kill, yet be
    The means that some one pity me.

Yet would I not that pity have
  From any other heart than hers,
Who first my wound of sorrow gave ;
  And if she still the cure defers,
    It was my fate that did assure
    A hand to wound, but none to cure.

IX.

A SIGH FROM OXFORD.

Go, and if thou chance to find
That is southwards bent a wind,
Take it upon any hire,
But be sure it do not tire :
If with love-sighs mix'd it be   5
Be secure 'twill carry thee ;
Spur it on, and make more haste,
Than the fleet that went out last ;
Do not stay to curl a rill,
Cleanse a corn, or drive a mill ;   10
Nor to crisp a lock, or turn it :
Thou hast fire, and so may'st burn it.
   For thy lodging do not come
In a bagpipe or a drum :
In the belly of some lute   15
That hath struck Apollo mute ;
Or a gentle lady's ear,
That might dream, whilst thou art there,
Of such vows as thou dost carry,
There for one night thou may'st tarry ;   20
Whisper there thy message to her ;
And if she have any wooer,
In her sleep perhaps she may
Speak what she denies the day,

10.—*Cleanse a corn, i.e.*, winnow.

And instruct thee to reply   25
To my Cælia more than I.
For thy lodging, the next day,
Do not thankless go away ;
Give the lute a test of air,
That a poet's sigh lay there ;   30
And inform it with a soul
Of so high divine control,
That whoever hears it next
Shall be with a Muse perplex'd ;
And a lawyer shall rehearse   35
His demurs and pleas in verse.
    In the Lady's Lab'rinth leave
Not a sound that may deceive ;
Drive it thence ; and after see
Thou there leave some part of thee,   40
By which she may well descry
Any lover's forgery :
For it never will admit
Ought that is not true as it.
    When that office thou hast done,   45
And the lady lastly won,
Let the air thou left'st the girl,
Turn a drop, and then a pearl ;
Which I wish that she should wear
For a pendant in her ear ;   50
And its virtue still shall be,
To detect all flattery.
Could I give each monarch such,

None would say I sigh'd too much.
When thy largess thou hast given, 55
(My best sigh next that for heaven)
Make not any longer stay;
Kiss thine hostess, and away.
    If thou meet, as thou dost stir,
Any Sigh a passenger, 60
Stand upon thy guard, and be
Jealous of a robbery;
For the Sighs that travel now
Bear not so much truth as thou;
Those may rob thee to supply 65
That defect of constancy
Which their masters left to be
Fill'd by what was stol'n from thee:
Yet adventure, for in sooth
Few dare meddle now with truth; 70
'Tis a coin that will not pay
For their meat or horses' hay;
'Tis cried down, and such a coin
As no great thief will purloin.
    Petty foot-Sighs thou may'st meet, 75
From the Counter or the Fleet
To a wife or mistress sent,
That her lover's means hath spent,
Of such ones beware, for those,
Much spent on their masters' woes, 80
May want of that store which thou
Carriest to my Cælia now:

And so rob thee, and then spend thee,
So as I did ne'er intend thee ;
With dishonour thou shalt move   85
To beg an alms, not get a love.
Shun them, for they have no ruth,
And know that few are hang'd for truth :
Nay, the laws have been more brief
To jail that theft, more than a thief ;   90
The Hue and Cry will not go post
For the worth which thou hast lost.
Yet for Faith and Truth betray'd
Countries heretofore have paid.

   Wary be, and fearing loss,   95
Like those of the Rosy-Cross,
Be not seen, but hie thee on
Like an inspiration ;
And as air, ascending higher,
Turns to drops, or else to fire :   100
So when thou art nearer come
To my star, and to thy home,
If thou meet a Sigh, which she
Hath but coldly sent to me,
Kiss it, for thy warmer air   105
Will dissolve into a tear ;
As the steam of roses will
At the cold top of a still :
Nor shalt thou be lost ; her eyes
Have Apollo's faculties ;   110
Their fair rays will work amain,

And turn thee to a Sigh again.
  What thou art yet closely shroud,
Rise up like a fleecy cloud ;
And as thou dost so aspire   115
To her element of fire,
(Which afar its forces dart,
And exhal'd thee from my heart,)
Make thine own shape, just as we
Fashion clouds by phantasy ;   120
Be a Cupid, be a Heart
Wounded, and her rays the dart ;
Have a chasma too, and there
Only let our vows appear :
Lastly, I would wish thee be   125
Such a cloud resembling me,
That Ixion-like she might
Clasp thee with his appetite ;
Yet more temperate and chaste,
And whilst thou art so embrac'd,   130
And afforded some sweet sips,
From her Muse-inspiring lips,
Vanish ! and then slip by art
Through those rubies to her heart.
Wind it round, and let it be   135
Thoughtless of all earth but me ;
Grow acquainted with that air,
Which doth to her heart repair ;

123.—*Chasma*, chasm.

And so temper and so blisse it,
And so fan it, and so kiss it,   140
That the new-born rose may be
Not so truly chaste as she.
    With that Regent, from that hour,
Leiger lie Ambassador :
Keep our truce unbroke, prefer   145
All the suits I send to her :
Get dispatches, that may stand
With the good of either hand ;
So that thou be bold and true,
Never fear what may ensue ;   150
For there is no policy
Like to that of honesty.
    Get into her minion thought,
Howsoever dearly bought ;
And procure that she dispense   155
To transport some kisses thence :
These are rarities and dear,
For like hers I meet none here.
    This thy charge is ; then begone
With thy full commission :   160
Make her mine, and clear all doubts ;
Kill each jealousy that sprouts ;
Keep the honour of thy place ;
Let no other Sigh disgrace
    ·Thy just worth, and never sit   165

139.—*Blisse*, bless.
144.—*Leiger*, a resident ambassador.

To her, though [s]he bribe for it.
  And when I shall call thee home,
To send another in thy room ;
Leave these thoughts for agents there :
  First, I think her pure and chaste,   170
As the ice congealed last ;
Next, as iron (though it glows)
Never melts but once, and flows ;
So her love will only be
Fluent once, and that to me :   175
Lastly, as the glowworm's might
Never kindled other light,
I believe that fire which she
Haply shows in loving me,
Never will encourage man,   180
(Though her love's meridian
Heat him to it) once to dare
To mention love, though unaware ;
Much less fire a Sigh that may
Incorporate with my fair ray.   185
  I have read of two erewhile,
Enemies burnt in one pile ;
That their flames would never kiss,
But made a several pyramis.
Let all Sighs that come to thee,   190
By thy love enlighten'd be ;
If they join and make one flame,
Be secure from me they came.
If they separate, beware,

There is craft that would ensnare ;   195
Mine are rarefied and just ;
Truth and love : the others lust.
   With this charge, farewell, and try
What must be my destiny :
Woo, secure her ; plead thy due ;   200
This Sigh is not so long as true :
And whoever shall incline
To send another after mine,
Though he have more cunning far
Than the Juggler Gondomar,   205
All his sleights, and all his faults,
Hollowness of heart, and halts ;
By thy chaster fire will all
Be so wrought diaphanal ;
She shall look through them, and see   210
How much he comes short of me :
Then my Sigh shall be approv'd,
And kiss that heart whom I have lov'd.

X.

A HAPLESS shepherd on a day
   Yode to St. Michael's Mount,
And spent more tears upon the way
   Than all the sands could count.

205.—*Gondomar*, Diego Sarmiento de Acuañ, Count Gon-
domar, ambassador from the Court of Spain to London, 1617-23,
by whose intrigues Sir Walter Raleigh was beheaded in 1618.
  207.— *Halts*, bad qualities.

Full was the sea, so were the eyes
Of this unhappy lover,
Yet without oar or wind in skies,
His sighs did waft him over.

XI.

CÆLIA is gone, and now sit I
As Philomela, on a thorn,
Turn'd out of Nature's livery,
Mirthless, alone, and all forlorn ;
Only she sings not, while my sorrows can
Afford such notes as fit a dying swan.
So shuts the marigold her leaves
At the departure of the sun ;
So from honeysuckle sheaves
The bee goes when the day is done.
So sits the turtle when she is but one ;
So is all woe ; as I, now she is gone.
To some few birds kind Nature hath
Made all the summer as one day,
Which once enjoy'd, cold winter's wrath,
As night, they sleeping pass away :
Those happy creatures are that know not yet
The pains to be depriv'd, or to forget.
I oft have heard men say there be
Some that with confidence profess
The helpful Art of Memory ;
But could they teach Forgetfulness,

I'd learn and try what further art could do
To make me love her and forget her too.
 Sad Melancholy that persuades
 Men from themselves to think they be
 Headless or other bodies' shades,
 Hath long and bootless dwelt with me ;
For could I think she some Idea were,
I still might love, forget, and have her here ;
 But such she is not : nor would I,
 For twice as many torments more,
 As her bereaved company
 Hath brought to those I felt before ;
For then no future time might hap to know,
That she deserv'd, or I did love her so.
 Ye hours then but as minutes be,
 (Though so I shall be sooner old,)
 Till I those lovely graces see,
 Which but in her can none behold :
Then be an age that we may never try
More grief in parting, but grow old and die.

II. ODES, SONGS, AND SONNETS.

AN ODE.

I.

AWAKE, fair Muse ; for I intend
    These everlasting lines to thee,
And, honour'd Drayton, come and lend
    An ear to this sweet melody :
For on my harp's most high and silver string
To those Nine Sisters whom I love, I sing.

    This man through death and horror seeks
        Honour by the victorious steel ;
    Another in unmapped creeks
        For jewels moors his winged keel.
The clam'rous Bar wins some, and others bite
At looks thrown from a mushroom favourite.

    But I, that serve the lovely Graces,
        Spurn at that dross which most adore ;
    And titles hate like painted faces,
        And heart-fed care for evermore.

Those pleasures I disdain which are pursu'd
With praise and wishes by the multitude.

 The bays, which deathless Learning crowns,
  Me of Apollo's troop installs :
 The satyrs following o'er the downs
  Fair nymphs to rustic festivals,
Make me affect (where men no traffic have)
The holy horror of a savage cave.

 Through the fair skies I thence intend,
  With an unus'd and powerful wing,
 To bear me to my journey's end :
  And those that taste the Muses' spring,
Too much celestial fire have at their birth
To live long time like common souls in earth.

 From fair Aurora will I rear
  Myself unto the source of floods ;
 And from the Ethiopian bear,
  To him as white as snowy woods ;
Nor shall I fear (from this day taking flight)
To be wound up in any veil of night.

 Of Death I may not fear the dart,
  As is the use of human state ;
 For well I know my better part
  Dreads not the hand of Time or Fate.

Tremble at Death, Envy, and Fortune who
Have but one life : Heaven gives a poet two.

All costly obsequies away,
　Marble and painting too, as vain ;
My ashes shall not meet with clay,
　As those do of the vulgar train.
And if my Muse to Spenser's glory come,
No king shall own my verses for his tomb.

II.

A ROUND.

All.

Now that the Spring hath fill'd our veins
　With kind and active fire,
And made green liv'ries for the plains,
　And every grove a quire :

Sing we a song of merry glee,
　And Bacchus fill the bowl.
1. Then here's to thee ;　2. And thou to me
　And every thirsty soul.

Nor Care nor Sorrow e'er paid debt,
　Nor never shall do mine ;
I have no cradle going yet,
　Not I, by this good wine.

No wife at home to send for me,
　　No hogs are in my ground,
No suit in law to pay a fee,
　　Then round, old Jocky, round.

All.

Shear sheep that have them, cry we still,
　　But see that no man 'scape
　　　　To drink of the sherry,
　　　　That makes us so merry,
And plump as the lusty grape.

III.

Unhappy Muse, that nothing pleasest me,
But tir'st thyself to reap another's bliss,
She that as much forbears thy melody,
As fearful maidens do the serpent's hiss,
Doth she not fly away when I would sing?
Or doth she stay, when I with many a tear
Keep solemn time to my woes' uttering ;
And ask what wild birds grant to lend an ear
O hapless tongue, in silence ever live,
And ye, my founts of tears, forbear supply :
Since neither words, nor tears, nor Muse can give
Ought worth the pitying such a wretch as I.
　　Grieve to yourselves, if needs you will deplore,
　　Till tears and words are spent for evermore.

IV.

UNHAPPY I, in whom no joy appears,
And but for sorrow of all else forlorn ;
Mishaps increasing faster than my years,
As I to grieve and die were only born.
Dark sullen night is my too tedious day ;
In it I labour when all others rest,
And wear in discontent those hours away,
Which make some less deserving greater blest.
The rose-cheek'd morn I hate, because it brings
A sad remembrance of my fairer fair,
From whose dear grave arise continual springs,
Whose misty vapours cloud the lightsome air.
   And only now I to my love prefer
   Those clouds which shed their rain, and weep for
   her.

V.

THIRSIS' PRAISE OF HIS MISTRESS.[a]

ON a hill that grac'd the plain
Thirsis sat, a comely swain,
   Comelier swain ne'er grac'd a hill :
Whilst his flock, that wander'd nigh,
Cropp'd the green grass busily,
   Thus he tun'd his oaten quill :

[a] From *England's Helicon ; or, the Muses' Harmony*, 1614, 8vo.

Ver hath made the pleasant field
Many sev'ral odours yield,
   Odours aromatical :
From fair Astra's cherry lip
Sweeter smells for ever skip,
   They in pleasing passen all.

Leavy groves now mainly ring
With each sweet bird's sonneting,
   Notes that makes the echoes long :
But when Astra tunes her voice,
All the mirthful birds rejoice,
   And are list'ning to her song.

Fairly spreads the damask rose,
Whose rare mixture doth disclose
   Beauties pencils cannot feign ;
Yet if Astra pass the bush,
Roses have been seen to blush,
   She doth all their beauties stain.

Phœbus, shining bright in sky,
Gilds the floods, heats mountains high
   With his beams' all-quick'ning fire :
Astra's eyes, most sparkling ones,
Strikes a heat in hearts of stones,
   And enflames them with desire.

Fields are blest with flow'ry wreath,
Air is blest when she doth breathe,

Birds make happy ev'ry grove,
She, each bird, when she doth sing:
Phœbus heat to earth doth bring,
She makes marble fall in love.

Those blessings of the earth we swains do call,
Astra can bless those blessings, earth and all.

CÆLIA.

SONNETS.

I.

Lo, I the man that whilom lov'd and lost,
Not dreading loss, do sing again of love;
And like a man but lately tempest-toss'd,
Try if my stars still inauspicious prove:
Not to make good that poets never can
Long time without a chosen mistress be,
Do I sing thus; or my affections ran
Within the maze of mutability;
What last I lov'd was beauty of the mind,
And that lodg'd in a temple truly fair,
Which ruin'd now by death, if I can find
The saint that liv'd therein some otherwhere,
I may adore it there, and love the cell
For entertaining what I lov'd so well.

2.

WHY might I not for once be of that sect,
Which hold that souls, when Nature hath her right,
Some other bodies to themselves elect ;
And sunlike make the day, and license night ?
That soul, whose setting in one hemisphere
Was to enlighten straight another part ;
In that horizon, if I see it there,
Calls for my first respect and its desert ;
Her virtue is the same and may be more ;
For as the sun is distant, so his power
In operation differs, and the store
Of thick clouds interpos'd make him less our.
   And verily I think her climate such,
   Since to my former flame it adds so much.

3.

FAIREST, when by the rules of palmistry
You took my hand to try if you could guess
By lines therein if any wight there be
Ordain'd to make me know some happiness ;
I wish'd that those characters could explain,
Whom I will never wrong with hope to win ;
Or that by them a copy might be ta'en,
By you alone what thoughts I have within.
But since the hand of Nature did not set
(As providently loath to have it known)
The means to find that hidden alphabet,
Mine eyes shall be th' interpreters alone ;

By them conceive my thoughts, and tell me, fair,
If now you see her, that doth love me there ?

4.

So sat the muses on the banks of Thames,
And pleas'd to sing our heavenly Spenser's wit,
Inspiring almost trees with pow'rful flames,
As Cælia when she sings what I have writ :
Methinks there is a spirit more divine,
An elegance more rare when ought is sung
By her sweet voice, in every verse of mine,
Than I conceive by any other tongue :
So a musician sets what some one plays
With better relish, sweeter stroke, than he
That first compos'd ; nay, oft the maker[a] weighs
If what he hears, his own, or other's be.
   Such are my lines : the highest, best of choice,
   Become more gracious by her sweetest voice.

5.

WERE'T not for you, here should my pen have rest
And take a long leave of sweet poesy ;
Britannia's swains, and rivers far by west,
Should hear no more mine oaten melody ;
Yet shall the song I sung of them awhile
Unperfect lie, and make no further known

---

[a] *Maker*, composer.

The happy loves of this our pleasant Isle ;
Till I have left some record of mine own.
You are the subject now, and, writing you,
I well may versify, not poetize :
Here needs no fiction : for the graces true
And virtues clip not with base flatteries.
   Here could I write what you deserve of praise,
   Others might wear, but I should win the bays.

6.

SING soft, ye pretty birds, while Cælia sleeps,
And gentle gales play gently with the leaves ;
Learn of the neighbour brooks, whose silent deeps
Would teach him fear, that her soft sleep bereaves.
Mine oaten reed, devoted to her praise,
(A theme that would befit the Delphian lyre)
Give way, that I in silence may admire.
Is not her sleep like that of innocents,
Sweet as herself; and is she not more fair,
Almost in death, than are the ornaments
Of fruitful trees, which newly budding are ?
   She is, and tell it, Truth, when she shall lie
   And sleep for ever, for she cannot die.

7.

FAIREST, when I am gone, as now the glass
Of Time is mark'd how long I have to stay,

Let me entreat you, ere from hence I pass,
Perhaps from you for evermore away,
Think that no common love hath fir'd my breast,
Nor base desire, but virtue truly known,
Which I may love, and wish to have possess'd,
Were you the high'st as fair'st of any one ;
'Tis not your lovely eye enforcing flames,
Nor beauteous red beneath a snowy skin,
That so much binds me yours, or makes you fame's,
As the pure light and beauty shrin'd within :
  Yet outward parts I must affect of duty,
  As for the smell we like the rose's beauty.

8.

As oft as I meet one that comes from you,
And ask your health, not as the usual fashion,
Before he speaks, I doubt there will ensue,
As oft there doth, the common commendation :
Alas, think I, did he but know my mind
(Though for the world I would not have it so)
He would relate it in another kind,
Discourse of it at large, and yet but slow ;
He should th' occasion tell, and with it too
Add how you charg'd him he should not forget ;
For thus you might, as sure some lovers do,
Though such a messenger I have not met :
  Nor do I care, since 'twill not further move me:
  Love me alone and say alone you love me.

9.

TELL me, my thoughts (for you each minute fly,
And see those beauties which mine eyes have lost,)
Is any worthier love beneath the sky?
Would not the cold Norwegian mix'd with frost
(If in their clime she were) from her bright eyes
Receive a heat, so pow'rfully begun,
In all his veins and numbed arteries,
That would supply the lowness of the sun?
I wonder at her harmony of words,
Rare (and as rare as seldom doth she talk)
That rivers stand not in their speedy fords,
And down the hills the trees forbear to walk:
   But more I muse why I should hope in fine
   To get a Love, a Beauty so divine.

10.

To get a Love and Beauty so divine,
(In these so wary times) the fact must be
Of greater fortunes to the world than mine;
Those are the steps to that felicity;
For love no other gate hath than the eyes,
And inward worth is now esteem'd as none;
Mere outsides only to that blessing rise,
Which Truth and Love did once account their own;
Yet as she wants her fairer, she may miss
The common cause of love, and be as free
From earth, as her composure heavenly is;
If not, I restless rest in misery,

And daily wish, to keep me from despair,
Fortune my mistress, or you not so fair.

II.

FAIR Laurel, that the only witness art
To that discourse, which underneath thy shade
Our grief-swoll'n breasts did lovingly impart,
With vows as true as e'er Religion made :
If (forced by our sighs) the flame shall fly
Of our kind love, and get within thy rind,
Be wary, gentle bay, and shriek not high,
When thou dost such unusual fervour find ;
Suppress the fire ; for should it take thy leaves,
Their crackling would betray us, and thy glory
(Honour's fair symbol) dies ; thy trunk receives
But heat sufficient for our future story:
   And when our sad misfortunes vanquish'd lie,
   Embrace our fronts in sign of memory.

12.

HAD not the soil that bred me further done,
And fill'd part of those veins which sweetly do,
Much like the living streams of Eden, run,
Embracing such a Paradise as you ;
My Muse had fail'd me in the course I ran,
But that she from your virtues took new breath,
And from your eyes such fire that, like a swan,
She in your praise can sing herself to death.

Now could I wish those golden hours unspent,
Wherein my fancy led me to the woods,
And tun'd soft lays of rural merriment,
Of shepherds' loves and never-resting floods :
   For had I seen you then, though in a dream,
   Those songs had slept, and you had been my theme.

13.

NIGHT, steal not on too fast : we have not yet
Shed all our parting tears, nor paid the kisses,
Which four days' absence made us run in debt,
(O, who would absent be where grow such blisses?)
The Rose, which but this morning spread her leaves,
Kiss'd not her neighbour flower more chaste than we :
Nor are the timely ears bound up in sheaves
More strict than in our arms we twisted be ;
O who would part us then, and disunite
Two harmless souls, so innocent and true,
That were all honest love forgotten quite,
By our example men might learn anew !
   Night severs us, but pardon her she may,
   And will once make us happier than the day.

14.

DIVINEST Cælia, send no more to ask
How I in absence do ; your servant may
Be freed of that unnecessary task :
For you may know it by a shorter way.

I was a shadow when I went from you ;
And shadows are from sickness ever free.
My heart you kept (a sad one, though a true)
And nought but memory went home with me.
Look in your breast, where now two hearts you have,
And see if they agree together there :
If mine want aid, be merciful and save,
And seek not for me any other where :
  Should my physician question how I do,
  I cannot tell him, till I ask of you.

EXPLICIT.

AMOUR.[a]

Like to the world my love I find to be,
Like to the earth my faith itself doth show,
And like the thrilling winds my sighs do blow :
Like to the fire my burning jealousy,
And as a rock my heart in constancy.
Ardent affection is like to the Summer ;
My fear cold Winter, senses all benummer,
And like the Spring is memory in me.
Like to the waters are my eye-spent showers,
My thoughts of April are the fading flowers,
My flame like to the Sun is rightly ta'en,
Like to the boundless heaven desire hath been.

[a] This and the two following poems are printed for the first time from the MS. in the Library of Salisbury Cathedral.

My hopes like to the moon do wax and wane ;
But Autumn yet in me was never seen.

———

LOOK as a bough cut lately from the rind
And thrown into the fire, ere it consume
It combats with the heat in noise and fume,
And sparkles forth his moisture and his wind.
So since my heart was fir'd by you, I find
Uncessant tears so welled fro mine eyes,
And from my breast such heavy sighs arise
Striving to quell the ardour which (unkind)
You pass and scarcely notice take it burns.
Is senseless wood so deem'd whenas it mourns
To be no more ?   O blame not then my heart
That would be read in characters of woe.
You are the fire embracing every part.
Can any choose but plain that's pained so ?
If such there be, he truly merits love
Even from the widow of a Turtle-dove.

SONNET.

FOR her gait if she be walking,
Be she sitting I desire her
For her state's sake, and admire her
For her wit if she be talking.
    Gait and state and wit approve her ;
    For which all and each I love her.

Be she sullen, I commend her
For a modest.   Be she merry,
For a kind one her prefer I.
Briefly everything doth lend her
   So much grace and so approve her,
   That for everything I love her.

III.—EPISTLES.

AN EPISTLE.

DEAR soul, the time is come, and we must part,
Yet, ere I go, in these lines read my heart ;
A heart so just, so loving, and so true,
So full of sorrow and so full of you ;
That all I speak, or write, or pray, or mean, 5
And (which is all I can) all that I dream,
Is not without a sigh, a thought for you,
And as your beauties are, so are they true.

 Seven summers now are fully spent and gone,
Since first I lov'd, lov'd you, and you alone ; 10
And should mine eyes as many hundreds see,
Yet none but you should claim a right in me ;
A right so plac'd that time shall never hear
Of one so vow'd, or any lov'd so dear.

 When I am gone (if ever prayers mov'd you) 15
Relate to none that I so well have lov'd you ;
For all that know your beauty and desert,
Would swear he never lov'd, that knew to part.
 Why part we then ? That spring which but this
   day
Met some sweet river, in his bed can play, 20

And with a dimple[d] cheek smile at their bliss,
Who never know what separation is.
The amorous vine with wanton interlaces
Clips still the rough elm in her kind embraces :
Doves with their doves sit billing in the groves,   25
And woo the lesser birds to sing their loves;
Whilst hapless we in grieful absence sit,
Yet dare not ask a hand to lessen it.

AN EPISTLE

*Occasioned by the most intolerable jangling of the
Papists' bells on All Saints' Night, the eve of All
Souls' Day, being then used to be rung all night
(and all as if the town were on fire) for the souls
of those in Purgatory.*

**WRITTEN FROM THOUARS TO SAUMUR, TO MR.
BRYAN PALMES.**

PALMES and my friend, this night of Hallantide,
Left all alone, and no way occupied :
Not to be idle, though I idle be
In writing verse, I send these lines to thee :
Ask me not how I can be left alone,   5
For all are here so in devotion,
So earnest in their prayers for the dead,

1.—*Hallantide*, All Saints' Day, a west country form of
Hallowtide.   For the custom of ringing bells on Allhallow Eve
see BRAND, *Pop. Antiq.*, ed. Bohn, i. 394-5.

And with their *De profundis* so far led,
And so transported, poor night-seeing fowls,
In their oraisons for all Christian souls,   10
That knowing me for one but yesterday,
Maybe they dreamt me dead, and for me pray.
This may conjectur'd be the reason why
I have this night with me no company,
I mean of that religion ; for indeed   15
But to consort with one that says his creed
In his own mother-tongue, this day for them
Were such a crime, that nor Jerusalem,
Not yet Rome's voyage, for which I am sorry,
Could free these friends of mine from purgatory.   20
And had I gone to visit them maybe
They at my entrance might have taken me,
If that I spoke in English, for some one
Of their good friends, new come from Phlegethon ;
And so had put them to the pains to woo   25
My friend friar Guy and Bonaventure too
To publish such a miracle of theirs
By ringing all the bells about mine ears.
    But peace be to their bells, say I, as is
Their prayer every day *pax defunctis ;*   30
For I am sure all this long night to hear
Such a charavary,* that if there were

* Tinkling of kettles and pans.

24.—*Phlegethon*, a river in the Lower World, which ran
with fire instead of water.
26.—*Friar Guy.* See Note. *Bonaventure,* Giovanni
Fidanza, the "seraphic doctor" (1221-1274).

All the Tom Tinkers since the world began,
Inhabiting from Thule to Magellan ;
And those that beat their kettles, when the moon 35
Dark'ning the sun, brings on the night ere noon :
I think all those together would not make
Such a curs'd noise as these for all souls' sake.
Honest John Helmes,* now by my troth I wish,
Although my popish hostess hath with fish 40
Fed me three days, that thou wert here with speed,
And some more of thy crew, not without need,
To teach their bells some rhyme or tune in swinging,
For sure they have no reason in their ringing.

   For mine own part, hearing so strange a coil, 45
Such discord, such debate, and such turmoil,
In a high steeple, when I first came hither,
And had small language, I did doubt me whether
Some had the Tow'r of Babel new begun,
And God had plagued them with confusion : 50
For which I was not sorry, for I thought
To catch some tongue among them, and for nought.
   But being much deceiv'd, good Lord ! quoth I,
What pagan noise is this? One that stood by,
Swore I did wrong them, for he me advis'd 55
The bells upon his knowledge were baptiz'd.
My friend, quoth I, y'are more to blame by far,
To see poor Christian creatures so at jar,
And seek not to accord them ; as for me,

* A good
ringer.

45.—*Coil*, disturbance.

Although they not of my acquaintance be,   60
Nor though we never have shook hands as yet,
Out of my love to peace, not out of debt,
See there's eight soulz, or ten, it makes not whether ;
Get them some wine and see them drink together :
Or if the sexton cannot bring them to it,   65
As he will sure have much ado to do it ;
Tell him he shall be thank'd, if so he strives
With special care to take away their knives ;
And for their cause of stir that he record it,
Until a gen'ral Council do accord it.   70
Till when, I'll hold, whate'er the Jesuits say :
Although their Church err not, their steeple may.

W. B.

AN EPISTLE THROWN INTO A RIVER IN
A BALL OF WAX.

Go, gentle paper ; happy, happier far
Than he that sends thee, with this character :
Go, view those blessed banks, enriched by
A fair but faithless maiden's company ;
And if consorted with my tears of brine,   5
Which, gentle flood, add waves to those of thine,
Thou chance to touch the sand in thy progression,
Made valuable by her steps' impression :

63.—*Soulz*, soules-turnois, silver coins, ten of which made a
shilling.

Stay, stay thy course ; and fortunate from danger
Dwell there, where my ill-fate makes me a stranger.
If, faithful paper which hold'st nought of Art,   [10
Thou come into her hands who kills my heart ;
And she demand thee how I spend my hours,
Tell her, O tell her ! how in gloomy bowers,
In caverns yet unknown even to the sun,   15
And places free from all confusion
Except my thoughts, there sit I girt with fears ;
Where day and night I turn myself to tears,
Only to wash away that stain which she
Hath (careless) thrown upon her constancy ;   20
And if, touch'd with repentance, she bedew
Thee with some crystal drops, I would she knew
Her sorrows or the breaking of the dart
Heals not her wounded faith, nor my slain heart.
And my just griefs of all redress bereaven   25
Shall ever witness before men and heaven,
That as she is the fair'st and most untrue
Of those that ever man or read or knew,
So am I the most constant without mate
Of all that breathe, and most affectionate ;   30
Although assured that nor my love nor faith
Shall reap one joy but by the hand of death.

AN EPISTLE.

HASTEN, O hasten, for my love's sake haste :
The Spring already hath your Beachworth grac'd.
What need you longer stay to grace it more ;
Or add to that which had enough before?
The heavens admit no suns : why should your seat 5
Have two, then, equal good and as complete ?
Hasten, O hasten then ; for till I see
Whom most I love, 'tis Winter still with me
I feel no Spring ; nor shall I, till your light
Repel my too-too long and lonely night :   10
Till you have quicken'd with your happy shine
A drooping discontented heart of mine,
No mirth, but what is forc'd, shall there be plac'd.
Hasten, O hasten then: for love's sake haste.
　　So longing Hero oftentimes was wont   15
Upon the flow'ry banks of Hellespont
To walk, expecting when her love should land,
As I have done on silver Isis' strand.
　　I ask the snowy swans, that swim along,
Seeking some sad place for their sadder song,   20
Whether they came from Mole, or heard her tell
What worth doth near her wanton river dwell ;

2.—*Beachworth*, i.e., Betchworth in Surrey, the original
seat of the Brownes.

And naming you, the gentle spotless birds,
As if they understood the power of words,
To bend their stately necks do straight agree ;   25
And honouring the name, so answer me.
   Those being gone, I ask the crystal brook,
Since part of it unwillingly had took
An ever-leave of that more happy place
Than pleasant Tempe, which the gods did grace ;   30
The stream I ask'd, if when it lately left
Those daisied banks, and griev'd to be bereft
So sweet a channel, you did mean to stay
Still in that vale whence they were forc'd away ;
Hereat the wave a little murmur makes,   35
And then another wave that overtakes ;
And then a third comes on, and then another,
Rolling themselves up closely each to other—
(As little lads, to know their fellow's mind,
While he is talking, closely steal behind ;)   40
I ask them all, and each like murmur keeps ;
I ask another, and that other weeps.
What they should mean by this, I do not know,
Except the mutt'rings and the tears they show
Be from the dear remembrance of that site   45
Where, when they left you, they forsook delight.
   That this the cause was, I perceived plain ;
For going thence, I thither came again
What time it had been flood, a pretty while ;
And then the dimpled waters seem'd to smile ;   50
As if they did rejoice and were full fain,

That they were turning back to Mole again.
　In such-like thoughts, I spend the tedious day ;
But when the night doth our half-globe array
In mournful black, I leave the curled stream,　　55
And by the kindness of a happy dream,
Enjoy what most I wish ; yourself and such,
Whose worth, whose love, could I as highly touch
As I conceive, some hours should still be spent
To raise your more than earthly monument.　　60
In sleep I walk with you, and do obtain
A seeming conf'rence : but, alas, what pain
Endures that man, which evermore is taking
His joys in sleep, and is most wretched waking ?
　To make me happy then, be you my sun,　　65
And with your presence clear all clouds begun ;
My mists of melancholy will outwear,
By your appearing in our hemisphere ;
Till which, within a vale as full of woe,
As I have ever sung, or eye can know,　　70
Or you can but imagine, reading this,
Inthralled lies the heart of him that is

Careless of all others' love

without your respect,

W. B.

From an Inner Temple,
than the Inner Temple,
May the third, 1615.

FIDO : AN EPISTLE TO FIDELIA.

SITTING one day beside a silver brook,
Whose sleepy waves unwillingly forsook
The strict embraces of the flow'ry shore,
As loath to leave what they should see no more :
I read (as fate had turn'd it to my hand)   5
Among the famous lays of fairy land,
Belphœbe's fond mistrust, whenas she met
Her gentle Squire with lovely Amoret.
And laying by the book, poor lad, quoth I,
Must all thy joys, like Eve's posterity,   10
Receive a doom, not to be chang'd by suit,
Only for tasting the forbidden fruit ?
Had fair Belphœbe licens'd thee some time
To kiss her cherry lip, thou didst a crime ;
But since she for thy thirst no help would bring,   15
Thou lawfully might'st seek another spring ;
And had those kisses stol'n been melting sips,
Ta'en by consent from Amoret's sweet lips,
Thou might'st have answer'd, if thy love had spied,
How others gladly gave what she denied ;   20
But since they were not such, it did approve
A jealousy not meriting thy love,
And an injustice offer'd by the maid
In giving judgment ere she heard thee plead.

6.—*The famous lays*, Spenser's *Faëry Queen.*

I have a Love, (and then I thought of you,   25
As Heaven can witness I each minute do,)
So well assur'd of that once promis'd faith,
Which my unmoved Love still cherisheth,
That should she see me private with a dame,
Fair as herself, and of a house whose name,   30
From Phœbus' rise to Tagus where he sets,
Hath been as famous as Plantagenet's ;
Whose eyes would thaw congealed hearts of ice ;
And as we now dispute of Paradise,
And question where fair Eden stood of old,   35
Among so many sweet plots we behold,
Which by the arms of those brave rivers been
Embraced which of yore did keep it in :
So were she one, who did so much abound
In graces, more than ever mortal crown'd,   40
That it might fitly for a question pass,
Where or wherein her most of beauty was.
I surely could believe, nay, I durst swear,
That your sweet goodness would not stoop to fear,
Though she might be to any that should win it   45
A Paradise without a serpent in it.
    Such were my thoughts of you, and thinking so,
Much like a man, who running in the snow
From the surprisal of a murd'rous elf,
Beats out a path, and so betrays himself,   50
I in security was further gone,
And made a path for your suspicion
To find me out.   Time being nigh the same,

When thus I thought, and when your letters came.
   But, oh, how far I err'd, how much deceiv'd   55
Was my belief ! yourself, that have bereav'd
Me of that confidence, my love had got,
Judge if I were an infidel or not ;
And let me tell you, fair, the fault was thine,
If I did misbelieve, and none of mine.   60
   That man which sees, as he along doth pass
Some beaten way, a piece of sparkling glass,
And deems far off that it a diamond is,
Adds to the glass by such a thought of his ;
But when he finds it wants, to quit his pain,   65
The value soon returns to him again.
   If in the ruder North some country clown,
That stands to see the king ride through the town,
Spying some gay and gold-belaced thing,   [70
Should cry, See, neighbours, yonder comes the king :
And much mistaken both in state and age,
Points at some lord, and for a lord a page :
Is not that lord or page beholding much
To him that thinks them worthy to be such
He took them for ?   And are not you to me   75
Indebted much, since my credulity
Made you the same I thought you, and from thence
Rais'd an assurance of your confidence ?
These were the thoughts of you I still was in,
Nor shall your letters so much of me win ;   80
I will not trust mine eyes so much to think
Your white hand wrote with such a staining ink ;

Or if I ever take it for your hand,
I sure shall think I do not understand
In reading as you meant, and fall from thence ·   85
To doubt if points perverted not the sense !
For such a constant faith I have in thee,
That I could die even in that heresy.
  In this belief of you I stand as yet,
And think as those that follow Mahomet :   90
He merits much that doth continue still
In his first faith, although that faith be ill.
  A vain inconstant dame, that counts her loves
By this enamell'd ring, that pair of gloves,
And with her chamber-maid when closely set,   95
Turning her letters in her cabinet,
Makes known what tokens have been sent unto her,
What man did bluntly, who did courtly woo her ;
Who hath the best face, neatest leg, most lands,
Who for his carriage in her favour stands.   100
Op'ning a paper then she shows her wit
On an epistle that some fool had writ :
Then meeting with another which she likes,
Her chambermaid's great reading quickly strikes
That good opinion dead, and swears that this   105
Was stol'n from Palmerin or Amadis.
Next come her sonnets, which they spelling read,
And say the man was very much afraid
To have his meaning known, since they from thence
(Save Cupid's darts) can pick no jot of sense ;   110
And in conclusion, with discretion small,

Scoff this, scorn that, and so abuse them all.
If I had thought you such an empty prize,
I had not sought now to apologize,
Nor had these lines the virgin paper stain'd   115
But, as my Love, unspotted had remain'd ;
And sure I think to what I am about
My ink than it was wont goes slower out,
As if it told me I but vaguely writ
To her that should, but will not, credit it.   120
   Yet go, ye hopeless lines, and tell that fair,
Whose flaxen tresses with the wanton air
Entrap the darling boy, that daily flies
To see his sweet face in her sweeter eyes ;
Tell my Fidelia, if she do aver   125
That I with borrow'd phrases courted her,
Or sung to her the lays of other men ;
And like the cag'd thrush of a citizen,
Tir'd with a note continually sung o'er
The ears of one that knew that all before.   130
If thus she think, (as I shall ne'er be won
Once to imagine she hath truly done,)
Let her then know, though now a many be
Parrots, which speak the tongue of Arcadie,
Yet in themselves not so much language know,   135
Nor wit sufficient for a Lord Mayor's show.
I never yet but scorn'd a taste to bring
Out of the channel when I saw the spring,
Or like a silent organ been so weak,
That others' fingers taught me how to speak.   140

The sacred Nine, whose powerful songs have made
In wayless deserts trees of mighty shade
To bend in admiration, and allay'd
The wrath of tigers with the notes they play'd,
Were kind in some small measure at my birth,   145
And by the hand of Nature to my earth
Lent their eternal heat, by whose bright flame
Succeeding time shall read and know your name,
And pine in envy of your praises writ,   .
Though now your brightness strive to lessen it.   150
Thus have I done, and like an artist spent
My days to build another's monument ;
Yet you those pains so careless overslip,
That I am not allow'd the workmanship.
Some have done less, and have been more re-
          warded ;   155
None hath lov'd more, and hath been less regarded :
Yet the poor silkenworm and only I
Like parallels run on to work and die.
Why write I then again, since she will think
My heart is limned with another's ink ?   160
Or if she deem these lines had birth from me,
Perhaps will think they but deceivers be,
And, as our flattering painters do impart,
A fair made copy of a faithless heart,
O, my Fidelia, if thou canst be won   165
From that mistrust my absence hath begun,
Be now converted, kill those jealous fears,
Credit my lines : if not, believe my tears,

Which with each word, nay, every letter, strove
That in their number you might read my love.   170
And where (for one distracted needs must miss)
My language not enough persuasive is,
Be that supplied with what each eye affords,
For tears have often had the power of words.
Grant this, fair saint, since their distilling rain   175
Permits me not to read it o'er again.
For as a swan more white than Alpine snow,
Wand'ring upon the sands of silver Po,
Hath his impression by a fuller sea
Not made so soon as quickly wash'd away :   180
Such in my writing now the state hath been,
For scarce my pen goes of the ink yet green,
But floods of tears fall on it in such store,
That I perceive not what I writ before.
Can any man do thus, yet that man be   185
Without the fire of love and loyalty ?
Know then in breach of Nature's constant laws,
There may be an effect and yet no cause.
Without the sun we may have April showers,
And   wanting   moisture   know   no   want   of
          flowers ;   190
Causeless the elements could cease to war :
The seaman's needle to the Northern star
Without the loadstone would for ever move.
If all these tears can be and yet no love :
If you still deem I only am the man,   195
Which in the maze of love yet never ran :

Or if in love I surely did pursue
The favour of some other, not of you ;
Or loving you, would not be strictly tied
To you alone, but sought a saint beside :   2co
Know then by all the virtues we enthrone,
That I have lov'd, lov'd you, and you alone.
Read o'er my lines where truthful passion mov'd,
And Hate itself will say that I have lov'd.
Think on my vows which have been ever true,   205
And know by them that I affected you.
Recount my trials, and they will impart
That none is partner with you in my heart.
Lines, vows, and trials will conclude in one,
That I have lov'd, lov'd you, and you alone.   210
Lines, seek no more then to that doubtful fair,
And ye, my vows, for evermore forbear :
Trials to her prove never true again ;
Since lines, vows, trials strive all but in vain.
Yet when I writ, the ready tongue of Truth   215
Did ever dictate, not deceiving youth.
When I have sworn my tongue did never err
To be my heart's most true interpreter,
And proof confirm'd when you examin'd both,
Love caused those lines, and constancy that
        oath ;   220
And shall I write, protest (you prove) and then
Be left the most unfortunate of men ?
Must truth be still neglected ? faith forgot ?
And constancy esteem'd as what is not ?

Shall dear regard and love for ever be   225
Wrong'd with the name of lust and flattery?
It must; for this your last suspicion tells,
That you intend to work no miracles.

W. B.

IV.—ELEGIES.

AN ELEGY ON MR. WILLIAM HOPTON.

WHEN shall mine eyes be dry?   I daily see
Projects on foot ; and some have fall'n on me :
Yet (with my fortune) had they ta'en away
The sense I have to see a friend turn clay ;
They had done something worth the name of spite ; 5
And (as the grim and ugly veil of night,
Which hides both good and bad) their malice then
Had made me worthless more the love of men
Than are their manners.   I had died with those,
Who once entomb'd shall scarce be read in prose : 10
But whilst I have a tear to shed for thee,
A star shall drop, and yet neglected be.
For as a thrifty pismire from the plain,
Busily dragging home some little grain,
Is in the midway to her pretty chamber   15
Fatally wept on by some drop of amber,
Which straight congeal'd (to recompense her doom)
The instrument to kill becomes her tomb ;
And such a one that she may well compare
With Egypt's monarchs for a sepulchre.   20

So as I homewards wend to meet with dust,
Bearing this grief along, and it is just,
Each eye that knew, and knowing held thee dear,
On these sad lines shall shed so true a tear :
It shall beget a second : that, a third :   25
And propagate so many, that the bird
Of Araby shall lack a sun to burn her,
Ere I shall want a tomb, or thou a mourner.
For in those tears we will embalmed be,
And prove such remoras to memory,   30
That some malicious at our fame grown sick
Shall die, and have their dust made into brick ;
And only serve to stop some prison's holes,
That hides as wretched bodies as their souls.
When (though the earth benight us at our noon,) 35
We there will lie like shadows in the moon ;
And every dust within our graves shall be
A star to light us to posterity.
   But (hapless Muse), admit that this may come,
And men may read I wept upon his tomb ;   40
What comfort brings it me ?   Princes have tried
To keep their names, yet scarce are known they died,
So weak is brass and marble ; and I pierce
His memory, while that I write this verse ;
Since I (his living monument) indite   45
And moulder into dust the while I write.

30.—*Remoras*, sea-lampreys or suckstones, believed to check
the course of ships by clinging to their keels.

Such is the grief thy loss hath brought on me,
I cut some life off in each line on thee :
The cold stone that lies on thee I survey,
And, looking on it, feel myself turn clay ;   50
Yet grieve not but to think, when I am gone,
The marble will shed tears, when I shed none.
This vexeth me, that a dead stone shall be
My rival in thy loss and memory ;
That it should both outweep me and rehearse,   55
When I am dust, thy glory in my verse.
    And much good may it do thee, thou dead stone,
Though not so dead as he thou liest upon.
Thou may'st instruct some after-age to say
This was the last bed whereon Hopton lay ;   60
Hopton, that knew to choose and keep a friend :
That scorn'd as much to flatter as offend :
That had a soul as perfect as each limb,
That serv'd learn'd Pembroke, and did merit him ;
    And to name Hopton with his master is   65
    More than a tomb, although a pyramis.

AN ELEGY ON THE COUNTESS DOWAGER
OF PEMBROKE.

TIME hath a long course run since thou wert clay ;
Yet hadst thou gone from us but yesterday,
We in no nearer distance should have stood,
Than if thy fate had call'd thee ere the flood ;

And I that knew thee, shall no less cause have   5
To sit me down and weep beside thy grave
Many a year from hence than in that hour
When, all amazed, we had scarce the power
To say that thou wert dead.   My latest breath
Shall be a sigh for thee ; and when cold death   10
Shall give an end to my just woes and me,
I consecrate to thy dear memory
So many tears, if on thy marble shed,
Each hand might write with them, who there lies
        dead :
And so much grief, that some from sickness free   15
Would gladly die to be bewail'd like thee.
   Yet (could I choose) I would not any knew
That thou wert lost but as a pearl of dew,
Which in a gentle evening mildly cold
Fall'n in the bosom of a marigold,   20
Is in her golden leaves shut up all night,
And seen again when next we see the light.
   For should the world but know that thou wert
      gone,
Our age, too prone to irreligion,
Knowing so much divinity in thee,   25
Might thence conclude no immortality.
And I believe the Puritans themselves
Would be seduc'd to think, that ghosts and elves
Do haunt us yet in hope that thou wouldst deign
To visit us, as when thou liv'd'st again.   30
   But more, I fear, (since we are not of France,

Whose gentry would be known by ignorance)
Such wits and nobles as could merit thee,
And should read this, spite of all penalty
Might light upon their studies, would become   35
Magicians all, and raise thee from thy tomb.
   Nay, I believe, all are already so ;
And now half mad or more with inward woe,
Do think great Drake maliciously was hurl'd
To cast a circle round about the world,   40
Only to hinder the magicians' lore;
And frustrate all our hopes to see thee more.
   Pardon my sorrow : is that man alive,
Who for us first found out a prospective
To search into the moon, and hath not he   45
Yet found a further skill to look on thee?
     Thou goodman, who thou be'st, that e'er hast
        found
The means to look on one so good, so crown'd,
For pity find me out ! and we will trace
Along together to that holy place   50
Which hides so much perfection ; there will we
Stand fix'd and gaze on her felicity.
And should thy glass a burning one becon
And turn us both to ashes on her tomb ;
Yet to our glory, till the latter day,   55
Our dust shall dance like atoms in her ray.
   And when the world shall in confusion burn,
And kings with peasants scramble at an urn ;
Like tapers new blown out, we, blessed then

Will at her beams catch fire and live again. 60
   But this is sense, and some one (may be) glad
That I so true a cause of sorrow had,
Will wish all those whom I affect might die,
So I might please him with an elegy.
   O let there never line of wit be read 65
To please the living, that doth speak thee dead ;
Some tender-hearted mother, good and mild,
Who on the dear grave of her only child
So many sad tears hath been known to rain,
As out of dust could mould him up again ; 70
And with her plaints enforce the worms to place
Themselves like veins so neatly on his face
And every limb ; as if that they were striving
To flatter her with hope of his reviving :
She should read this ; and her true tears alone 75
Should copy forth these sad lines on the stone
Which hides thee dead.   And every gentle heart
That passeth by should of his tears impart
So great a portion, that (if after times
Ruin more churches for the clergy's crimes,) 80
When any shall remove thy marble hence,
Which is less stone than he that takes it thence,
Thou shalt appear within thy tearful cell,
Much like a fair nymph bathing in a well :
But when they find thee dead so lovely fair, 85
Pity and Sorrow then shall straight repair,
And weep beside thy grave with cypress crown'd,
To see the second world of beauty drown'd ;

And add sufficient tears, as they condole,
Would make thy body swim up to thy soul.   90
   Such eyes should read the lines are writ on thee ;
But such a loss should have no elegy
To palliate the wound we took in her.
Who rightly grieves admits no comforter.
   He that had ta'en to heart thy parting hence,   95
Should have been chain'd in Bethlem two hours
              thence ;
And not a friend of his e'er shed a tear,
To see him for thy sake distracted there ;
But hugg'd himself for loving such as he,
That could run mad with grief for losing thee.   100
   I, hapless soul, that never knew a friend
But to bewail his too untimely end ;
Whose hopes, cropp'd in the bud, have never come,
But to sit weeping on a senseless tomb,
That hides not dust enough to count the tears,   105
Which I have fruitless spent, in so few years :
   I, that have trusted those that would have given
For our dear Saviour and the Son of heaven,
Ten times the value Judas had of yore,
Only to sell him for three pieces more :   110
I that have lov'd and trusted thus in vain,
Yet weep for thee : and till the clouds shall deign
To shower on Egypt more than Nile e'er swell'd,
These tears of mine shall be unparallel'd.   [115
   He that hath love enjoy'd, and then been cross'd,
Hath tears at will to mourn for what he lost ;

He that hath trusted, and his hope appears
Wrong'd but by death, may soon dissolve in tears ;
But he, unhappy man, whose love and trust
Ne'er met fruition, nor a promise just :   120
For him, unless, like thee, he deadly sleep,
'Tis easier to run mad than 'tis to weep.
 And yet I can ! Fall then, ye mournful showers ;
And as old Time leads on the winged hours,
Be you their minutes : and let men forget 125
To count their ages from the Plague of Sweat,
From Eighty-eight, the Powder Plot, or when
Men were afraid to talk of it again ;
And in their numeration, be it said,
Thus old was I, when such a tear was shed, 130
And when that other fell a comet rose,
And all the world took notice of my woes.
Yet, finding them past cure, as doctors fly
Their patients past all hope of remedy,
No charitable soul will now impart   135
One word of comfort to so sick a heart ;
But as a hurt deer beaten from the herd,
Men of my shadow almost now afear'd,
Fly from my woes, that whilom wont to greet me,
And well-nigh think it ominous to meet me. 140
 Sad lines, go ye abroad : go, saddest Muse :
And as some nation formerly did use
To lay their sick men in the streets, that those
Who of the same disease had 'scap'd the throes,
Might minister relief as they went by   145

To such as felt the selfsame malady ;
So, hapless lines, fly through the fairest land ;
And if ye light into some blessed hand,
That hath a heart as merry as the shine
Of golden days, yet wrong'd as much as mine ;   150
Pity may lead that happy man to me,
And his experience work a remedy
To those sad fits which, spite of Nature's laws,
Torture a poor heart that outlives the cause.

But this must never be, nor is it fit   155
An ague or some sickness less than it,
Should glory in the death of such as he,
That had a heart of flesh, and valued thee.

Brave Roman ! I admire thee, that wouldst die
At no less rate than for an empery :   160
Some massy diamond from the centre drawn
For which all Europe were an equal pawn,
Should, beaten into dust, be drunk by him,
That wanted courage good enough to swim
Through seas of woe for thee ; and much despise 165
To meet with death at any lower price.
Whilst grief alone works that effect in me ;
And yet no grief but for the loss of thee.

Fortune, now do thy worst, for I have got
By this her death so strong an antidote,   170
That all thy future crosses shall not have
More than an angry smile.   Nor shall the grave
Glory in my last day.   These lines shall give
To us a second life, and we will live

To pull the distaff from the hands of Fate ;	175
And spin our own threads for so long a date,
That death shall never seize upon our fame,
Till this shall perish in the whole world's flame.

ON AN INFANT UNBORN, AND THE MOTHER DYING IN TRAVAIL.

WITHIN this grave there is a grave entomb'd :
Here lies a mother and a child enwomb'd ;
'Twas strange that Nature so much vigour gave
To one that ne'er was born to make a grave.
Yet, an injunction stranger, Nature will'd her,
Poor mother, to be tomb to that which kill'd her ;
And not with so much cruelty content,
Buries the child, the grave, and monument.
Where shall we write the epitaph ? whereon ?
The child, the grave, the monument is gone ;
Or if upon the child we write a staff,
Where shall we cut the tomb's own epitaph ?
Only this way is left ; and now we must,
As on a table carpeted with dust,
Make chisels of our fingers, and engrave
An epitaph both on the child and grave
Within the dust: but when some days are gone,
Will not that epitaph have need of one ?
I know it will ; yet grave it there so deep,

That those which knew the loss, and truly weep,
May shed their tears so justly in that place,
Which we before did with a finger trace,
That filling up the letters, they shall lie
As inlaid crystal to posterity :
Where, as on glass, if any write another,
Let him say thus : Here lies a hapless mother,
Whom cruel fate hath made to be a tomb,
And keeps in travail till the Day of Doom.

ON THE RIGHT HONOURABLE CHARLES, LORD HERBERT OF CARDIFF AND SHURLAND.

If there be a tear unshed
On friend, or child, or parent dead,
Bestow it here ; for this sad stone
Is capable of such alone.
Custom showers swell not our deeps,
Such as those his marble weeps ;
Only they bewail his herse,
Who unskill'd in powerful verse,
To bemoan him slight their eyes,
And let them fall for elegies.

All that sweetness, all that youth
All that virtue, all that truth
Can or speak, or wish, or praise,

Was in him in his few days.
His blood of Herbert, Sidney, Vere,
Names great in either hemisphere,
Need not to lend him of their fame :
He had enough to make a name ;
And to their glories he had come,
Had Heaven but given a later tomb.
But the Fates his thread did spin
Of a sleave so fine and thin
Minding still a piece of wonder,
It untimely broke in sunder ;
And we of their labours meet
Nothing but a winding-sheet.
What his mighty prince hath lost :
What his father's hope and cost :
What his sister, what his kin,
Take too all the kingdom in :
'Tis a sea wherein to swim,
Weary faint, and die with him.
O let my private grief have room,
Dear Lord, to wait upon thy tomb ;
And since my weak and saddest verse
Was worthy thought thy grandam's herse,
Accept of this ! Just tears my sight
Have shut for thee—dear Lord—good night.

Et longum formose, vale, vale, inquit, Iolla.

AN EPICED ON MR. FISHBOURNE.

As some, too far inquisitive, would fain
Know how the Ark could so much life contain ;
Where the ewe fed, and where the lion lay,
Both having den and pasture, yet all sea :
When fishes had our constellations true,   5
And how the hawk and partridge had one mew ;
So do I wonder, in these looser times,
When men commit more villanies than rhymes,
How honour'd Fishbourne, in his lesser Ark,
Could so much immortality embark ;*   10
And take in man too.   How his good thoughts lay
With wealth and hazard both of them at sea :
How when his debtors thought of longer owing,
His chiefest care was of that sum's bestowing
In pious uses.   But to question all ;   15
Did this rich man come to an hospital
To curb the incomes, or to beg the leads,
Or turn to straw more charitable beds ?
Or gaz'd he on a prison with pretence,
More to enthrall than for a prayer thence ?   20
Or on the Levites' part, the churches' living,
Did he e'er look without the thought of giving ?
No : as the Angel at Bethesda he
Came never in the cells of charity,
Unless his mind by Heaven had fraughted bin   25
To help the next poor cripple that came in ;

* He gave £20,000 to pious uses.

And he came often to them ; and withal
Left there such virtue since his funeral,
That, as the ancient prophet's buried bones
Made one to know two resurrections :   30
So after death it will be said of him,
Fishbourne revived this man, gave that a limb :
Such miracles are done in this sad age,
And yet we do not go in pilgrimage.
    When by the graves of men alive he trod,   35
Prisons where souls and bodies have abode
Before a judgment ; and, as there they lie,
Speak their own epitaphs and elegy :
Had he a deaf ear then ? threw he on more
Irons or actions than they had before ?   40
Nay : wish'd he not, he had sufficient worth
To bid these men, dead to the world, come forth ?
Or since he had not, did not he anon
Provide to keep them from corruption ?
Made them new shrouds (their clothes are sure no
        more,   45
Such had the desert wanderers heretofore)
Embalm'd them, not with spice and gums, whereby
We may less noisome, not more deadly lie ;
But with a charitable food, and then
Hid him from thanks to do the like agen.   50
Methinks I see him in a sweet repair,
Some walk, not yet infected with the air
Of news or libel, weighing what may be,
After all these, his next good legacy ;

Whether the Church that lies within his ken,   55
With her revenues feeds or beasts or men?
Whether, though it equivocally keep
A careful shepherd and a flock of sheep,
The patron have a soul, and doth entreat
His friends more to a sermon than his meat?   60
In fine, if church or steeple have a tongue,
Bells by a sexton or a wether rung?
Or where depopulations were begun,
An almshouse were for men by it undone?
Those, Fishbourne, were thy thoughts, the pulse of
   these   65
Thou felt'st, and hast prescrib'd for the disease.
Some thou hast cur'd, and this thy Gilead balm
Hath my præludium to thy Angel's Psalm.
 And now, ye oracles of Heaven, for whom
He hath prepar'd a candle, stool, and room,   70
That to St. Mary's, Paul's, or elsewhere come,
To send us sighing, and not laughing home;
Ye, that the hour may run away more free,
Bribe not the clerk, but with your doctrine me;
Keep ye on wing his ever honour'd fame,   75
And though our learned Mother want his name,
'Twas modesty in him that his dear BROWNE*
Might have place for his charity, and crown
Their memories together.   And though his
The City got, the Universities   80
Might have the other's name.   You need not call
A herald to proclaim your funeral.

* His part-
ner

Nor load your graves with marble, nor expend
Upon a statue more than on a friend ;
Or make stones tell a lie to after times,   85
In prose inscriptions, or in hired rhymes.
For whilst there shall a church unruin'd stand,
And five blest souls as yours preserve the land ;
Whilst a good preacher in them hath a room,
You live, and need nor epitaph nor tomb.   90

AN ELEGY ON SIR THOMAS OVERBURY,

POISONED IN THE TOWER OF LONDON.

HAD not thy wrong, like to a wound ill cur'd,
Broke forth in death, I had not been assur'd
Of grief enough to finish what I write ;
These lines, as those which do in cold blood fight,
Had come but faintly on ; for ever he   5
That shrines a name within an elegy,
Unless some nearer cause do him inspire,
Kindles his bright flame at the funeral fire.
For passion, after less'ning her extent,
Is then more strong, and so more eloquent.   10
   How pow'rful is the hand of Murther now !
Was't not enough to see his dear life bow

10.—Here the MS. copy terminates; the remainder is given
from the ninth impression of Sir T. Overbury's *The Wife*
(1616).

Beneath her hate ? but crushing that fair frame,
Attempt the like on his unspotted fame?
O base revenge ! more than inhuman fact !   15
Which (as the Romans sometime would enact
No doom for parricide, supposing none
Could ever so offend) the upright throne
Of Justice salves not : leaving that intent
Without a name, without a punishment.   20
  Yet through thy wounded fame, as thorough these
Glasses which multiply the species,
We see thy virtues more ; and they become
So many statues sleeping on thy tomb,
Wherein confinement new thou shalt endure,   25
But so as, when to make a pearl more pure
We give it to a dove, in whose womb pent
Some time, we have it forth most orient.
  Such is thy lustre now that venom'd spite
With her black soul dares not behold thy light,   30
But banning it, a course begins to run
With those that curse the rising of the sun.
The poison, that works upwards now, shall strive
To be thy fair fame's true preservative.
And witchcraft, that can mask the upper shine,   35
With no one cloud shall blind a ray of thine.
  And as the Hebrews in an obscure pit
Their holy fire hid, not extinguish'd it,
And after time, that broke their bondage chain,

15.—*Fact*, crime.   19.—*Salves*, remedies.

Found it, to fire their sacrifice again :   40
So lay thy worth some while, but being found,
The Muses' altars plentifully crown'd
With sweet perfumes by it new kindled be,
And offer all to thy dear memory.
   Nor have we lost thee long : thou art not gone, 45
Nor canst descend into oblivion.
But twice the sun went round since thy soul fled,
And only that time men shall term thee dead :
Hereafter, rais'd to life, thou still shalt have
An antidote against the silent grave.   50

W. B.
Int : Temp.

AN ELEGY

*On the untimely death of his ever honoured and as
much beloved as lamented Friend, Mr. Thomas
Ayleworth of the Middle Temple, slain at
Croydon, and there buried.*

   Is goodness shortest liv'd ? doth Nature bring
Her choicest flowers but to adorn the spring ?
Are all men but as tarriers ? first begun,
Made and together put to be undone ?
Will all the rank of friends in whom I trust,   5
Like Sodom's trees, yield me no fruit but dust ?
Must all I love, as careless sparks that fly
Out of a flint, but show their worth and die ?
Will Nature ever to things fleeting bow ?

Doth she but, like the toiling hind at plough,   10
Sow to be in'd? then I'll begin a lore
Hard to be learn'd, love still to wail no more ;
I ever will affect that good, which he
Made the firm steps to his eternity.
I will adore no other light than shines   15
From my best thoughts, to read his life ; the mines
Of richest India shall not buy from me
That book one hour wherein I study thee.
A book, wherein men's lives so taxed bin
That all men labour'd death to call it in.   20
What now as licens'd is dispers'd about,
Is no true copy, or the best left out.
No ornaments I'll love brought from the Change,
But what's in it, and in the Court more strange,
Virtue ; which clad thee well, and I may have,   25
Without the danger of a living grave.
I will not wish Fortune should make of me
A worshipp'd golden calf, as most rich be ;
But let her, for all lands else, grant me this,
To be an inmate in that house now his.   30
One stone will serve, one epitaph above,
So one shall be our dust, as was our love.
　　O, if privation be the greatest pain,
Which wretched souls in endless night sustain,
What mortal torment can be worse than his,   35
That by enjoying, knows what losing is ?

11.—*In'd*, gathered, as the harvest.

Yet such is mine.   Then if with sacred fire
A passion ever did a Muse inspire ;
Or if a grief-sick heart hath writ a line
Than Art or Nature could more genuine,   40
More full of accents sad ; let it appear
In what I write, if any drop a tear,
To this small payment of my latest debt
He witness is, that 'twas not counterfeit.

  May this be never known to hearts of stone,   45
That measure all men's sorrows by their own ;
And think no flood should ever drown an eye,
That hath not issue from an injury
Of some misfortune, tending more the loss
Of goods than goodness.   Let this hapless cross 50
Alone be read, and known by such as be
Apt to receive that seal of misery,
Which his untimely death prints on my heart.

  And if that fatal hand, which did the part
That Fate should have perform'd, shall ever chance,
Either of purpose or through ignorance,   [55
To touch this paper may it rose-like wither ;
Or as the plant sentida shrink together !
Let him not read it ; be the letters dim,
Although the ordinary give it him !   60
Or let the words transpose them and impart
A crying anagram for his desert.
Or may this ink, now dry, grow green again,

58.—*Sentida*, the Sensitive Plant.

As wounds, before the murd'rer, of the slain.
So these sad lines shall, in the Judge's eye,　　　65
Be his accuser and mine elegy.

　But vain are imprecations.　And I fear
Almost to show him in a character,
Lest some accursed hand the same should stain,
Or by depraving murder him again.　　　70

　Sleep then, sweet soul ; and if thy virtues be
In any breast, by him we'll portrait thee.
If thou hadst liv'd where heathen gods have reign'd,
Thy virtues thee a deity had gain'd.
But now more blest !　And though thy honour'd
　　　shrine　　　75
Be unadorn'd by stone, or Indian mine :
Yet whilst that any good to earth is lent,
Thou canst not lie without a monument.

AN EPITAPH ON HIM.

HERE wither'd lies a flower, which blown,
Was cropp'd as soon as it was known ;
The loss was great, and the offence,
Since one unworthy took it hence.
W. BROWNE.

AN ELEGY.

Is Death so great a gamester, that he throws
Still at the fairest, and must I still lose ?

Are we all but as tarriers first begun,
Made and together put to be undone?
Will all the rank of friends, in whom I trust,   5
Like Sodom's trees yield me no fruit but dust?
Must all I love, as careless sparks that fly
Out of a flint, but show their worth and die?
   O, where do my for ever losses tend?
I could already by some buried friend   10
Count my unhappy years; and should the sun
Leave me in darkness, as her loss hath done,
By those few friends I have yet to entomb,
I might, I fear, account my years to come.
What need our canons then be so precise   15
In registers for our nativities?
They keep us but in bonds, and strike with fears
Rich parents, till their children be of years;
For should they lose and mourn, they might, as I,
Number their years by every elegy.   20
These books to sum our days might well have stood
In use with those that liv'd before the Flood,
When she indeed that forceth me to write,
Should have been born, had Nature done her right;
And at five hundred years been less decay'd,   25
Than now at fifteen is the fairest maid.
But Nature had not her perfection then,
Or being loath for such long-living men,
To spend the treasure which she held most pure,
She gave them women apter to endure;   30
Or providently knowing there were more

Countries and islands which she was to store,
Nature was thrifty, and did think it well,
If for some one part each one did excel :
As this for her neat hand, that for her hair,   35
A third for her sweet eyes, a fourth was fair :
And 'tis approv'd by him, who could not draw
The Queen of Love till he a hundred saw.
Seldom all beauties met in one, till she,
All other lands else stor'd, came finally   40
To people our sweet Isle : and seeing now
Her substance infinite, she 'gan to bow
To lavishness in every nuptial bed,
And she her fairest was that now is dead ;
Dead as a blossom forced from the tree,   45
And if a maiden, fair and good as she,
Tread on thy grave.   O let her there profess
Herself for evermore an anchoress.
Let her be deathless ! let her still be young !
Without this means we have no verse nor tongue 50
To say how much I lov'd, or let us see
How great our loss was in the loss of thee.
Or let the purple violet grow there,
And feel no revolution of the year ;
But full of dew with ever-drooping head,   55
Show how I live, since my best hopes are dead.

   Dead ! as the world to virtue.   Murd'rers, thieves
Can have their pardons, or at least reprieves.
The sword of Justice hath been often won
By letters from an execution.   60

Yet vows nor prayers could not keep thee here,
Nor shall I see, the next returning year,
Thee with the roses spring and live again.
Th'art lost for ever, as a drop of rain
Fall'n in a river ! for as soon I may   65
Take up that drop, or meet the same at sea,
And know it there, as e'er redeem thee gone,
Or know thee in the grave, when I have one.
   O ! had that hollow vault, where thou dost lie,
An echo in it, my strong fantasy   70
Would draw me soon to think her words were thine,
And I would hourly come, and to thy shrine
Talk as I often used to talk with thee,
And frame my words that thou might'st answer me
As when thou liv'd'st : I'd sigh, and say I love,   75
And thou should'st do so too, till we had mov d
With our complaints to tears each marble cell
Of those dead neighbours which about thee dwell.
   And when the holy father came to say
His orisons, I'd ask him if the day   80
Of miracles were past, or whether he
Knew any one whose faith and piety
Could raise the dead ; but he would answer, none
Can bring thee back to life ; though many one
Our cursed days afford, that dare to thrust   85
Their hands profane to raise the sacred dust
Of holy saints out of their beds of rest.
   Abhorred days !   O may there none molest
Thy quiet peace ! but in thy ark remain

Untouch'd, as those the old one did contain,   90
Till he that can reward thy greatest worth,
Shall send the peaceful Dove to call thee forth.

ON A TWIN AT TWO YEARS OLD DEAD
OF A CONSUMPTION.

DEATH ! thou such a one hast smit,
Any stone can cover it ;
'Twas an envy more than sin,
If he had not been a twin,
To have kill'd him, when his herse
Hardly could contain a verse.
Two fair sisters, sweet and young,
Minded as a prophet's tongue,
Thou hadst kill'd, and since with thee
Goodness had no amity :
Nor could tears of parents save
So much sweetness from the grave ;
Sickness seem'd so small to fit him,
That thou should'st not see to hit him ;
And thou canst not truly say,
If he be dead or flown away.

AN ELEGIE

ON THE NEVER

INOVGH BEWAILED DEATH

of the VVorthy, Vertuous, glory of
thefe, and wonder for enfuing times,

HENRY, PRINCE of
WALES.

Ouid de Trift. Lib. 1. Eleg. 3.
Quocumq; adfpiceres, luctus, gemitufq; fonabant.

Virgil. Eclog. 3.
Et longùm formosè vale, vale, inquit, Iola.

LONDON:
Printed by *T. S.* for RICHARD MORE, and are to
be fould at his fhoppe in Saint Dunftones
Church-yard. 1613.

AN ELEGY

ON THE BEWAILED DEATH OF THE TRULY
BELOVED AND MOST VIRTUOUS HENRY,
PRINCE OF WALES.

WHAT time the world, clad in a mourning robe,
A stage made for a woful tragedy,
When showers of tears from the celestial globe
Bewail'd the fate of sea-lov'd Brittany ;
When sighs as frequent were as various sights,   5
When Hope lay bed-rid, and all pleasures dying,
        When Envy wept,
        And Comfort slept,
When Cruelty itself sat almost crying ;
Nought being heard but what the mind affrights : 10
   When Autumn had disrob'd the Summer's pride,
   Then England's Honour, Europe's Wonder, died.

O saddest strain that e'er the Muses sung !
A text of woe for Grief to comment on ;
Tears, sighs and sobs, give passage to my tongue, 15
Or I shall spend you till the last is gone ;
And then my heart, in flames of burning love,
Wanting his moisture, shall to çinders turn.
        But first by me,
        Bequeathed be,   20

To strew the place wherein his sacred urn
Shall be enclos'd.   This might in many move
  The like effect : who would not do it when
  No grave befits him but the hearts of men ?

The man whose mass of sorrows have been such,   25
That, by their weight, laid on each several part,
His fountains are so dry, he but as much
As one poor drop hath left, to ease his heart :
Why should he keep it, since the time doth call
That he ne'er better can bestow it in ?   30
              If so he fears
              That other tears
In greater number greatest prizes win,
Know, none gives more than he who giveth all :
  Then he which hath but one poor tear in store,   35
  Oh, let him spend that drop and weep no more !

Why flows not Helicon beyond her strands ?
Is Henry dead, and do the Muses sleep ?
Alas ! I see each one amazed stands ;
Shallow fords mutter, silent are the deep :   40
Fain would they tell their griefs, but know not where.
All are so full, nought can augment their store.
              Then how should they
              Their griefs display
To men so cloy'd they fain would hear no more,   45
Though blaming those whose plaints they cannot
          hear ?

And with this wish their passions I allow,
May that Muse never speak that's silent now !

Is Henry dead ? alas ! and do I live
To sing a screech-owl's note that he is dead ?   50
If any one a fitter theme can give,
Come, give it now, or never to be read :
But let him see it do of horror taste,
Anguish, destruction ; could it rend in sunder
        With fearful groans   55
        The senseless stones,
Yet should we hardly be enforc'd to wonder,
Our former griefs would so exceed their last :
  Time cannot make our sorrows ought completer,
  Nor   add   one   grief   to   make   our   mourning
     greater.   60

England stood ne'er engirt with waves till now,
Till now it held part with the Continent.
Aye me ! some one, in pity, show me how
I might in doleful numbers so lament,
That any one, which lov'd him, hated me,   65
Might dearly love me for lamenting him.
       Alas, my plaint
       In such constraint
Breaks forth in rage, that though my passions swim,
Yet are they drowned ere they landed be.   70
  Imperfect lines : oh, happy were I hurl'd
  And cut from life as England from the world.

O ! happier had we been, if we had been
Never made happy by enjoying thee.
Where hath the glorious eye of Heaven seen   75
A spectacle of greater misery?
Time, turn thy course, and bring again the spring !
Break Nature's laws ! search the records of old !
        If ought e'er fell
        Might parallel   80
Sad Albion's case : then note when I unfold
What seas of sorrow she is plunged in :
  Where storms of woe so mainly have beset her,
  She hath no place for worse, nor hope for better.

Britain was whilom known, by more than fame,   85
To be one of the islands fortunate :
What frantic man would give her now that name,
Lying so rueful and disconsolate ?
Hath not her wat'ry zone, in murmuring,
Fill'd every shore with echoes of her cry ?   90
        Yes, Thetis raves,
        And bids her waves
Bring all the nymphs within her Empery
To be assistant in her sorrowing.
  See where they sadly sit on Isis' shore,   95
  And rend their hairs as they would joy no more.

Isis, the g'ory of the Western world,
When our heröe, honour'd Essex, died,

Strucken with wonder, back again she hurl'd,
And fill'd her banks with an unwonted tide.   100
As if she stood in doubt if it were so,
And for the certainty had turn'd her way.
   Why do not now
   Her waves reflow ?
Poor nymph, her sorrows will not let her stay,   105
Or flies to tell the world her country's woe.
 Is that the cause, fair maid ? then stay and know
 Bad news are swift of wing, the good are slow.

Sometime a tyrant held the reins of Rome,
Wishing to all the city but one head,   110
That all at once might undergo his doom,
And by one blow from life be severed.
Fate wish'd the like on England, and 'twas given,
(O miserable men enthrall'd to Fate !)
   Whose heavy hand,   115
   That never scann'd
The misery of kingdoms ruinate :
(Minding to leave her of all joy bereaven)
 With one sad blow (alas ! can worser fall ?)
 Hath given this little Isle her funeral.   120

O ! come, ye blessed imps of Memory,
Erect a new Parnassus on his grave.
There tune your voices to an elegy,
The saddest note that e'er Apollo gave :

Let every accent make the stander-by   125
Keep time unto your songs with dropping tears,
                 Till drops that fell
                 Have made a well
To swallow him which still unmoved hears :
And though myself prove senseless of your cry,   130
    Yet gladly should my light of life grow dim
    To be entomb'd in tears are wept for him.

When last he sicken'd then we first began
To tread the Labyrinth of Woe about,
And by degrees we further inward ran,   135
Having his thread of life to guide us out.
But Destiny no sooner saw us enter
Sad Sorrow's maze, immured up in night,
                 Where nothing dwells
                 But cries and yells   140
Thrown from the hearts of men depriv'd of light,
When we were almost come into the centre,
    Fate, cruelly to bar our joys returning,
    Cut off our thread and left us all in mourning.

Olympius Nemesianus, Eclog. 2.

Tum verò ardentes flammati pectoris æstus
Carminibus dulcique parant relevare querela.

                     Deflevit W. B.
                        Inter : Templ :

V.—VISIONS.

1.

SITTING one day beside the banks of Mole,
Whose sleepy stream by passages unknown
Conveys the fry of all her finny shoal,
As of the fisher she were fearful grown;
I thought upon the various turns of time,
And sudden changes of all human state;
The fear mix'd pleasures of all such as climb
To fortunes merely by the hand of fate,
Without desert.   Then weighing inly deep
The griefs of one whose nearness makes him mine,
Wearied with thoughts, the leaden god of sleep
With silken arms of rest did me entwine:
  While such strange apparitions girt me round,
  As need another Joseph to expound.

2.[a]

[a] This "Vision" is wanting in the MS., though a space was left for it.

3.

I SAW a silver swan swim down the Lea,
Singing a sad farewell unto the vale,
While fishes leapt to hear her melody,
And on each thorn a gentle nightingale
And many other birds forbore their notes,
Leaping from tree to tree, as she along
The panting bosom of the current floats,
Rapt with the music of her dying song :
When from a thick and all-entangled spring
A neatherd rude came with no small ado,
Dreading an ill presage to hear her sing,
And quickly struck her tender neck in two ;
   Whereat the birds, methought, flew thence with speed,
   And inly griev'd for such a cruel deed.

4.

WITHIN the compass of a shady grove
I long time saw a loving turtle fly,
And lastly pitching by her gentle love,
Sit kindly billing in his company :
Till, hapless souls, a falcon, sharply bent,
Flew towards the place where these kind wretches stood,
And sev'ring them, a fatal accident,
She from her mate flung speedy through the wood ;

And 'scaping from the hawk, a fowler set
Close and with cunning underneath the shade,
Entrapp'd the harmless creature in his net,
And nothing moved with the plaint she made,
   Restrain'd her from the groves and deserts wide,
   Where, overgone with grief, poor bird, she died.

5.

A ROSE, as fair as ever saw the North,
Grew in a little garden all alone ;
A sweeter flower did Nature ne'er put forth,
Nor fairer garden yet was never known :
The maidens danc'd about it morn and noon,
And learned bards of it their ditties made ;
The nimble fairies by the pale-fac'd moon
Water'd the root and kiss'd her pretty shade.
But well-a-day, the gard'ner careless grew ;
The maids and fairies both were kept away,
And in a drought the caterpillars threw
Themselves upon the bud and every spray.
   God shield the stock ! if heaven send no supplies,
   The fairest blossom of the garden dies.

6.

DOWN in a valley, by a forest's side,
Near where the crystal Thames rolls on her waves,
I saw a mushroom stand in haughty pride,
As if the lilies grew to be his slaves ;

The gentle daisy, with her silver crown,
Worn in the breast of many a shepherd's lass ;
The humble violet, that lowly down
Salutes the gay nymphs as they trimly pass :
These, with a many more, methought, complain'd
That Nature should those needless things produce,
Which not alone the sun from others gain'd
But turn it wholly to their proper use .
　　I could not choose but grieve that Nature made
　　So glorious flowers to live in such a shade.

7.

A GENTLE shepherd, born in Arcady,
That well could tune his pipe, and deftly play
The nymphs asleep with rural minstrelsy,
Methought I saw, upon a summer's day,
Take up a little satyr in a wood,
All masterless forlorn as none did know him,
And nursing him with those of his own blood,
On mighty Pan he lastly did bestow him ;
But with the god he long time had not been,
Ere he the shepherd and himself forgot,
And most ingrateful, ever stepp'd between
Pan and all good befell the poor man's lot :
　　Whereat all good men griev'd, and strongly swore
　　They never would be foster-fathers more.

VI.—EPIGRAMS.

It happen'd lately at a fair, or wake,
After a pot or two or such mistake,
Two iron-soled clowns, and bacon-sided,
Grumbled : then left the forms which they bestrided,
And with their crab-tree cudgels, as appears,
Thresh'd, as they use, at one another's ears :
A neighbour near both to their house and drink,
Who, though he slept at sermons, could not wink
At this dissension, with a spirit bold
As was the ale that arm'd them, strong and old,
Stepp'd in and parted them ; but Fortune's frown
Was such that there our neighbour was knock'd down.
For they, to recompense his pains at full,
Since he had broke their quarrel, broke his skull.
People came in, and rais'd him from his swound ;
A chirurgeon then was call'd to search the wound,
Who, op'ning it, more to endear his pains,
Cried out, Alas ! look, you may see his brains.
Nay, quoth the wounded man, I tell you free,
Good Mr. Surgeon, that can never be ;
   For I should ne'er have meddled with this brawl
   If I had had but any brains at all.

ON AN HOUR-GLASS.

THE truest hour-glass lies ; for, you'll confess,
All holes grow bigger, and the sand grows less.

ON THE COUNTESS OF SOMERSET'S PICTURE.

THE pitied fortune most men chiefly hate,
And rather think the envied fortunate :
Yet I, if Misery did look as she,
Should quickly fall in love with Misery.

ON JOHN TOOTH.

HERE lieth in sooth
Honest John Tooth ;
Whom Death on a day
From us drew away.

TO DON ANTONIO, KING OF PORTUGAL.

BETWEEN thee and thy kingdom late with force
Spain happily hath sued a divorce ;
And now thou may'st, as Christ did once of his,
Say, that thy kingdom not of this world is.

[MAN.]

Like to a silkworm of one year,
Or like a wronged lover's tear,
Or on the waves a rudder's dint,
Or like the sparkles of a flint,
Or like to little cakes perfum'd,
Or fireworks made to be consum'd ;
Even such is man, and all that trust
In weak and animated dust.
The silkworm droops ; the tear's soon shed;
The ship's way lost ; the sparkle dead ;
The cake is burnt ; the firework done ;
And man as these as quickly gone.

[KISSES.]

Give me three kisses, Phillis ; if not three,
Give me as many as thy sweet lips be ;
You gave and took one, yet deny me twain,
Then take back yours, or give me mine again.

ON ONE BORN BLIND, AND SO DEAD.

Who (but some one like thee) could ever say,
He master'd Death from robbing him a day ?
Or was Death ever yet so kind to any ?
One night she took from thee, from others many,
And yet, to recompense it, in thy tomb
Gives thee a longer till the day of doom.

ON A ROPE-MAKER HANGED.

HERE lies a man much wronged in his hopes,
Who got his wealth backwards by making of ropes
It was his hard chance in his fortunes to falter,
For he liv'd by the rope, and died by the halter

VII.—EPITAPHS

AN EPITAPH ON MR. JOHN SMYTH, CHAPLAIN TO THE RIGHT HONOURABLE THE EARL OF PEMBROKE.

1624

Know thou, that tread'st on learned Smyth inurn'd,
Man is an hour-glass that is never turn'd ;
He is gone through ; and we that stay behind
Are in the upper glass, yet unrefin'd.
When we are fit, with him so truly just,
We shall fall down, and sleep with him in dust.

ON MRS. ANNE PRIDEAUX, DAUGHTER OF MR. DOCTOR PRIDEAUX, REGIUS PROFESSOR.

SHE DIED AT THE AGE OF SIX YEARS.

NATURE in this small volume was about
To perfect what in woman was left out ;
Yet fearful lest a piece so well begun
Might want preservatives, when she had done,
Ere she could finish what she undertook,
Threw dust upon it, and shut up the book

AN EPITAPH ON MR. WM. HOPTON.

READER, stay, and read a truth :
Here lies Hopton, goodness, youth.
Drop a tear, and let it be
True as thou would'st wish for thee ;
Shed one more, thou best of souls ;
Those two tears shall be new poles :
By the first we'll sail and find
Those lost jewels of his mind ;
By the latter we will swim
Back again, and sleep with him.

AN EPITAPH ON SIR JOHN PROWDE,

LIEUTENANT-COLONEL TO SIR CHARLES MORGAN,
SLAIN AT THE SIEGE OF GROLL,[a] AND BURIED
AT ZUTPHEN, 1627.

AFTER a march of twenty years and more,
I set me down on Yssel's[b] warlike shore ;
There now I lie intrench'd, where none can seize me,
Until an host of angels come to raise me.
War was my mistress, and I courted her
As Semele was by the Thunderer :

---

[a] *Groll*, now Croenlo.
[b] *Yssel*, a river of Holland flowing by Zutphen.

The mutual tokens 'twixt us two allow'd
Were bullets wrapt in fire, sent in a cloud ;
One I received, which made my pass so far,
That honour laid me in the bed of war.

IN OBITUM M S, X° MAIJ, 1614.

MAY ! Be thou never grac'd with birds that sing,
         Nor Flora's pride !
In thee all flowers and roses spring,
         Mine only died.   W. B.

ON MR. VAUX, THE PHYSICIAN.

STAY ! this grave deserves a tear ;
'Tis not a corse, but life lies here :
May be thine own, at least some part,
And thou the walking marble art.
   'Tis Vaux ! whom Art and Nature gave
A power to pluck men from the grave ;
When others' drugs made ghosts of men,
His gave them back their flesh agen ;
'Tis he lies here, and thou and I
May wonder he found time to die ;
So busied was he, and so rife,
Distributing both health and life.

Honour his marble with your tears,
You, to whom he hath added years ;
You, whose life's light he was about
So careful, that his own went out.
    Be you his living monument ! or we
    Will rather think you in the grave than he.

ON ONE DROWNED IN THE SNOW.

WITHIN a fleece of silent waters drown'd,
Before I met with death a grave I found ;
That which exil'd my life from her sweet home,
For grief straight froze itself into a tomb.
One only element my fate thought meet
To be my death, grave, tomb, and winding-sheet ;
Phœbus himself my epitaph had writ ;
But blotting many, ere he thought one fit,
He wrote until my tomb and grave were gone,
And 'twas an epitaph, that I had none ;
For every man that pass'd along the way
Without a sculpture read that there I lay.
    Here now, the second time, entomb'd I lie,
And thus much have the best of destiny :
Corruption, from which only one was free,
Devour'd my grave, but did not feed on me,
    My first grave took me from the race of men ;
    My last shall give me back to life agen.

ON MR. JOHN DEANE, OF NEW COLLEGE.

LET no man walk near this tomb,
That hath left his grief at home.
Here so much of goodness lies,
We should not weep tears, but eyes,
And grope homeward from this stone
Blind for contemplation
How to live and die as he.
Deane, to thy dear memory
With this I would offer more,
Could I be secur'd before
They should not be frown'd upon
At thy resurrection.
    Yet accept upon thy herse
My tears far better than my verse.
They may turn to eyes and keep
Thy bed untouch'd whilst thou dost sleep.

AN EPITAPH.[a]

FAIR Canace this little tomb doth hide,
Who only seven Decembers told and died.
O cruelty ! O sin ! yet no man here
Must for so short a life let fall a tear ;
Than death the kind was worse, what did infect
First seiz'd her mouth, and spoil'd her sweet aspect :

[a] Imitated from Martial, Epig. 91, Lib. xi., Aeolidos Canace
jacet hoc tumulata sepulcro, etc.

A horrid ill her kisses bit away,
And gave her almost lipless to the clay.
If Destiny so swift a flight did will her,
It might have found some other way to kill her ;
But Death first struck her dumb, in haste to have
　　her,
Lest her sweet tongue should force the Fates to save
　　her.

ON MR. FRANCIS LEE OF THE TEMPLE, GENT.

NATURE having seen the Fates
Give some births untimely dates,
And cut off those threads before
Half their web was twisted o'er,
Which she chiefly had intended
With just story should be friended,
Underhand she had begun,
From those distaffs half way spun,
To have made a piece to tarry,
As our Edward should, or Harry.
　But the fatal Sisters spying
. What a fair work she was plying,
Curstly[a] cut it from the loom,
And hid it underneath this tomb.

[a] *Curstly*, maliciously.

MY OWN EPITAPH.

LOADEN with earth, as earth by such as I,
In hope of life, in Death's cold arm I lie ;
Laid up there, whence I came, as ships near spilt
Are in the dock undone to be new built.
Short was my course, and had it longer bin,
I had return'd but burthen'd more with sin.
Tread on me he that list ; but learn withal,
As we make but one cross, so thou must fall,
To be made one to some dear friend of thine,
That shall survey thy grave, as thou dost mine.
   Tears ask I none, for those in death are vain,
The true repentant showers which I did rain
From my sad soul, in time to come will bring
To this dead root an everlasting spring.
   Till then my soul with her Creator keeps,
   To waken in fit time what herein sleeps.

WM. BROWNE. 1614.

ON HIS WIFE, AN EPITAPH.

THOU need'st no tomb, my wife, for thou hast one,
To which all marble is but pumex stone ;
Thou art engrav'd so deeply in my heart,
It shall outlast the strongest hand of Art.
Death shall not blot thee thence, although I must
In all my other parts dissolve to dust ;

For thy dear name, thy happy memory,
May so embalm it for eternity,
That when I rise, the name of my dear wife
Shall there be seen as in the book of life.

ON THE COUNTESS DOWAGER OF PEMBROKE.

UNDERNEATH this sable herse
Lies the subject of all verse :
Sidney's sister, Pembroke's mother :
Death, ere thou hast slain another,
Fair, and learn'd, and good as she,
Time shall throw a dart at thee.

Marble piles let no man raise
To her name : for after days
Some kind woman born as she,
Reading this, like Niobe
Shall turn marble, and become
Both her mourner and her tomb.

ON THE RIGHT HONOURABLE SUSAN, COUNTESS OF MONTGOMERY.

THOUGH we trust the earth with thee,
We will not with thy memory ;
Mines of brass or marble shall
Speak nought of thy funeral ;

They are verier dust than we,
And do beg a history :
In thy name there is a tomb,
If the world can give it room ;
　For a Vere and Herbert's wife
　Outspeaks all tombs, outlives all life.

AN EPITAPH ON MRS. EL:Y.

UNDERNEATH this stone there lies
More of beauty than are eyes ;
Or to read that she is gone,
Or alive to gaze upon.

She in so much fairness clad,
To each grace a virtue had ;
All her goodness cannot be
Cut in marble.　Memory
Would be useless, ere we tell
In a stone her worth.　Farewell !

ON MR. TURNER OF ST. MARY-HALL.

I ROSE, and coming down to dine,
I Turner met, a learn'd divine ;
'Twas the first time that I was bless'd
With sight of him, and had possess'd

His company not three hours space,
But Oxford call'd him from that place.
Our friendship was begun, for Arts,
Or love of them, can marry hearts.
But see whereon we trust : eight days
From thence, a friend of mine thus says :
Turner is dead ; amaz'd, thought I,
Could so much health so quickly die?
And have I lost my hopes to be
Endear'd to so much industry?
O man ! behold thy strength, and know
Like our first sight and parting, so
Are all our lives, which I must say
Was but a dinner, and away.

ON GOODMAN HURST OF THE GEORGE
AT HORSHAM,

DYING SUDDENLY WHILE THE EARL OF NOTTING-
HAM LAY THERE, 26 AUGUST, 1637.

SEE what we are : for though we often say,
We are like guests that ride upon the way,
Travel and lodge, and when the morn comes on,
Call for a reck'ning, pay, and so are gone—
We err ; and have less time to be possess'd,
For see ! the host is gone before the guest.

Here lies kind Tom, thrust out of door,
Nor high nor low, nor rich nor poor ;
He left the world with heavy cheer,
And never knew what he made here.

VIII.—PARAPHRASES, &c.

1.

TELL me, Pyrrha, what fine youth,[a]
　　All perfum'd and crown'd with roses,
To thy chamber thee pursu'th,
　　And thy wanton arm encloses ?

2.

What is he thou now hast got,
　　Whose more long and golden tresses
Into many a curious knot
　　Thy more curious finger dresses ?

3.

How much will he wail his trust,
　　And, forsook, begin to wonder,
When black winds shall billows thrust,
　　And break all his hopes in sunder !

4.

Fickleness of winds he knows
　　Very little that doth love thee ;
Miserable are all those
　　That affect thee ere they prove thee.

[a] Imitated from Horace :—Quis multa gracilis, etc.　Carm.
lib. i. 5.

5.

I, as one from shipwreck freed,
  To the ocean's mighty ranger
Consecrate my dropping weed,
  And in freedom think of danger.

THE HAPPY LIFE.[a]

O BLESSED man ! who, homely bred,
In lowly cell can pass his days,
Feeding on his well-gotten bread ;
And hath his God's not others' ways.

That doth into a prayer wake,
And rising, not to bribes or bands,
The power that doth him happy make,
Hath both his knees, as well as hands.

His threshold he doth not forsake,
Or for the city's cates, or trim ;
His plough, his flock, his scythe, and rake,
Do physic, clothe, and nourish him.

By some sweet stream, clear as his thought,
He seats him with his book and line ;
And though his hand have nothing caught,
His mind hath whereupon to dine.

[a] A paraphrase of Horace :—Beatus ille, qui procul negotiis
etc. Epodon lib., Ode 2.

He hath a table furnish'd strong,
To feast a friend, no flattering snare,
And hath a judgment and a tongue
That know to welcome and beware.

His afternoon spent as the prime
Inviting where he mirthful sups;
Labour, or seasonable time,
Brings him to bed and not his cups.

Yet, ere he take him to his rest,
For this and for their last repair,
He, with his household meek address'd,
Offer their sacrifice of prayer.

If then a loving wife he meets,
Such as a good man should lie by,
Bless'd Eden is betwixt these sheets.
Thus would I live, thus would I die.

IN URBEM ROMAM QUALIS EST HODIE.

QUI Romam in media quæris novus advena Roma,
   Et Romæ in Româ nil reperis mediâ:
Aspice murorum moles præruptaque saxa
   Obrutaque horrenti vasta theatra situ:
Hæc sunt Roma. Viden' velut ipsa cadavera tantæ
   Urbis adhuc spirant imperiosa minas?

Vicit ut hæc mundum visa est se vincere : vicit,
  A se non victum ne quid in orbe foret.
Nunc victa in Roma victrix Roma illa sepulta est,
  Atque eadem victrix victaque Roma fuit.
Albula Romani nunc restat nominis index
  Quæque etiam rapidis fertur in æquor aquis.
Disce hinc quid possit Fortuna : immota labascunt ;
  Et quæ perpetuo sunt agitata manent.

ON ROME AS IT IS NOW.

THOU, who to look for Rome, to Rome art come,
And in the midst of Rome find'st nought of Rome ;
Behold her heaps of walls, her structures rent,
Her theatres overwhelm'd, of vast extent ;
Those now are Rome.   See how those ruins frown,
And speak the threats yet of so brave a town.
By Rome, as once the world, is Rome o'ercome,
Lest ought on earth should not be quell'd by Rome :
Now conqu'ring Rome doth conquer'd Rome inter ;
And she the vanquish'd is and vanquisher.
To show us where she stood there rests alone
Tiber ; yet that too hastens to be gone.
    Learn hence what fortune can.   Towns glide
        away ;
And rivers, which are still in motion, stay.

IX.—MISCELLANEOUS PIECES.

ON A DREAM.

VAIN dreams, forbear, ye but deceivers be ;
For as, in flatt'ring glasses, women see
More beauty than possess, so I in you
Have all I can desire, but nothing true.
Who would be rich, to be so but an hour,   5
Eats a sweet fruit to relish more the sour ;
If, but to lose again, we things possess,
Ne'er to be happy is a happiness.
Men walking in the pitchy shades of night
Can keep their certain way, but if a light   10
O'ertake and leave them, they are blinded more,
And doubtful go that went secure before :
For this, though hardly, I have oft forborne
To see her face fair as the rosy morn ;
Yet mine own thoughts in night such traitors be,   15
That they betray me to that misery.
    Then think no more of her ! as soon I may
Command the sun to rob us of a day ;

Or with a sieve repel a liquid stream,
As lose such thoughts or hinder but a dream.   20
  The lightsome air as eas'ly hinder can
A glass to take the form of any man
That stands before it, as or time or place
Can draw a veil between me and her face ;
Yet by such thoughts my torments hourly strive ; 25
For, as a prisoner by his prospective,
By them I am inform'd of what I want :
I envy none now but the ignorant.
He that ne'er saw of whom I dream'd last night,
Is one born blind, that knows no want of light ; 30
He that ne'er kiss'd those lips, yet saw her eyes,
Is Adam living still in Paradise.
But if he taste those sweets, as hapless I,
He knows his want and meets his misery.
An Indian rude that never heard one sing   35
A heavenly sonnet to a silver string,
Nor other sounds, but what confused herds
In pathless deserts make, or brooks, or birds,
Should he hear Syms the sweet pandora touch
And lose his hearing, straight he would as much 40
Lament his knowledge, as do I my chance,
And wish he still had liv'd in ignorance.
I am that Indian, and my soothing dreams
In thirst have brought me but to painted streams,
Which not allay, but more increase desire.   45
 A man, near frozen with December's ire,
 Hath from a heap of glowworms as much ease

As I can ever have by such as these.
  O leave me then ! and strongest memory
Keep still with those that promise-breakers be :   50
Go ! bid the debtor mind his payment-day,
Or help the ignorant-devout to say
Prayers they understand not. Lead the blind,
And bid ingrateful wretches call to mind
Their benefactors ! And if Virtue be,   55
As still she is, trod down with misery,
Show her the rich, that they may free her want,
And leave to nurse the fawning sycophant :
Or if thou seest fair Honour careless lie
Without a tomb, for after memory,   60
Dwell by the grave, and teach all those that pass
To imitate, by showing who it was.
  This way, Remembrance, thou may'st do some
     good,
And have due thanks ; but he that understood
What throes thou bring'st on me, would say I
     miss   65
The sleep of him that did the pale moon kiss,
And that it were a blessing thrown on me,
Sometimes to have the hated lethargy.
  Then, dark Forgetfulness, that only art
The friend of lunatics, seize on that part   70
Of memory which nightly shows her me,
Or suffer still her waking fantasy,

58.—Leave, cease.

Even at the instant that I dream of her.
To dream the like of me, that we may err
In pleasure's endless maze without offence ;   75
And both connex, as souls in innocence.

LYDFORD JOURNEY.

I OFT have heard of Lydford law,
How in the morn they hang and draw,
  And sit in judgment after :
At first I wonder'd at it much ;
But now I find their reason such,   5
  That it deserves no laughter.

They have a castle on a hill ;
I took it for an old windmill,
  The vanes blown off by weather ;
Than lie therein one night, 'tis guess'd,   10
'Tis better to be ston'd or press'd,
  Or hang'd, now choose you whether.

Ten men less room within this cave
Than five mice in a lanthorn have ;
  The keepers they are sly ones :   15
If any could devise by art
To get it up into a cart,
  'Twere fit to carry lions.

When I beheld it, Lord ! thought I,
What justice and what clemency   20
  Hath Lydford, when I spy all !
They know none there would gladly stay,
But rather hang out of the way,
  Than tarry for his trial.

The Prince a hundred pounds hath sent   25
To mend the leads and planchings rent
  Within this living tomb :
Some forty-five pounds more had paid
The debts of all that shall be laid
  There till the day of doom.   30

One lies there for a seam of malt,
Another for three pecks of salt,
  Two sureties for a noble ;
If this be true, or else false news,
You may go ask of Mr. Crewes,*   35
  John Vaughan, or John Doble.†

Near to the men that lie in lurch,
There is a bridge, there is a church,
  Seven ashes, and an oak ;
Three houses standing, and ten down ;   40
They say the parson hath a gown,
  But I saw ne'er a cloak.

* The Steward. *Marginal Note in Westcote's Survey* and *Prince's Worthies of Devon.*

† Attorneys of the Court. —*Ibid.*

26.—*Planchings*, flooring, or sometimes a (boarded ?) ceiling ; it is still in general use in South Devon in these senses.

Whereby you may consider well,
That plain simplicity doth dwell
　　At Lydford without bravery ;　　　45
For in that town, both young and grave
Do love the naked truth, and have
　　No cloaks to hide their knavery.

This town's enclos'd with desert moors,
But where no bear nor lion roars,　　　50
　　And nought can live but hogs :
For, all o'erturn'd by Noah's flood,
Of fourscore miles scarce one foot's good,
　　And hills are wholly bogs.

And near hereto's the Gubbins' cave ;　　　55
A people that no knowledge have
　　Of law, or God, or men :
Whom Cæsar never yet subdued ;
Who've lawless liv'd ; of manners rude ;
　　All savage in their den.　　　60

By whom,—if any pass that way,
He dares not the least time to stay,
　　For presently they howl ;
Upon which signal they do muster
Their naked forces in a cluster,　　　65
　　Led forth by Roger Rowle.

The people all, within this clime,
Are frozen up all winter time ;
　　Be sure I do not fain ;

And when the summer is begun   70
They lie like silkworms in the sun,
   And come to life again.

One told me, in King Cæsar's time,
The town was built of stone and lime,
   But sure the walls were clay :   75
For they are fall'n, for ought I see,
And since the houses were got free,
   The town is run away.

O Cæsar, if thou there didst reign,
Whilst one house stands, come there again ; 80
   Come quickly, while there is one :
If thou but stay a little fit,
But five years more, they may commit
   The whole town into prison.

To see it thus much griev'd was I ;   85
The proverb says, Sorrow is dry,
   So was I at this matter :
When by great chance, I know not how,
There thither came a strange stray'd cow,
   And we had milk and water.   90

Sure I believe it then did rain
A cow or two from Charles his wain,
   For none alive did see
Such kind of creatures there before,
Nor shall from hence for evermore,   95
   Save pris'ners, geese, and we.

To nine good stomachs, with our whig,
At last we got a tithing pig ;
  This diet was our bounds :
And that was just as if 'twere known,   100
One pound of butter had been thrown
  Amongst a pack of hounds.

One glass of drink I got by chance,
'Twas claret when it was in France ;
  But now from that nought wider :   105
I think a man might make as good
With green crabs boil'd with Brazil wood
  And half a pint of cider.

I kiss'd the Mayor's hand of the town,
Who, though he wear no scarlet gown,   110
  Honours the Rose and Thistle :
A piece of coral to the mace,
Which there I saw to serve the place,
  Would make a good child's whistle.

At six o'clock I came away,   115
And pray'd for those that were to stay,
  Within a place so arrant,
Wild and ope to winds that roar :
By God's grace I'll come there no more,
  Unless by some tin warrant.   120

W. B.

97.—*Whig*, sour whey.
107.—*Brazil wood*, which produces a red dye.

[ON THE MARRIAGE OF CHARLES I.
AND HENRIETTA MARIA.[a]]

UXOR, at illa parùm ; regnum jam ducitur : ipsis
   Reginæ in thalamis Gallia sponsa jacet.
Conjugio Gens illa tuæ sociata Britannæ est,
   Te dignumque torum Fœdere, Cæsar, habes.
Quæris et hinc sobolem ? fælices ecce triumphos
   Præ manibus, Natos hos tuus ambit Amor.
Néve perire queas, ditet Maria Britannos
   Perpetuo Carolo, proleque vive Pater.

GUILIEL. BROWNE,

Mag. Art. é Col. Exon.

[DEVOTIONAL VERSES.]

BEHOLD, O God, in rivers of my tears
I come to thee : bow down thy blessed ears
To hear me wretch, and let thine eyes which sleep
Did never close, behold a sinner weep :
Let not, O God, my God, my faults, though great
And numberless, between thy mercy's seat
And my poor soul be thrown ! since we are taught
Thou, Lord, remember'st thine if thou be sought.
I come not, Lord, with any other merit
Than what I by my Saviour Christ inherit :

* Contributed to *Epithalamia Oxoniensia*, 1625.

Be then his wounds my balm ; his stripes my bliss ;
My crown his thorns ; my death be lost in his.
And thou, my blest Redeemer, Saviour, God,
Quit my accompts, withhold the vengeful rod.
O beg for me ! my hopes on thee are set ;
And Christ forgive, as well as pay the debt.
The living fount, the life, the way, I know,
And but to thee, O whither should I go?
All other helps are vain : grant thine to me,
For in thy cross my saving health must be.
O hearken then what I with faith implore,
Lest sin and death sink me for evermore.
Lastly, O God, my ways direct and guide ;
In death defend me, that I never slide ;
And at the doom let me be raised then,
To live with thee ; sweet Jesus, say Amen.

X.—COMMENDATORY VERSES.

TO HIS WORTHY AND INGENIOUS FRIEND THE AUTHOR.[a]

So far as can a swain, who than a round
   On oaten-pipe no further boasts his skill,
I dare to censure the shrill trumpet's sound,
   Or other music of the sacred hill :
The popular applause hath not so fell,
   Like Nile's loud cataract, possess'd mine ears
But others' songs I can distinguish well
   And chant their praise despised virtue rears :
Nor shall thy buskin'd Muse be heard alone
   In stately palaces ; the shady woods
By me shall learn't, and echoes one by one
   Teach it the hills, and they the silver floods.
Our learned shepherds that have us'd tofore
   Their happy gifts in notes that woo the plains
By rural ditties will be known no more ;
   But reach at fame by such as are thy strains.

---

[a] Prefixed to *The Ghost of Richard the Third*, 1614, by Christopher Brooke.

And I would gladly (if the Sisters' spring
   Had me enabled) bear a part with thee,
And for sweet groves, of brave heroës sing,
   But since it fits not my weak melody,
It shall suffice that thou such means dost give,
That my harsh lines among the best may live.

W. BROWNE,
Int. Temp.

TO MY HONOURED FRIEND MR DRAYTON.[a]

ENGLAND'S brave genius, raise thy head, and see,
We have a Muse in this mortality
Of virtue yet survives ; all met not death,
When we entomb'd our dear Elizabeth.
Immortal Sidney, honour'd Colin Clout,
Presaging what we feel, went timely out.
Then why lives Drayton, when the times refuse
Both means to live, and matter for a Muse?
Only without excuse to leave us quite,
And tell us, Durst we act, he durst to write.
   Now, as the people of a famish'd town,
Receiving no supply, seek up and down
For mouldy corn, and bones long cast aside,
Wherewith their hunger may be satisfied :

---

[a] Prefixed to the second part of Drayton's *Polyolbion*, 1622.

(Small store now left) we are enforc'd to pry
And search the dark leaves of antiquity
For some good name, to raise our Muse again,
In this her crisis, whose harmonious strain
Was of such compass, that no other nation
Durst ever venture on a sole translation ;
Whilst our full language, musical and high,
Speaks as themselves their best of poesy.

   Drayton, amongst the worthiest of all those
The glorious laurel, or the Cyprian rose
Have ever crown'd, doth claim in every line
An equal honour from the sacred Nine :
For if old Time could, like the restless main,
Roll himself back into his spring again,
And on his wings bear this admired Muse
For Ovid, Virgil, Homer, to peruse,
They would confess, that never happier pen
Sung of his loves, his country, and the men.

WILLIAM BROWNE.

UPON THIS WORK OF HIS BELOVED
FRIEND THE AUTHOR.[a]

I AM snapp'd already, and may go my way ;
The poet-critic's come ; I hear him say,
This youth's mistook, the author's work's a play.

---

[a] Prefixed to *The Duke of Milan*, a tragedy by Philip
Massinger, 1623. Subscribed "W. B." only, these and the
lines which follow have been also assigned to William Basse.

He could not miss it ; he will straight appear
At such a bait ; 'twas laid on purpose there
To take the vermin, and I have him here.

Sirrah, you will be nibbling ; a small bit,
A syllable, when yo' are i' the hungry fit,
Will serve to stay the stomach of your wit.

Fool ; knave ; what's worse? for worse cannot
          deprave thee.
And were the divel now instantly to have thee,
Thou canst not instance such a work to save thee,

'Mongst all the ballets which thou dost compose,
And what thou styl'st thy poems, ill as those,
And, void of rhyme and reason, thy worse prose.

Yet like a rude Jack-sauce in poesy,
With thoughts unbless'd and hand unmannerly,
Ravishing branches from Apollo's tree :

Tnou mak'st a garland (for thy touch unfit)
And boldly deck'st thy pig-brain'd sconce with it,
As if it were the supreme head

The blameless Muses blush, who no. allow
That reverend order to each vulgar brow ;
Whose sinful touch profanes the holy bough.

Hence, shallow prophet, and admire the strain
Of thine own pen, or thy poor copesmate's[a] vein :
This piece too curious is for thy coarse brain.

Here wit (more fortunate) is join'd with art,
And that most sacred frenzy bears a part,
Infus'd by nature in the poet's heart.

Here may the puny-wits themselves direct ;
Here may the wisest find what to affect ;
And kings may learn their proper dialect.

On, then, dear friend; thy pen thy name shall spread;
And shouldst thou write while thou shalt not be read,
Thy Muse must labour when thy hand is dead.

W. B.

THE AUTHOR'S FRIEND TO THE READER.[b]

THE printer's haste calls on ; I must not drive
My time past six, though I begin at five.
One hour I have entire ; and 'tis enough.
Here are no gipsy jigs, no drumming stuff,
Dances, or other trumpery to delight,
Or take, by common way, the common sight.

---

[a] *Copesmate*, companion.
[b] These lines are prefixed to *The Bondman: An Ancient Story*, by Philip Massinger, 1624.

The author of this poem, as he dares
To stand th' austerest censure, so he cares
As little what it is.   His own best way
Is to be judge and author of his play.
It is his knowledge makes him thus secure ;
Nor does he write to please, but to endure.
And, reader, if you have disburs'd a shilling
To see this worthy story, and are willing
To have a large increase ; if rul'd by me,
You may a merchant and a poet be.
'Tis granted for your twelvepence you did sit,
And see, and hear, and understand not yet.
The author, in a Christian pity, takes
Care of your good, and prints it for your sakes.
That such as will but venter sixpence more
May know what they but saw and heard before ;
'Twill not be money lost, if you can read,
(There's all the doubt now) but your gains exceed,
If you can understand, and you are made
Free of the freest and the noblest trade.
  And in the way of poetry, now-a-days,
  Of all that are call'd works, the best are plays.

W. B.

NOTES.

NOTES TO VOL. I.

P. 3. EDWARD, LORD ZOUCH.—Born in 1556, the only son of George, Lord Zouch, of Haringworth, Northamptonshire. Succeeded to the peerage in 1569. From 1612 until his death in 1625 he resided principally at Bramshill House, Hampshire. He was also a patron of Ben Jonson. Browne likewise dedicated to him *The Shepherd's Pipe* (1614).

P. 9. JOHN SELDEN, the eminent jurist, legal antiquary, and Oriental scholar (born 1584: died 1654). On terms of friendship with Browne, Ben Jonson, Drayton, and Camden. In 1613 he supplied a series of notes, enriched by an immense number of quotations and references to the first eighteen songs of Drayton's *Poly-Olbion*. He has English verses before the edition of Drayton's *Poems* published in 1619.

P. 10. MICHAEL DRAYTON (born 1563: died 1631). He died in the parish of St. Dunstan in the West, London, his estate being administered to by his brother Edmund Drayton on 17 January, 1631-2 (*Commissary Court of London, Book* 1627-38). In his *Elegy*, or rather Epistle to Henry Reynolds (1627), he mentions the two Beaumonts (Francis Beaumont and Sir John Beaumont) and William Browne as his "dear companions," "bosom friends," and "rightly-born poets." He also addressed an *Elegy* to Browne "of the evil time" (1627). Browne has introduced him as "our second Ovid" in his eulogy of the English poets in the second song of the second book of *Britannia's Pastorals*, ll. 287-92, refers to him as "honour'd Drayton" in an *Ode* (vol. ii., p. 211), and wrote commendatory verses before the second part of his *Poly-Olbion* (vol. ii. p. 313).

VOL. II.   Y

P. 12. EDWARD HEYWARD, born in 1594, the eldest son of Richard Heyward, gent., of Reepham, Norfolk. Admitted of the Inner Temple in 1604, he was called to the Bar in 1618. A man of great learning, the friend of Browne, Selden, Ben Jonson, Drayton, and other distinguished persons. Both the editions of *Titles of Honor* (1614 and 1631) are dedicated to him by Selden, who calls him his "most beloved friend and chamber-fellow." One of Selden's executors and one of the four persons to whom Richard Milward, Selden's amanuensis, inscribed that great scholar's *Table-Talk*, not printed until 1689. He has lines prefixed to Jonson's *Works* (1616), and some verses before Drayton's *The Barons' Wars* (1619). Died on 25th September, 1658.

P. 13. CHRISTOPHER BROOKE (died 1628). An intimate friend of Browne, with whom he published, in 1613, elegies on the death of Prince Henry. Browne had an exaggerated opinion of Brooke's poetic capacity, and eulogizes him far beyond his deserts in the second song of the second book of *Britannia's Pastorals*, ll. 303-22. In the fifth eclogue of the *Shepherd's Pipe* (1614), which is inscribed to Brooke, Browne urges him to attempt more ambitious poetry than the pastorals which he had already completed. In response to this appeal Brooke wrote his *Ghost of Richard the Third* (1614), a lame flight, before which Browne has commendatory verses. Brooke addressed in turn an eclogue to Browne, also printed in the *Shepherd's Pipe*. "Cuttie" or "Cuddy" is the pastoral name which he adopted for himself.

P. 13. FR: DYNNE. This was Francis Dynne, of Deptford, who became a member of the Inner Temple in 1610, and was called to the Bar in 1620. He has also commendatory verses before Christopher Brooke's *The Ghost of Richard the Third* (1614).

P. 14. THO. GARDINER. Thomas Gardiner, third son of Michael Gardiner, successively rector of Littlebury, Essex, and of Greenford Magna, Middlesex. He was admitted of the Inner Temple in 1609, called to the Bar in 1618, and held the recordership of London from 1635 to 1643, when he was discharged "for long absence." For his loyalty he received knighthood in 1641; but in February, 1646-7, he had to mortgage his lands in Oxfordshire to the usurer Hugh Audley, and lost them (*cf.* his will in P. C. C. 369, Berkley, with that of Audley, P. C. C. 134, Laud). Resided latterly at Cuddesdon, Oxfordshire, where he was buried in 1652. Upon Browne's admission to the Inner Temple, in March 1611-12, Gardiner became one of his sureties.

P. 15. W. FERRAR. William Ferrar, third son of Nicholas Ferrar, an eminent Lond n merchant, who was interested in the adventures of Hawkins, Drake, and Raleigh, and brother of the well-known Nicholas Ferrar (1592-1637), of Little Gidding, in Huntingdonshire. Entered the Middle Temple on 10 May, 1610. Died young, at sea. Wither introduces him, under the pastoral name of "Alexis," in *The Shepherd's Hunting*, and addresses the fifth eclogue to him; therein "Roget" (Wither) urges "Alexis" to write poetry, which diffidence had hitherto prevented him from doing. Browne pays a graceful tribute to his memory in the first song of the second book of *Britannia's Pastorals*, ll. 241-318.

P. 15. FR: OULDE. Francis Oulde, a native of Rowton, Shropshire. Admitted student of the Inner Temple in 1608; called to the Bar in 1618.

P. 38, l. 578. *Are apter to receive*, etc. Both editions read *as*.

P. 41, l. 662. *False tables wrought by Alcibiades.* They represented a god or goddess without, and a Silenus or deformed piper within. Erasmus has a curious dissertation on "Sileni Alcibiadis" in his *Adagia*.

P. 44, ll. 735-36—

> *Nor shall this help their sheep, whose stomach fails,*
> *By tying knots of wool near to their tails.*

A kindred superstition to this appears to have prevailed forty years ago in the district of Buchan, Aberdeenshire, where, according to a correspondent of *Notes and Queries* (1st Ser., vol. iv. pp. 380-1), the housewives were accustomed to tie a piece of red worsted thread round their cows' tails on turning them out to grass for the first time in the spring. It secured their cattle, they believed, from an evil eye, from being "elf-shot" by fairies, and from other mishaps. —*Hazlitt.* Both editions have "stomachs."

P. 56, l. 277. *May never evet nor the toad*, etc. Imitated by Henry Vaughan in his address "To the River Isca" in *Olor Iscanus*, 1651, p. 2:

> May the evet and the toad
> Within thy banks have no abode,
>
> .   .   .   .   .   .

> In all thy journey to the main
> No nitrous clay, nor brimstone-vein
> Mix with thy streams, but may they pass
> Fresh as the air and clear as glass.

P. 57, ll. 280–5.

> *May'st thou ne'er happen in thy way*
> *On nitre or on brimstone mine,*
> *To spoil thy taste !* this spring of thine
> Let it of nothing taste but earth,
> And salt-conceived in their birth
> Be ever fresh ! *Let no man dare*
> *To spoil thy fish, make lock or ware.*

Imitated from Fletcher's *Faithful Shepherdess* [1610], Act iii., Sc. 1. Milton, in his *Comus*, 1637 (MILTON, *Poems*, ed. Warton, pp. 250–1), was also indebted to Fletcher's pastoral. The lines in Roman type are thus explained by Dr. Brinsley Nicholson, in a learned note communicated to *Notes and Queries*, 4th Ser., xii., 301 : " Marina wishes that the waters of the river god, salt-conceived in their mother sea, may, in losing their saltness, receive only the savour given by purer earth uncontaminated with nitre, brimstone, and the like."

Dr. Nicholson remarks further : " The words *spring, it*, and then *their birth*, read awkwardly to our ears, and as ' its ' is not used by Browne, *their* may be a misprint for *her*. But the text may be defended by two lines just above :—

> Whilst I into my spring do dive
> To see that *they* do not deprive
> The meadows near, which much do thirst,

where the plural refers to the waters that issue from the spring, their springing place."

P. 59, ll. 353–82. *There stood the elm*, etc. Browne is here imitating his favourite Spenser. Cf. *The Faëry Queen*, Bk. I., Canto I., Stanzas 8–9.

P. 60, ll. 369–70—

> *The tamarisk there stood,*
> *For housewives' besoms only known most good.*

Both editions read " bosoms," for which I have substituted " besoms."

P. 63, l. 456. *Apelles' half-done table.* Apelles, the most celebrated of Greek painters, flourished in the latter part of the fourth century B.C. That he painted on movable panels is evident from the frequent mention of *tabulæ* with reference to his pictures. After his death no one could be found to complete his picture of Aphrodite intended for the Coans, which he averred should surpass his best picture, the Aphrodite Anadyomene.

P. 67, l. 574. *And have a form and heart, but yet no passion.* Both editions read "a passion." I adopt Mr. Hazlitt's correction.

P. 69, l. 628. *Dragon's blood.* The dragon's blood known to Browne would be the dark-coloured resin, valuable in medicine for its tonic astringent properties, but more generally used as a colouring matter, which is yielded in part by the Dracæna Draco from the surface of the leaves and from the cracks in its trunk. A woodcut of the "Dragon tree" and its fruit is given by Gerard (*Herbal*, 1597, p. 1339). It is also obtained from other trees, such as Calamus Draco, Pterocarpus Draco, etc. Browne may likewise have had in his mind the following passage from Topsell :—" That ancient Cinnabaris, made by commixture of the blood of Elephants and Dragons both together, which alone is able and nothing but it, to make the best representation of blood in painting . . . . it hath [also] a most rare and singular virtue against all poisons " (*The History of Four-footed Beasts*, 1607, p. 199).

P. 72, l. 691, and p. 73, l. 717. *An aged rock.* Probably, as Mr. Shelly suggests, Mary Tavy Rock, "a grey crag that lies in the bed of the river about three miles above Tavistock."

P. 73, ll. 711-12.

> *. . . . his work not seeming fit*
> *To walk in equipage with better wit.*

The expression to " walk " or " march in equipage " is not uncommon. Nashe, in the preface to Greene's *Menaphon* (1589), writes: " And in truth (Master Watson except, whom I mentioned before) I know not almost any of late days that hath showed himself singular in any special Latin Poem, whose *Amintas* and translated *Antigone* may *march in equipage of honour with any of our ancient Poets.*" Marston, in verses " in praise of his Pigmalion " (1598), has

> " Stanzas like odd bands
> Of voluntaries and mercenarians ;

> Which like soldados of our warlike age,
> *March rich bedight in warlike equipage.*"

Shakespeare, in Sonnet XXXII., uses a similar expression :—

> "Had my friend's muse grown with this growing age,
> A dearer birth than this his love had brought,
> *To march in ranks of better equipage.*"

(*Cf.* review of Dr. Thomas Tyler's edition cf Shakespeare's Sonnets in *Athenæum*, 26 July, 1890, p. 123.)

P. 73, l. 729. *Here digs a cave at some high mountain's foot.* Though there is no "high mountain," properly so called, along the whole course of the river, the allusion, observes Mr. Shelly, "may be to the Virtuous Lady Cave, where the Walkham joins the Tavy, about four miles below Tavistock, and where the banks of the river, particularly the west bank, are very steep and lofty."

P. 74, ll. 736-7.

> *Helps down an abbey, then a natural bridge*
> *By creeping underground he frameth out.*

The "abbey" alluded to is probably that at Tavistock, " by whose ruins," says Risdon, a contemporary of Browne, " you may now aim at the antique magnificence thereof." (*Survey of Devon*, ed. 1811, p. 213.)

There is no "natural bridge," strictly speaking, formed by the Tavy, but "between Crowndale and Virtuous Lady Mine, two or three miles below Tavistock," remarks Mr. Shelly, "the river passes through a narrow channel between steep banks.'

P. 79, l. 872. *Had-I-wists.—"Had I known*. A common exclamation of those who repented of anything unadvisedly undertaken. . . . . Sometimes used much like a substantive in the sense of repentance."—Nares's *Glossary*.

P. 82, l. 15. *And the maid help.* Both editions have "maids."

P. 86, l. 132. *Sought out*, etc. Both editions have "sought ought."

P. 94, ll. 315-40. *When turning head, he not a foot would stir*, etc. It will be noticed that Browne speaks of the hind in both genders. A similar deviation from strict syntax occurs in the description of the wounded swan in Song 5 (p. 141, ll. 129-41).

P. 108, l. 95. *On craggy rocks, or steepy hills*, etc. The 8vo edition has "steepy stils," an obvious misprint. I retain the reading of the folio.

P. 109, l. 140. *Out of the covert of an ivy tod.* The word "tod," meaning a thick tuft or bush, is misprinted "rod" in both editions. The error is noticed in Nares's *Glossary*, ed. Halliwell and Wright, ii. 888.

P. 117, ll. 353-4.

> Or to a mead a wanton river dresses
> With richest collars of her turning esses.

The winding of a river is here quaintly compared by Browne to the collar of SS, or esses, which was bestowed on knights of the garter, the chief justices, and other exalted personages.

P. 118, l. 391. *Poor Aletheia, long despis'd of all.* My friend Mr. A. H. Bullen points out to me that this episode owes much of its general treatment to John Day's prose tract, *Peregrinatio Scholastica or Learning's Pilgrimage* (*Cf.* Day's Works, ed. Bullen, 1881).

P. 119, ll. 395-400. *In winter's time,* etc. Browne appears to have had in his mind, as Mr. Hazlitt suggests, the song in Shakespeare's *Love's Labour's Lost*, 1598 :—

> When icicles hang by the wall,
> And Dick the shepherd blows his nail.

P. 121, l. 474.

> *Unhappy, unreliev'd, yet unredress'd !*

Both editions read "undressed," which, in the annotated copy in the Library of Salisbury Cathedral, is corrected to "unredress'd."

P. 122, l. 486. *That he might till those lands were fallow laid.* Both editions have "were," but *where* may be the right reading, the word "laid" being, as often, intransitive.

P. 129, ll. 683 *seq.* *Next him a great man sat,* etc. The permanence of Essex's popular reputation as a sturdy champion of British interests against Spain was attested in 1624 by the publication of *Robert, Earl of Essex, his Ghost sent from Elysium to the Nobility, Gentry, and Commonalty of England,* a warning against Prince Charles's Spanish marriage, and the maintenance of peaceful relations with Spain (Mr. Sidney Lee, in *Dict. Nat. Biog.*).

P. 130, ll. 692-3.

> *He sung the outrage of the lazy drone*
> *Upon the lab'ring bee.*

A poem attributed to Essex, " It was a time when silly bees could speak," was printed in Dowland's *Third Book of Songs and Airs* (1603), but in Egerton MS. 923, f. 5, the authorship is assigned to Essex's secretary, Henry Cuffe.

P. 131, l. 728. *A surly bear.* Leicester was popularly believed to have poisoned the Earl of Essex's father in Dublin (1576).

P. 132, l. 746. *Quelling his rage with faithless Gerion.* The allusion (which is borrowed from Spenser, *Faëry Queen*, Bk. V., c. 10, 11) refers to Gerion, or Geryon, of Gadês (Cadiz), a monster with three bodies (or, in other words, a king over three kingdoms) slain by Hercules. The three kingdoms over which Philip reigned were Spain, Germany, and the Netherlands.

P. 141, ll. 129-41. *But as a snowy swan,* etc. See note on Song 3, ll. 315-40 (p. 326).

P. 142, l. 152. *Which spoil'd her fishers' nets and fishes' breed.* Both editions read " her sister's nets." The sense is preserved by substituting " fishers," according to the emendation proposed in the copy in Salisbury Cathedral Library.

P. 142, l. 154. *A royal youth,* etc. Henry [Frederick], Prince of Wales. Eldest son of James I. Born February 19, 1593-4 ; died November 6, 1612. His unexpected death occasioned an extra-ordinary deluge of elegies and lamentations in prose and verse. (See List in Nichols's *Progresses of James I.*, pp. 504-12.)

P. 151, ll. 381-2.

> *Thou, by whose hand the sacred Trine did bring*
> *Us out of bonds, from bloody Bonnering.*

A reference to the religious persecutions which took place during Edmund Bonner's occupancy of the see of London (1540-1558). The bishop was held in such detestation that, according to Sir John Harington (*Brief View*, p. 16), men would say of any ill-favoured, fat fellow in the street, "There goes Bonner."

P. 151, l. 395. *The mulberry (his black from Thisbe taking).* According to the legend, Pyramus, the lover of Thisbe, a maiden of Babylon, imagining that she had been murdered, made away with himself under a mulberry-tree. Thisbe, on finding his body, likewise killed herself. Thenceforth the fruit of the mulberry-tree was as the colour of blood.

P. 167, l. 810. *Makes poor her garments to enrich her bed.* The conceit is borrowed from Sidney's *Arcadia*, book ii. (ed. 1613, p. 115):—"These words wan no further of Pamela, but that telling her they might talk better as they lay together, they *impoverished their clothes to enrich their bed.*"

P. 168, l. 846. *The shrill chanting of her teery-lerry.* *Cf.* Shakespeare :—

The lark, that tirra lirra chants.— *Wint. Tale*, iv. 2.

P. 175. WILLIAM, EARL OF PEMBROKE. Born in 1580, the eldest son of Henry Herbert, second earl, by his third wife Mary, third daughter of Sir Henry Sidney and sister of Sir Philip Sidney. He succeeded to the earldom January 19, 1600–1, and died April 10, 1630. Sharing the literary tastes of his mother and uncle, he wrote verse himself, and was, according to Aubrey, "the greatest Mæcenas to learned men of any peer of his time or since." Browne lived with him for some time at his seat, Wilton House, near Salisbury.

P. 177. JOHN GLANVILL. A kinsman of Browne's. Born at Kilworthy, near Tavistock, in 1586, the second son of Sir John Glanvill, Knt., Judge of the Common Pleas. Called to the Bar at Lincoln's Inn about 1610. Successively M.P. for, and recorder of Plymouth and Bristol. Became eminent in his profession and prominent as a politician, for a while on the popular side. Made serjeant-at-law in 1637. Subsequently he adhered to the King, and was created a king's serjeant in 1640 and knighted in 1641. He fell into the hands of the Parliament and was imprisoned in the Tower in 1645. Dying in 1661, he was buried at Broad Hinton, Wiltshire.

P. 178. THO. WENMAN. Born in 1596, the eldest son of Sir Richard Wenman, Knt., of Thame Park, Oxfordshire, who was made an Irish peer by the title of Viscount Wenman in 1629. Admitted a student of the Inner Temple in 1613. Succeeded to the peerage in April, 1640. One of the commissioners to carry the propositions for peace to the King at Oxford in 1644 ; again named commissioner for the treaty at Uxbridge in the same year, and for the treaty at Newport in 1648. One of the adventurers in Ireland on the reduction of that kingdom by the English Parliament. Died in 1664.

P. 179. W. HERBERT. William Herbert, probably son of William Herbert of Glamorgan. Seems to have matriculated at Christ Church, Oxford, on October 17, 1600, at the age of 17. He was apparently in attendance on Prince Henry soon after James I.'s accession. Wrote a long poem entitled, *A Prophesie of Cadwallader* (1604). Contributed also verses " in laudem authoris " to Peter Erondelle's *French Garden* (1608).

P. 181. JOHN DAVIES OF HEREF[ORD], poet and writing-master, was born about 1565 and died in 1618. He contributed the third eclogue appended to the *Shepherd's Pipe*: it is entitled, " An Eclogue between young Willy the singer of his native Pastorals and old Wernocke his friend." Browne, in turn, paid a high compliment to Davies in the second song of this (the second) Book of *Britannia's Pastorals*, ll. 323-6.

P. 181. CAROLUS CROKE. Born in 1591, the third son of Sir John Croke, Knt., Judge of the King's Bench, Charles Croke matriculated at Christ Church, Oxford, on June 8, 1604 (B.A. 1608, M.A. 1611, B. and D.D. 1625). Entered the Inner Temple in 1609, and held the professorship of Rhetoric at Gresham College, London, from 1613 to 1619. Took orders, and became rector of Waterstock, Oxfordshire (1616), fellow of Eton College (1617–21), and rector of Agmondisham, Buckinghamshire (1621). Fled to Ireland during the Civil War, and died at Carlow, near Dublin, on April 10, 1657. Contributed a copy of sapphics to the *Epithalamia* (1613), published on the marriage of Prince Frederick and the Princess Elizabeth, daughter of James I.

P. 182. UNTON CROKE. Born about 1594, the fourth son of Sir John Croke, Knt., judge of the King's Bench. Matriculated from Christ Church, Oxford, on March 2, 1609-10. Appointed deputy-steward of the University in February, 1619–20. Admitted a student of the Inner Temple in 1609 ; called to the Bar in 1616, and made a bencher in 1635. M.P. for Wallingford in 1626, and again in the Short Parliament of 1640. Actively aided the Parliamentarians, and enjoyed the favour of Cromwell, by whom he was promoted serjeant-at-law in 1654. Died January 28, 1670-1.

P. 182. ANTH. VINCENT. Eldest son of Sir Francis Vincent, bart., of Stoke D'Abernon, Surrey. Upon the outbreak of the Civil War he declared for the King, and suffered in his fortune. Died in 1642. He was connected with Devonshire by his marriage to

Elizabeth, daughter of Sir Arthur Acland, of Killerton, in that county.

P. 183. JOHN MORGAN. One of the ten sons of George Morgan of Pencraig, near Caerleon, Monmouthshire. Became a student of the Inner Temple in 1610. Died young.

P. 183. THO. HEYGATE. Eldest son of Thomas Heygate, of Hayes, Middlesex. Admitted a student of the Inner Temple in 1613.

P. 184. AUGUSTUS CÆSAR. Born in 1598, the second son of Sir Thomas Cæsar, Knt., baron of the exchequer. Admitted a student of the Inner Temple in 1609. Matriculated at St. Edmund Hall, Oxford, on October 23, 1612. Contributed verses to the *Epithalamia* (1613) on the marriage of Prince Frederick to Elizabeth, daughter of James I., and to the *Justa Funebria* on Sir Thomas Bodley (1613). Died young.

P. 185. G. WITHER. George Wither, the poet (born June 11, 1588 ; died May 2, 1667). He has introduced Browne as " Willy " in his fine poem, *The Shepherd's Hunting* (1615), and speaks of him as one—

> " Who, at twice ten, hath sung more,
> Than some will do at fourscore."

Elsewhere he refers to Browne as—

> " that gentle swain
> Who wons by Tavy, on the Western plain."

Wither was author of the second and fourth Eclogues appended to the *Shepherd's Pipe* : in the one Christopher Brooke and Browne are figured under the names of " Cuttie " and " Willy "; the other he dedicates " to his truly loving and worthy friend, Mr. W. Browne." Browne, besides eulogizing Wither in company with John Davies of Hereford, in the second song of this (the second) Book of *Britannia's Pastorals*, ll. 323-6, has introduced him under the pastoral name of " Roget " in the first Eclogue of the *Shepherd's Pipe*.

P. 185. W. B. Apparently the initials of William Basse, the poet. He was a retainer to Sir Richard, afterwards Viscount Wenman, of Thame Park, Oxfordshire, whose son, Thomas, was contemporary with Browne at the Inner Temple, and also wrote verses prefixed to this (the second) Book of *Britannia's Pastorals*. The lines before Massinger's *Bondman* (1624), signed W. B., are variously attributed to Basse and to Browne. Basse died at Thame

Park, his estate being administered to by his only child, Elizabeth, wife of John Brooke, on 20 March, 1653-4 (*Administration Act Book, P. C. C.*). It is just possible that Basse and Browne were kinsmen. In her will, dated 10 September, 1624 (*P. C. C.*, 88, *Byrde*), Anne Basse, widow of William Basse, one of the proctors of the Prerogative Court of Canterbury, names as her executrix her daughter Elizabeth, wife of Ambrose Browne, Esq., of Betchworth Castle, Surrey.

P. 186. BEN JONSON. Born about 1573 ; died in 1637. Browne has introduced a laudatory notice of Jonson in the second song of this (the second) Book of *Britannia's Pastorals*, ll. 293-302.

P. 191, marginal note. *Petunt Classem*, etc. The exact words of Galfridus are as follows : " Nec mora, petivit suorum assensu classem suam, et replevit eam universis divitiis vel deliciis quas acquisiverat, et ipsam ingressus est : prosperis quoque ventis pro-missam insulam exigens, in Totonesio littore applicuit." (*Historia Britonum*, ed. Giles, p. 20.)

P. 196, ll. 241-318. *Glide soft, ye silver floods*, etc. A tribute to the memory of William Ferrar ("Alexis"). *See* Note at page 323.

P. 202, ll. 391-2. *Tom the Miller with a golden thumb*, etc. I have sought diligently for mention of this ballad in the various collections of old ballads and in the *Registers of the Stationers' Company*, but without success.

P. 202, l. 400. *Martial will show for coin in 's crabbed woman.* The allusion may be to Martial's coarse epigram " In Vetustillam," epig. 93, lib. iii.

P. 217, ll. 771-96. *Now great Hyperion*, etc. The unpleasant allusion to the "sweating" of the steeds (ll. 778-9) and the prosaic introduction of "conduit-pipes" in the description of the rivulets (l. 783) serve to mar this otherwise fine picture of the approach of Night. The "conduit-pipes" were probably suggested to Browne by the upper and lower conduit which formerly existed in the main street of Tavistock. They were "places of general resort with all the old and young women and children in the neighbourhood. There they gathered to fill their water-buckets, to chat or wash their clothes." (MRS. BRAY, *The Tamar and the Tavy*, iii. 18.)

P. 223, l. 947. *Delightful Saluste.* Guillaume de Saluste Du Bartas (born 1544, died 1590), author of *La Sepmaine*, a poem on the creation of the world, which was translated by Joshua Sylvester in 1598. Its religious tone and rather fanciful style made it a great favourite with English writers of the time, by whom the author was also designated the " divine Du Bartas," and placed on an equality with Ariosto.

P. 229, ll. 33–40. *Here from the rest a lovely shepherd's boy*, etc. Imitated from the description of Arcadia in the first book of Sir Philip Sidney's *Arcadia* (ed. 1613, p. 6). Browne has introduced a graceful eulogy on Sidney, and on the *Arcadia* in particular, in this very Song, ll. 247–80.

P. 235, ll. 193–222. *Shall I tell you whom I love?* etc. That this charming song was rightly appreciated as it circulated in MS. among the poet's friends is clear from the allusions to it by John Olney in his verses prefixed to Browne's *Shepherd's Pipe* (1614). It has been set to music by Dr. S. S. Wesley.

P. 239, l. 303. *Well-languag'd Daniel.* Samuel Daniel (1562–1619), from whose pleasing lines on *Ulysses and the Siren* (1605) Browne may have derived a hint for his *Inner Temple Masque.*

P. 245, ll. 443–5.

> *The griping carl*
> *That spoils our plains in digging them for marl.*

Risdon, in his *Survey of Devon* (edit. 1811, p. 5), which was written about 1630, says, "the south part of the shire is thin, standing upon somewhat a rocky soil ; but the most part of these rocks are a kind of marl, fruitful in dressing of ground." And Fuller, in his *Worthies* (edit. 1662, p. 245) says, under Devonshire, "no shire shows more industrious or so many husbandmen, who by marl (blue and white), chalk, lime, ... and what not, make the ground both to take and keep a moderate fruitfulness." (Cited by Mr. Shelly in Hazlitt's edition.)

P. 250, ll. 599–604.

> *Here sat the lad, of whom I think of old*
> *Virgil's prophetic spirit had foretold*, etc.

The reference is to the pseudo-Virgilian epigram :—

> " Dum dubitat Natura marem faciatne puellam,
> Factus es, O pulcher, paene puella puer."

P. 288, ll. 727–8.

> *Whilst in a bush two nightingales together*
> *Show'd the best skill they had to draw me thither.*

Writing in 1832, Mrs. Bray says, "Browne's allusion to the night-ingale, in these lines, must either have been a poetical license, or some change must have taken place in the natural history of Devon since his day; as that bird is now unknown in our county." (*The Tamar and the Tavy*, ii. 8.)

P. 289, ll. 734-8.

> *Thetis with her brave company had won*
> *The mouth of Dart*, etc.

The Earme and Yealm are small streams that run down from Dartmoor and fall into the sea between Dartmouth and Plymouth. The Plym, accurately described in Bk. I. Song 5, l. 132, as the "sandy Plym," and the Tamar, fall into Plymouth Sound.—*Mr. Shelly in Hazlitt's edition.*

P. 290, l. 762, *seq. Walla, Tavy's fairest love.* The Walla-brook, that has its source just under Brent Tor, and runs through Kilworthy (in Browne's time belonging to the Glanvills) and Ines-combe, "sweet Ina's Coombe" (l. 1117), falling into the Tavy about half a mile above Tavistock.--*Mr. Shelly in Hazlitt's edition.*

"About half a mile from Tavistock," writes Mrs. Bray in 1833, "is the Walla Brook, a little stream of unpretending character, that, over a rocky bed, comes murmuring down the gentle descent of some sloping grounds, and unites itself with the Tavy nearly opposite to Rowdon woods. The Walla was till very lately over-hung by some vestiges of oak-trees so old and decaying that I could never look at them without fancying that in the days of Browne he had often reclined under their picturesque branches on the margin of the stream, and there, perhaps, employed his imagination in composing the beautiful episode called the 'Loves of the Walla and the Tavy.'" (*The Tamar and the Tavy*, iii. 2.)

The idea of this episode was probably suggested to Browne by Ovid's Egeria, who was transformed into a fountain (*Met.* xv. 482, *seq.*).

P. 290, ll. 775-80. *For as I oft have heard the wood-nymphs say,* etc. An allusion to the Devonshire legend that fairies and pixies steal honey from the hives of bees.

—— l. 777. *Then back did pull them.* Both editions have "Then black."

P. 300, l. 1033. *Upon a great adventure is it bound.* So Spenser of the Red Cross Knight :—"Upon a great adventure he was bond," *Faëry Queen*, Bk. i. c. i. st. 3.

P. 305, l. 1168. *Fair-check'd Etesia's yellow camomile.* By " Etesia " are personified the etesian gales, which blow during the dog-days (July–August), when the camomile attains its full bloom. Henry Vaughan, a lover of our poet, has celebrated a lady under the name of " Etesia " in several poems in his *Thalia Rediviva* (1678).

P. 312, l. 27. *That apt fabric.* Ordgar, Earl of Devonshire, founded the monastery of Tavistock about A.D. 961 (WILL. MALMESB., *De Gestis Pontific*, ed. Hamilton, p. 202). His son Ordulf is said to have completed it A.D. 981.

P. 312, ll. 35-7.

I'll strive to draw
The nymphs by Tamar, Tavy, Exe and Taw,
By Turridge, Otter, Ock, by Dart and Plym.

Of all these rivers, except the Exe and the Otter, which run through the eastern part of the county, it may be said, as Risdon says of one of them, the Ock, more generally called the Ockment,—" It fetcheth its fountain from the high and hungry hills of Dartmoor." —*Mr. Shelly.*

P. 314, l. 85. *Some wearied crow is set.* Both editions read " it set."

P. 319, l. 210. CORNISH MICHAEL, whose family name was Blaumpain, flourished about 1250, and was dean of Maestricht in Brabant (*Cf.* BOASE and COURTNEY, *Bibl. Cornub.*, i. 25, iii. 1072 ; BOASE, *Collect. Cornub.*, col. 554 ; CAMDEN, *Remains*, edit. 1870, p.9).

P. 319, ll. 211-12.

To see a swain unfold
The tragedy of Drake in leaves of gold.

Charles Fitzgeffrey (1575 ?-1638), a native of Fowey and rector of St. Dominick, Cornwall. in 1596 published at Oxford a spirited poem, entitled, *Sir Francis Drake, his honourable Life's Commendation and his tragical Death's Lamentation.*

P. 319, l. 213.

Then hear another Grenville's name relate.

In 1595 Gervase Markham published a poem called *The most Honorable Tragedy of Sir Richard Grinville, Knight.*

P. 320, l. 224. *The rock Main-Amber.* The Logan Rock, a rocking-stone which weighs about eighty tons, on the headland called Castle Treryn, in the parish of S. Levan, Cornwall. " Well worth the viewing," writes Carew, " is Mainamber. Mayne [Maen or Mean] is a rock; amber, as some say, signifieth Ambrose. And a great rock the same is, advanced upon some others of a meaner size with so equal a counterpeyze that the push of a finger will sensibly move it to and fro : but farther to remove it, the united forces of many shoulders are over-weak" (*Survey of Cornwall*, 1602, ed. 1769, p. 151ᵇ). In 1824 an ignorant naval lieutenant overthrew Main-Amber with nine of his men. He was forced to replace it, and deservedly lost his promotion.

P. 328, ll. 445–446.

> *And women, which before to love began*
> *Man without wealth, love wealth without a man.*

Cf. Sir John Davies' *Twelve Wonders of the World* (xii.) :—

> "'Titles and lands I like, yet rather fancy can
> A man that wanteth gold than gold that wants a man."

For other examples of this proverbial expression see note in Davison's *Poetical Rhapsody*, ed. Bullen, ii. 177.

P. 343, l. 848.

> . . . . *him that did the shady plane-tree love.*

Cf. Herodotus, vii. 27, 31.

P. 357, l. 219.

> *Music that lent feet to the stable woods.*

For "stable" the folio edition has "sable." I adopt the reading of the 8vo edition.

P. 360, l. 278. *Her nigh inhabitants.* For "nigh," the reading of the 8vo edition, the folio has "high.'

P. 373, l. 652.

> *Submissly prayen to the name of Pan.*

"Prayer," the reading of both editions, has been corrected to "prayen." .

P. 374, l. 68r.

> *And she begins to still and still her pace.*

For "to" both editions read "it."

P. 374, l. 687.

> *And harmless flocks of sheep,* etc.

Both editions read "as" for "and."

NOTES TO VOL. II.

P. 4. PHIL. PAPILLON. Philip Papillon, son of David Papillon, of Lubbenham, Leicestershire. Born January 1, 1620. First at Oriel College, Oxford, from which he migrated to Exeter College July 1, 1634, and matriculated on September 9 following. B.A. April 7, 1638; M.A. February 3, 1640-1. Died 1641. He published the tragedy of his friend and fellow-collegian, Samuel Hardinge, entitled, *Sicily and Naples* (1640), in defiance of the author's wish.

P. 4. P. S., COLL. EX. These initials represent either Peter (born 1595) or Paul (died 1644), respectively the eldest and the second sons of Sir John Speccott, Knt., of Thornbury, Devonshire. Both contributed verses to the *Threni Exoniensium* in 1613 on Lord Petre, and both became members of the Inner Temple in 1615.

P. 6. EDW. HALL. Born in Essex in 1621, the sixth son of Joseph Hall, successively bishop of Exeter and of Norwich. Matriculated at Exeter College, Oxford, in 1635. B.A. 1637, M.A. 1640. Elected Probationer Fellow in 1638. Died in 1643. Contributed also verses to *Coronæ Carolinæ Quadratura* (1636) and *Eucharistica Oxoniensia* (1641); also lines prefixed to *Sicily and Naples* (1640), a tragedy written by his friend and fellow-collegian Samuel Hardinge.

The preceding lines, entitled, "On the Author of Britannia's Peerless Pastorals," are written in the same hand, according to Beloe, and therefore may have been likewise by Hall.

P. 7. JO. DYNHAM. John Dynham, born in 1585, the eldest son of John Dynham, of Wortham, in the parish of Lifton, Devonshire. Matriculated at Oxford from Exeter College on March 23,

1603-4. B.A. 1606. Rector of St. Mary Major, Exeter, 1613-22. Died 1641.

P. 11. SAM. HARDINGE. Born about 1618, the son of Robert Hardinge, of Ipswich, Suffolk. In 1634 he became a sojourner of Exeter College, Oxford, and took his B.A. degree in 1638. He afterwards became chaplain to some nobleman, and died "about the beginning, or in the heat of, the Civil War." He wrote an unacted tragedy in verse and prose, entitled, *Sicily and Naples; or, the Fatal Union*, which was published in 1640, without his consent, by his fellow-collegian, Philip Papillon.

P. 12. CHR. GEWEN. Christopher Gewen was born in 1617, the eldest son of Thomas Gewen, of Bradridge, in the parish of Boyton, Cornwall. Commoner of Exeter College, Oxford, May 12, 1634, to October 4, 1636; matriculated September 9, 1634. Admitted student of the Inner Temple in 1635

P. 13.

> *'Tis their wish each place could tell*
> *Thy conquests like St. Dunstan's well.*

An allusion to a passage in the fourth Eclogue of Wither's *The Shepherd's Hunting*, where "Roget" (Wither) says of "Willy" (Browne) :—

> It is known what thou canst do,
> For it is not long ago
> When that Cuddy, thou, and I,
> Each the other's skill to try,
> At St. Dunstan's charmed well
> (As some present there can tell),
> Sang upon a sudden theme,
> Sitting by the crimson stream.

"Cuddy" is Christopher Brooke. St. Dunstan's Well was in Tottenham Wood, Middlesex. (Robinson, *Hist. of Tottenham*, i. 19.) There is another well dedicated to the Saint at Mayfield Palace, Sussex.

P. 14. B. N. Nicholas Breton (1545?-1626?), who often reversed his initials, may possibly be the author of this poem ; it is quite in his style. Moreover, as the writer does not indicate (as the others are careful to do) that he was a member of Exeter College, he would appear not to have belonged to that particular group of Browne's friends. No one bearing the initials " B. N." was a

member of the College at that time, as the printed registers show
Beloe, however, remarks that the poem is written in the same hand
as that by Christopher Gewen.

Pp. 14, 15. ROBERT TAYLOR, or TAYLER. Of Exeter College,
Oxford. B.A. 1615; M.A. 1618. There seems to be no means of
identifying him with the Robert Taylor who wrote a play called,
The Hog hath lost his Pearl (1614). "The above acrostic is suc-
ceeded by two quotations from *The Shepherd's Calendar* of Spenser,
applied in compliment to Browne, and at the bottom is inscribed in
Robert Taylor's hand, Sic ignorans cecinit. Edm. Spencer."—
BELOE. Contributed verses to *Annæ Funebria Sacra* (1619).

P. 18. NICH. DOWNEY. Born in 1618, the son of the Rev.
Nicholas Downey, of Little Modbury, Devonshire. Matriculated
at Oxford from Exeter College on June 19, 1635. B.A. 1638–9 ;
M.A. 1641. Has also verses before *Sicily and Naples* (1640), a
tragedy written by his fellow-collegian, Samuel Hardinge.

P. 22. Perigot. A pseudonym.

P. 25, ll. 51–2.

> *So shuts the marigold her leaves*
> *At the departure of the sun.*

Cf. Shakespeare :

> "The marigold that goes to bed wi' the sun,
> And with him rises weeping."
> *Wint. Tale*, iv. 3.

P. 26, l. 73.

> *For could I think she some idea were*, etc.

Here, as Mr. Hazlitt observes, the poet had in his thoughts the
collection of sonnets written by his friend Drayton under the name
of *Idea*, and printed in 1593. Browne elsewhere (*Brit. Past.*, Bk. I.,
Song 5) personifies England under a similar name—"Idya."

P. 29, ll. 159–234.

> *Vain dreams, forbear ! ye but deceivers be*, etc.

These lines occur as a separate poem, with variants, in Lansdowne
MS. 777.

P. 34, l. 290. *Sad mandragoras*. Mandragoras, popularly
called mandrakes, poisonous plants, natives of the Mediterranean
region. The root, from its occasional resemblance to the lower

part of the human body, was formerly supposed to possess an inferior kind of animal life, and the popular belief was that when torn from the ground it uttered such fearful groans, that the person who uprooted it went mad.

P. 40, ll. 430-449.

Yet one day's rest for all my cries ! etc.

The first and second stanzas of this song are likewise in Lansdowne MS. 777.   Both texts are exactly the same.

P. 41, ll. 463-492.

Love! when I met her, etc.

This song also occurs, with unimportant verbal variations, in Lansdowne MS. 777.

—— ll. 473-4.

She sat and listen'd, etc.

The Lansdowne MS. reads :—

> She sat and listen'd, for she loves the strain
> Of one whose songs would make a tiger tame.

P. 42, l. 486.   *The blood of elephants.*   "It is reported," writes Topsell, "that the blood of an Elephant is the coldest blood in the world, and that Dragons in the scorching heat of summer cannot get anything to cool them, except this blood." (*The History of Four-footed Beasts,* 1607, p. 199 ; also in the same author's *History of Serpents,* 1608, p. 169.)

P. 44, ll. 552-63.

I know that like to silkworms of one year, etc.

In Lansdowne MS., but in a different metre.

P. 48, ll. 654-5.

> . . . . *as in physic by some signature*
> *Nature herself doth point us out a cure.*

What is popularly known as the doctrine of signatures was a system for discovering the medicinal uses of a plant from something in its external appearance that resembled the disease it would cure, and proceeded upon the belief that God had in this indicated its especial virtues (*Cf.* Friend, *Flowers and Flower Lore,* ch. xii.).

P. 51, l. 733.   *A little mushroom,* etc.   Browne, like many of his contemporaries, was fond of girding at the supposed niggardliness of the Spaniards. He returns to the attack a little further on (p. 53, ll. 793-812). Shakespeare, in *Love's Labour's Lost*, has represented Don Adriano de Armado as lean and miserable through too sparing a diet. *Cf.* also Donne's 18th Epigram, "Supping Hours" (*Works*, ed. Grosart, ii. 270).

P. 51, l. 746. *Spinner's sleaves*, cobwebs.

P. 55, ll. 840-1.

That famous race,
Engender'd by the wind.

Cf. Virgil, *Georgics*, iii. 274-5.

P. 70, l. 198. *With her unto Cyprus strip*. The reading of the MS., "trip," is not only defective rhyme but defective sense. I have therefore altered the word to "strip," *i.e.*, go rapidly.

P. 77. *The Shepherd's Pipe*. Richard Brathwaite, an admirer of Browne and Wither, alludes to *The Shepherd's Pipe* in a poem entitled "Upon the general Sciolists or Poetasters of Britannie," which is included in his volume called *A Strappado for the Devil*, 1615. After abusing the low versifiers of the day, he thus honourably distinguishes them :—

Yet rank I not (as some men do suppose)
These worthless swains amongst the lays of those
Time-honour'd Shepherds (for they still shall be,
As they well merit, honoured of me)
Who bear a part, like honest faithful swains,
On witty Wither never-with'ring plains :
For these (though seeming Shepherds) have deserv'd
To have their names in lasting marble carv'd.
Yea, this I know, I may be bold to say,
Thames ne'er had swans that sang more sweet than they.
It's true, I may avow 't, that ne'er was song
Chanted in any age by swains so young
With more delight than was perform'd by them,
Prettily shadow'd in a borrow'd name.
And long may England's Thespian springs be known
By lovely Wither and by bonny Browne ;
Whilest solid Selden, and their Cuddy too,
Sing what our Swains of old could never do.

P. 79.   *To Edward, Lord Zouch.*   To him Browne had previously dedicated the First Book of *Britannia's Pastorals.* See note at p. 321.

P. 82.   E. Johnson.   Edward Johnson, the author of these execrable lines, was the eldest son of Sir Robert Johnson, Knt., of London.   Admitted of the Inner Temple in 1609, he was called to the bar in 1617, and became a bencher in 1635.

P. 84.   John Onley, of Tottenham, Middlesex.   He was admitted of the Inner Temple in 1605.   In these verses he evidently alludes to the charming song, " Shall I tell you whom I love ?" in Bk. 2, Song 2, of *Britannia's Pastorals,* particularly to the lines :—

> " Such she is : and if you know
>   Such a one as I have sung ;
> Be she brown, or fair, or so,
>   That she be but somewhile young."

P. 85.   *The First Eclogue,* a dialogue between Roget (Wither) and Willie (Browne), touches on the imprisonment of Wither in the Marshalsea, after the publication of *Abuses Stript and Whipt* in 1613.   In that satire were many passages thought to aim at living persons, which Roget (or Wither) alludes to in ll. 41–56.—Hazlitt.

P. 88, ll. 83–108.   *But in vain then shall I keep,* etc.   In both editions these lines form part of Willie's speech ; they clearly belong to Roget.

P. 109, l. 568.   *The charter of health.*   Metaphorically used for a " complete cure."   It may allude to the charm written on a scrap of parchment or paper which was given by quacks to their patients, to be worn about the person as a preventive against disease.

P. 119, l. 790.
> *That but jar as Skelton's reed.*

John Skelton, born about 1460, died in 1529.   Browne, by this disparaging allusion, does but scant justice to the vigour and versatility of Skelton's verse.   On the other hand, the graceful compliment (ll. 749–70) which he pays Occleve is far beyond that dull writer's deserts.

P. 119, *note.*   Thomas Occleve, or Hoccleve (1370 ?–1450 ?) was for twenty-four years a clerk in the privy seal office.   His poem of *Jonathas,* which, in printing for the first time, Browne somewhat modernized and abridged, is a close copy of the Early English version of the fable in the *Gesta Romanorum*, entitled, "De mulierum subtili decepcione," where the "emperor" is called "Darius," the wicked woman being nameless. The English version is entitled, "Godfridus, a wise Emperor," and the lady figures in it as "Felicia," which Occleve has changed to "Fellicula." The fiction may have come originally from the East, as traces of resemblance are to be found in the *Arabian Nights*. It also presents, perhaps, one of the oldest forms of the popular story of Fortunatus, respecting which see DOUCR, *Illustrations*, ii. 391.

P. 129, l. 59. *Flawns.* Usually interpreted "custards." Drayton, however, distinguishes between the two dainties :—

"With green cheese, clouted cream, with flawns and custards stor'd."
        —*Muses' Elysium* (1630), Sixth Nymphal, p. 56.

Kersey defines flawn as "a kind of dainty, made of fine flour, eggs, and butter."

P. 134. MR. THOMAS MANWOOD, second son of Sir Peter Manwood, K.B., of St. Stephen's, otherwise Hackington, near Canterbury, entered the Inner Temple in 1610, and graduated B.A. from Lincoln College, Oxford, on 5 June, 1611. Was drowned in France in 1613.

P. 134. *The fourth Eclogue.* This Elegy is also found in Lansdowne MS. 777, and in the Salisbury Cathedral Library MS. The more important variations are here noted :—

P. 134, l. 12.   And echo *out* his moan.—(Lansd. MS.)
P. 135, l. 16.   And mighty forests stood with sapless flanks.
                                —(Lansd. MS.)
——   l. 21.   Against the broad-spread *oaks*.—(Lansd. MS.)
——   l. 33.   Broke *lay* his tuneful pipe.
                                —(Lansd. & Salisb. MSS.)
P. 136, l. 55.   Green *fitteth best* a lover's heat.
                                —(Lansd. & Salisb. MSS.)
——   l. 64.   Cease with dear Philaret for evermore.
                                —(Lansd. MS.)
P. 137, l. 71.   Will all be spent *ere I have paid.*—(Lansd. MS.)
——   l. 89.   Though we poor shepherds all should strive.
                                —(Lansd. MS.)
P. 138, l. 93.   That can suppress *our griefs*.
                                —(Lansd. & Salisb. MSS.)

P. 138, l. 96. *Our* greatest loss of thee.—(Lansd. and Salisb. MSS.)

—— l. 100. Or else through *time* be rotten.—(Lansd. and Salisb. MSS.)

P. 138, l. 103. These have *their* sev'ral fixed date.—(Salisb. MS.)

P. 139, l. 117. So stands *our* mournful case.—(Lansd. and Salisb. MSS.)

—— l. 121. *And* though so long he liv'd not as he might.—(Salisb. MS., where "Yet," the reading of the printed text, is erased.)

—— l. 128. That *hath* more years allotted.—(Lansd. MS.)

—— l. 131. Bemoan *our* hapless loss of him.—(Lansd. and Salisb. MSS.)

—— l. 134. (Sweet soul!) this *comfort only* seizeth me.—(Lansd. and Salisb. MSS.)

—— l. 135. That so few years *did* make thee so much blest.—So Lansd. and Salisb. MSS. The printed text has *should*.

—— l. 141. So fled dear Philaret.—(Lansd. and Salisb. MSS.)

—— l. 143. While others have a longer time.—(Salisb. MS.)

P. 140, l. 147. 'Tis for myself I moan, and *I* lament.—(Lansd. and Salisb. MSS.)

—— l. 151. *And* glorious days seem ugly nights.—(Lansd. MS.)

—— ll. 154-6. *But briny tears distil*, etc. For these three lines the following are substituted in both Lansd. and Salisb. MSS. :—

> No bird his ditty move,
>   No pretty spring smi'e on the vales,
> No shepherd on his love.

—— ll. 163-4.

> Melt into tears if he unkind
> To rase it put his hand.

—(Lansd. and Salisb. MSS.) In the Salisb. MS. the lines as they stand in the printed text have been erased and the above substituted for them.

—— ll. 165-8. And thou, my loved Muse, etc. The reading of the Lansd. and Salisb. MSS. is quite different :

> Ye Nymphs of mighty woods,
>   With flowers his grave betrim,

> And humbly pray the earth he hath
> Would gently cover him.

In the Salisb. MS. the lines as they occur in the printed version are erased, and the above lines written over the erasure.

P. 141, l. 171. Then from the ground, etc. The printed text has "earth," for which I have substituted "ground," the reading of the Salisb. MS.

P. 142. This address is wanting in the Lansd. and Salisb. MSS.

P. 165. *Non* [Nec] *semper Gnosius arcu*, etc. The tag is from a panegyric on a certain Calpurnius Piso, the authorship of which has been variously attributed to Virgil, Ovid, Statius, Lucan, and Saleius Bassus.

P. 165. *The Inner Temple Masque.* I have adopted the following readings from the Hopton Hall MS. in preference to those of the Emmanuel College MS. :—

P. 167. *Dedication.* *Our* Society for *the* Society.

P. 172, ll. 49–50.

> And till some greater power her hand can stay,
> Whoe'er commands,
>
> for
>
> And till some greater hand her power can stay,
> Whoe'er command.

P. 175, l. 101.

> What doth each wind breathe as it fleets?
>
> for
>
> What doth each wind breathe us that fleets?

P. 179, l. 169. *Grillus.* See Index of Names, *s. v.*

P. 179, l. 173.

> No gin shall snare you,
>
> for
>
> Nor gin shall snare you.

P. 183, l. 227.

> Let not the sad chance of distressed Greeks
>
> for
>
> Let yet the sad chance of distressed Greeks.

P. 201, l. 8. *The fleet that went out last.* As "A Sigh from Oxford" was probably written in 1624 or 1625, the poet's reference, in these lines, may be, as Mr. Hazlitt suggests, to the fleet despatched by James I., under the command of Sir Robert Mansel, against the pirates of Algiers.   Mansel had also instructions to visit the Court of Spain. After considerable delay he set sail on October 12, 1620, and returned on August 3, 1621, without having accomplished aught. "Sir Robert Mansel and his fleet," writes John Chamberlain to Sir Dudley Carleton, "have done nothing but negociate with the pirates of Algiers for the liberation of some slaves. They had many discourtesies in Spain " (*Cal. State Papers*, Dom. Ser. 1619–23). An account of the voyage was published in 1621 by one of the Captains (J. Button). Or the allusion may be to the long-delayed expedition against Cadiz, 1625, for hindering which the Duke of Buckingham was severely blamed by Sir John Eliot in the House of Commons.

P. 209. *Cælia is gone*, etc. These verses are inserted in the first song of the third book of *Britannia's Pastorals*, ll. 45–86, Marina being there substituted for " Cælia."

P. 214, st. 3. *Not I, by this good wine*. MS. has *nor*.

P. 229. MR. BRYAN PALMES. Born in 1599, the eldest son of Sir Guy Palmes, knt., of Lindley, Yorkshire, and Ashwell, Rutlandshire. Matriculated at Oxford from Trinity College on March 17, 1614–15. Knighted on April 21, 1642. Forced to compound for his estate in 1647 for £681, and assessed in 1651 at £200. See Index of Names, *s. v.*

P. 230, l. 26. *My friend friar Guy*. Mr. Hazlitt's conjecture that allusion is here made to Guy, Bishop of Amiens, author of a poem on the battle of Hastings, who died about 1076, is unfortunate. Friar Guy was probably a monk of Thouars, who may have acted as Browne's cicerone, and probably begged of him for his convent.

P. 240, l. 106. *Palmerin or Amadis*. Translations of these favourite romances, *Palmerin of England*, *Palmerin d'Oliva*, and *Amadis de Gaula*, had been published by Anthony Munday. Browne seems to have had the following passage in his mind : – " She reads Greene's works over and over, but is so carried away with *The Mirror of Knighthood*, she is many times resolved to run out of herself, and become a Lady Errant."—Character of a Chambermaid, from Characters appended to *Sir Thomas Overbury his Wife*, the ninth impression, 1616. (Cited by Mr. Hazlitt.)

P. 246. MR. WILLIAM HOPTON. See Index of Names, *s. v.*

P. 248. THE COUNTESS DOWAGER OF PEMBROKE. Mary, third daughter of Sir Henry Sidney by Mary, eldest daughter of John Dudley, Duke of Northumberland. Born about 1555; died September 25, 1621. Sir Philip Sidney was her eldest brother.

P. 250, ll. 43-46. *Is that man alive*, etc. Galileo Galilei invented the telescope in 1609.

P. 253, l. 125. *The Plague of Sweat* was prevalent during 1582-3.

P. 256. CHARLES, LORD HERBERT OF CARDIFF AND SHURLAND. Eldest surviving son of Philip, fourth Earl of Pembroke, by his first wife Susan, third daughter of Edward Vere, Earl of Oxford. He was made Knight of the Bath at the coronation of Charles I., and was married at Christmas, 1634, to Mary, daughter of George Villiers, Duke of Buckingham, but died of the small-pox at Florence, in January, 1635.

P. 258. *An Epiced on Mr. Fishbourne.* This was Richard Fishbourne, citizen and mercer of London, who is said to have been found as an infant floating in a basket on the river which runs through Huntingdon. He was placed at Christ's Hospital, and subsequently acquired considerable wealth. To the Mercers' Company and the town of Huntingdon he was a generous benefactor. In 1617 he, along with his partner and brother-in-law, John Browne, gave the altar of St. Bartholomew, Broad Street Ward, two silver flagons, and during 1623-24 he acted as Surveyor-Accountant of St. Paul's School. He died in May, 1625, and by his desire was buried in the Mercers' chapel. In his published funeral sermon, preached by Nathaniel Shute, rector of St. Mildred in the Poultry, his legacies are enumerated. The Poet is not mentioned in his will, proved in P. C. C. (57, Clarke) on 14 May, 1625.

P. 260. *His dear Browne.* John Browne, citizen and merchant taylor of London, who died in 1629, his nuncupative will being proved on 28 April of that year (*P. C. C.* 34, *Ridley*). He was apparently not related to the Poet, but he and his partner, Richard Fishbourne, may have become known to him through their mutual friend, Thomas Gardiner, of the Inner Temple, who prefixed verses to the first book of *Britannia's Pastorals.* Gardiner was John Browne's cousin and executor. From him was also descended John Browne, Clerk of the Parliaments, 1640-48, and another of his connections, John Chalkhill, author of *Thealma and Clearchus,* was a party to a dispute over his will.

P. 263. *An Elegy on Mr. Thomas Ayleworth.* Thomas Ayleworth, the eldest son of Peter Ayleworth, of Kineton, Warwickshire, was admitted a member of the Middle Temple on January 24, 1605-6. He was a cousin of the Sir Thomas Eversfield, whose daughter, Timothy, Browne afterwards married. As may be gathered from the poem Ayleworth was stabbed in some affray.— "1615, June 21. Thomas Aylworth, gent., 'wounded the xvij. day of May, lay long languishing under the hands of surgeons unto the xx. day of June, and then died, and was buried the xxi. day, 1615, in the middle chancel in Croydon Church.'"—Entry in the Parish Register of Croydon, printed by Nichols (*Collectanea Topograph. et Genealog.* ii. 295).

P. 266. *An Elegy.* This poem was first printed under the title of *Elegeia* by F. G. Waldron in *A Collection of Miscellaneous Poetry* (1802) from a MS. in his possession dated 1625, the authorship being assigned to Donne. Dr. Grosart reprinted it in his edition of Donne's *Poems* (ii. 347-50) and gave it the title of "Lament for his Wife." The principal variants of Waldron's MS. may be here noted :—l. 2, *must I ever lose* for *must I still lose ;* l. 19, *should all lose* for *should they lose ;* l. 21, *those* for *these ;* l. 26, *than now at twenty* for *than now at fifteen ;* l. 29, *so pure* for *most pure ;* l. 32, *Countries which ask'd for people from her store* for *Countries and islands which she was to store ;* l. 36. *fine foot* for *sweet eyes ;* ll. 37-8 are wanting ; l. 39, *And seld'* for *Seldom ;* l. 40, *All others' lands* for *All other lands ;* l. 45, *Dead, as my joys for ever, ever be !* for *Dead as a blossom forced from the tree ;* l. 46, *woman* for *maiden ;* ll. 47-8, *Tread on her, grant O may she there become. A statue like Lot's wife, and be her tomb !* for *Tread on thy grave, O let her there profess Herself for evermore an anchoress ;* ll. 49–52 are entirely omitted ; l. 54, *know* for *feel ;* l. 57, *murders* for *murd'rers ;* l. 62, *Nor shall I see thee* for *Nor shall I see, the ;* l. 71, *win* for *draw ;* l. 73, *did* for *used ;* l. 74, *shouldst* for *might'st ;* l. 75, *lov'd* (which is of course the true reading) for *love ;* l. 80, *we'd* for *I'd ;* l. 82, *Knows* for *Knew ;* l. 83, *crimes* for *days.*

P. 267, l. 3. *Tarriers, i.e.,* terriers, hillocks, mounds.

P. 267, ll. 3-8. *Are we all but as tarriers first begun,* etc. These lines occur also as ll. 3-8 of the *Elegy on Thomas Ayleworth* (p. 263).

P. 279. *Visions.* Closely imitated from Spenser's "Visions of the World's Vanity" and his translation of "Visions of Bellay."

P. 284. *On the Countess of Somerset's Picture.* Frances, a younger daughter of Thomas Howard, first Earl of Suffolk, married, first, on January 15, 1606, Robert Devereux, third Earl of Essex, from whom she obtained a divorce in 1613 ; and secondly, in 1613, Robert Carr, Earl of Somerset. She was sent to the Tower in 1615, and convicted with her husband of the murder of Sir Thomas Overbury in 1613, Overbury having incurred her resentment by reflecting on her character. Pardoned, but kept in the Tower until January, 1622. Died August 23, 1632.

P. 284. *To Don Antonio, King of Portugal.* Dom Antonio (1531-1595), prior of Crato, illegitimate son of Louis, Duke of Beja. He assumed the crown of Portugal upon the death of Henry I. in 1580, but was easily defeated by the Duke of Alva at Alcantara, after which Philip II. of Spain was declared king of Portugal, and then began the "sixty years' captivity," as the domination of Spain over Portugal (from 1580 to 1640) was called.

P. 285. [*Man.*] Lines similar to these occur in the first song of the third book of *Britannia's Pastorals* (ll. 552-63).

P. 287. *On Mrs. Anne Prideaux*, etc. Her father, John Prideaux, born of humble parentage in 1578 at Stowford, in the parish of Harford, Devonshire, became rector of Exeter College, Oxford, in 1612, and regius professor of divinity in 1615. In December, 1641, he was consecrated bishop of Worcester. Died in 1650.

P. 288. Sir John Prowde. Son of Serle Proude, of Kent. Knighted in 1622.

P. 289. *In Obitum M. S.* See Introduction.

P. 289. *On Mr. Vaux, the Physician.* Perhaps Francis Vaux, or Vaulx, born in Gloucester in 1601, the son of James Vaux, gent., of Marston-Meysey, Wilts. He matriculated at Oxford from Broadgates Hall (afterwards Pembroke College) on December 12, 1623, and proceeded M.B. on April 28, 1626. His estate was administered to on February 5, 1631-2, by his widow Catherine (*Administration Act Book, P. C. C.*, 1631-33, f. 80).

P. 291. *On Mr. John Deane.* Born in 1596 or 1598, a native of Newbury, Berkshire. Admitted to Winchester College in 1610. Matriculated at Oxford as a scholar of New College in 1615, and elected fellow in 1617. Graduated B.C.L. on January 18, 1622–3. Died in 1626–7; buried in New College chapel.

P. 292. *On Mr. Francis Lee.* A kinsman of Browne's. Second son of Sir Francis Leigh, Knt., of Addington, Surrey, and grandson of Sir Olliph Leigh, Knt., of Addington and East Wickham, who married in 1578 Jane, daughter of Sir Thomas Browne, Knt., of Betchworth. Entered the Inner Temple in 1633. Died in 1637.

P. 294. *On the Countess Dowager of Pembroke.* These famous lines occur in exactly the same form in the middle seventeenth-century MS. in the Library of Trinity College, Dublin, and are there signed "William Browne." They appear to have been first printed in Osborne's *Traditional Memoirs on the Reign of King James*, in 1658 (p. 78), and were also included in the *Poems* of the Countess's son, William, Earl of Pembroke, and Sir Benjamin Rudyerd in 1660 (p. 66); but in neither volume is there any indication of the authorship. Writing about the same time Aubrey, in his *Natural History of Wiltshire* (ed. Britton, 1847, p. 90), cited the first sextain, and stated that the verses were "made by Mr. Browne, who wrote the *Pastorals*." But in 1756 Peter Whalley printed a garbled version of the first six lines in his edition of Ben Jonson's *Works* (vi. 297), giving as his reason that they were "universally assigned" to Jonson, and they appear in all editions of Jonson since Whalley's time, and are commonly attributed to him. The epitaph is certainly more effective as a single sextain ; and Mr. Hazlitt suggests that "whoever composed the original sextain, the addition is the work of another pen, namely, Lord Pembroke's." Still, it must be remembered that Browne has occasionally marred his work by not knowing when to stay his hand, and the epitaph, as it appears in the Lansdowne and Dublin MSS., reflects him at his best and at his worst.

It may be worth noting that Browne thus pointedly refers to this very epitaph in his *Elegy* on Charles, Lord Herbert of Cardiff and Shurland (p. 257), which is written in the same metre :—

> "And since my weak and saddest verse
>   Was worthy thought thy grandam's herse ;
>   Accept of this !"

——— ——— The variants of the Trinity College MS. are "killed" for "slain" (l. 4) and "his dart" for "a dart" (l. 6).

P. 294. *On Susan, Countess of Montgomery.* Third daughter of Edward Vere, 17th Earl of Oxford. Married in 1604 Philip, 1st Earl of Montgomery and Baron Herbert of Shurland. Her husband afterwards succeeded his brother William in the Earldom of Pembroke. Lady Montgomery died in January, 1628-9. Browne also commemorated the death of her son Charles (p. 256).

P. 295. *On Mr. Turner.* He was *Richard* Turner, born in 1607, the son of Richard Turner, of Hendon, Middlesex. Matriculated at Oxford from St. Mary Hall on October 17, 1623 (B.A. January 30, 1626-7 ; M.A. June 13, 1629). Vicar of Burford, Oxfordshire, 1626-7. Died in 1637.

P. 296. *On Goodman Hurst.* According to the Horsham register the baptismal name of this worthy was *Richard*, and his burial took place on August 28. The "George" Inn has long since disappeared ; it is not mentioned in the list of hostelries given in Howard Dudley's *History of Horsham*, 1836.

P. 300. *In Urbem Romam.* These lines are a translation by the Sicilian poet Janus Vitalis of Du Bellay's third sonnet in the series called *Antiquitez de Rome*, the greater part of which had been previously translated into English by Spenser. They are included in *Delitiæ CC. Italorum Poetarum*, 1608, edited by Ranutius Gherus (*i.e.*, Janus Gruterus), ii. 1433, where the title is simply "De Româ." Vitalis omits ll. 7-8 of his original, which are here supplied by Browne. In the *Delitiæ* the reading of ll. 11-12 is Albula Romani *restat nunc* nominis index, *Qui quoque nunc* rapidis fertur in æquor aquis.

P. 302. *On a Dream.* These lines are also inserted, with variants, in the first song of the third book of *Britannia's Pastorals*, ll. 159-234.

P. 305. *Lydford Journey.* The Cornish antiquary, William Hals, in a letter in the possession of William Chapple, the editor of Risdon's *Survey of Devonshire*, stated that this poem was written in 1644, after Browne had paid a visit to his friend Lieut.-Col. James Hals, who had been taken prisoner by the Royalists and confined in Lydford Castle in the custody of Sir Richard Grenville, and that Browne, "soon after his return to Tavistock," forwarded the verses to Hals (Mrs. BRAY, *The Tamar and the Tavy*, iii. 11). There is, however, no allusion in the poem to justify the conclusion that it was written in 1644 ; it had, in fact, been inserted by Westcote in his *View of Devonshire in* 1630 (ed. 1845, p. 360) in precisely the same form as that mentioned by Hals as being correct. Of Lydford, which is about seven miles from Tavistock, Westcote writes : " It hath neither fair nor market to comfort itself withal, and little fruitful land. It is only entrusted with the keeping of the prince's prisoners, for stannary causes " (p. 359). He adds that Browne's verses were " commonly sung by many a fiddler." Portions of them have become proverbial in Devonshire.

The chief variants of Westcote's version are as follows :—

Ll. 5–6 : *But since I find the matter such,*
  As it deserves no laughter.

L. 8, *some* for *an* ; l. 10, *to* for *than* ; l. 11, *'twere* for *'tis* ; l. 12 *ere you come hither* for *now choose you whether* ; l. 15, *too* for *they.*

Ll. 21–2 : *Hath Lydford castle's high hall!*
  I know none gladly there would stay.

L. 24, *a* for *the* ; l. 25, *Prince Charles* for *The Prince* ; l. 37 *Near these poor men* for *Near to the men* ; l. 38, *See a dire bridge, a little church* ; l. 39, *one* for *an* ; l. 41, *Rector* for *Parson* ; l. 51, *Or drown'd with snow or rain* ; l. 55, *'Twas* for *One* ; l. 59, *have* for *were* ; l. 64, *For if thou stay'st* a little fit ; l. 65, *will* for *may* ; l. 66, *to a* for *into* ; l. 87, *it much* for *that nought* ; l. 95, *in* for *the* ; l. 100, *Wide* and ope *the* winds *so* roar.

P. 307. Stanzas 9, 10, 11.
  This town's enclos'd with desert moors, etc.

These verses are not in the Lansdowne MS. nor in the copy in Prince's *Worthies of Devon* (1701). But they were in the author's original manuscript, Hals tells us, and they are given by Westcote. They afford the first reference to that singular tribe of savages the Gubbinses, of whom a graphic account may be found in Fuller's *Worthies* (edit. 1662, p. 248, art. " Devonshire "). They infested the borders of the moor, near Brent Tor, the district occupied by them being called Gubbins's land. Mrs. Bray, in her romance of *Warleigh*, and Kingsley in *Westward Ho !* have introduced the legend of the Gubbinses, and their leader, Roger Rowle.

P. 308. Stanza 16.
  Sure I believe it then did reign, etc.,
is not in Westcote or Prince.

CORRIGENDA.

Vol. I., p. 44, for "malum *cæcat*" (side-note) read "malum *cacat*."
I., 59, l. 355, read "pyramides" (quadrisyllable). I., 152, l. 408,
read "perfumèd Flora." I., 203, l. 409, for "left" read "lest."
Vol. II., p. 11, st. 14, for "lands" read "hands." II., 23, l. 8, for
"Then" read "Than." II., 269, l. 75, for "love" read "lov'd."

INDEX OF NAMES.

Woodfall & Kinder, Printers, 70 to 76, Long Acre, London, W.C.